The Rhetoric of
RHETORIC

The Quest for Effective Communication

Wayne C. Booth

Blackwell
Publishing

© 2004 by Wayne C. Booth

BLACKWELL PUBLISHING
350 Main Street, Malden, MA 02148-5020, USA
9600 Garsington Road, Oxford OX4 2DQ, UK
550 Swanston Street, Carlton, Victoria 3053, Australia

First published 2004 by Blackwell Publishing Ltd

2   2005

Library of Congress Cataloging-in-Publication Data

Booth, Wayne C.
    The rhetoric of rhetoric: the quest for effective communication / Wayne C. Booth.
        p. cm. – (Blackwell manifestos)
    Includes bibliographical references and index.
    ISBN 1-4051-1236-0 (hardcover: alk. paper) – ISBN 1-4051-1237-9 (pbk.: alk. paper)
    1. Rhetoric. I. Title. II. Series.

    P301.B594 2004
    808–dc22

                                                                2004003097

ISBN-13: 978-1-4051-1236-9 (hardcover: alk. paper) – ISBN-13: 978-1-4051-1237-6 (pbk.: alk. paper)

A catalogue record for this title is available from the British Library.

Set in 11.5 on 13.5 pt Bembo
by Kolam Information Services Pvt. Ltd, Pondicherry, India
Printed and bound in the United Kingdom
by TJ International, Padstow, Cornwall

The publisher's policy is to use permanent paper from mills that operate a sustainable forestry policy, and which has been manufactured from pulp processed using acid-free and elementary chlorine-free practices. Furthermore, the publisher ensures that the text paper and cover board used have met acceptable environmental accreditation standards.

For further information on
Blackwell Publishing, visit our website:
www.blackwellpublishing.com

The Rhetoric of RHETORIC

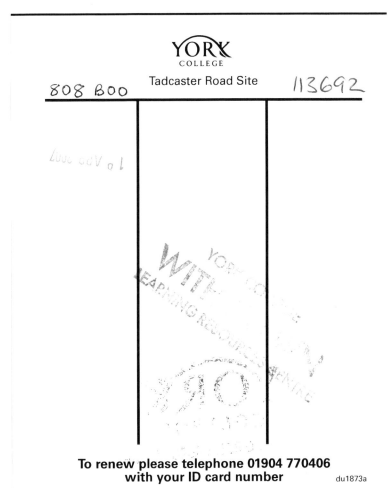

By the same author

The Rhetoric of Fiction, 1961
Now Don't Try to Reason with ME: Essays and Ironies for a Credulous Age, 1970
A Rhetoric of Irony, 1974
Modern Dogma and the Rhetoric of Assent, 1974
Critical Understanding: The Powers and Limits of Pluralism, 1979
The Vocation of a Teacher, 1988
The Company We Keep: An Ethics of Fiction, 1988
The Harper and Row Rhetoric: Writing as Thinking, Thinking as Writing (with Marshall Gregory), 1987; 2nd ed., 1991
The Art of Growing Older, 1992
The Craft of Research (with Joseph Williams and Gregory Colomb), 1995; 2nd ed., 2003
For the Love of It: Amateuring and Its Rivals, 1999

Books edited

The Knowledge Most Worth Having, 1967
The Harper and Row Reader (with Marshall Gregory), 1984

For my wife, Phyllis, thanking her for six decades of criticism
of my frequent failure to practice
listening–rhetoric

Contents

Preface   viii

Acknowledgments   xvi

Part I   Rhetoric's Status: Up, Down, and – Up?   **1**

1 How Many "Rhetorics"?   3
2 A Condensed History of Rhetorical Studies   23
3 Judging Rhetoric   39
4 Some Major Rescuers   55

Part II   The Need for Rhetorical Studies Today   **85**

5 The Fate of Rhetoric in Education   89
6 The Threats of Political Rhetrickery   107
7 Media Rhetrickery   129

Part III   Reducing Rhetorical Warfare   **149**

8 Can Rhetorology Yield More Than a Mere Truce,
  in Any of Our "Wars"?   153

Conclusion   171
Notes   173
Index of Names and Titles   189
Index of Subjects   201

Preface

In 1960, I was at a post-lecture reception in Oxford. Chatting over drinks with a don, I asked him what subject he taught.

"Chiefly eighteenth-century literature. What is *your* field?"
"Basically it's rhetoric, though I'm officially in 'English.' I'm trying to complete a book that will be called *The Rhetoric of Fiction*."
"Rhetoric!" He scowled, turned his back, and strode away.

Forty years later (summer 2003), I attended the semi-annual "Conference on Rhetoric and Composition" at Pennsylvania State University. This year it was entitled "Rhetoric's Road Trips: Histories and Horizons," with about 200 rhetoricians sharing views about rhetoric and rhetorical studies. Though many different definitions of rhetoric emerged, as always, it was clear that everyone there took rhetorical studies seriously, and would have felt even more startled by the Oxford scholar's response than I had been in 1960. But just imagine how surprised – even annoyed – he would be now if he stumbled upon that conference, or the many other annual conferences about rhetoric. There has been an amazing outburst of attention to rhetoric, though most academics in other fields are unaware of it. Too many academics view the study of rhetoric as at the bottom of the ladder: it is merely fussing with cheap persuasion.

So the point of this "manifesto" will be both to celebrate the recent flowering of studies and to lament their confinement to a tiny garden in a far corner of our academic and public world. Since we are all flooded daily with rhetoric, admirable and contemptible, we are in desperate need of serious rhetorical study, everywhere. Of course it is true, as chapter 4 will illustrate, that scholars in many fields are studying rhetorical issues, though under other "communication" terms. But too often they are unaware of how much they might learn about their basic questions by studying not just this or that branch of thoughtful communication – philosophy, symbiotics, linguistics, sociology, psychology, language studies – but *rhetoric*.

That claim would probably annoy the Oxford don even more than did my use of the term back then, and he would still be joined by various academics today. Many still view all rhetoric as what Stephen Spender described in those days: "Rhetoric is the art of deception, isn't it? And when you become good at using rhetoric on other people you eventually and all unknowingly use it on yourself."[1] Even some of those who engage in its study often treat it as, at best, the art of manipulation of audiences, or of promoting a reality or truth discovered through other means: a kind of icing to a cake that is produced by real thought. For some it sinks even lower, becoming little better than the crippled servant of true thinkers.[2] Just glance through the following four selections from the hundreds I have collected, echoing Spender, or Bertrand Russell's dismissal of Lytton Strachey's style as "unduly rhetorical," used only to "touch up the picture" and "make the lights and shades more glaring."

- "Impoverished students deserve solutions, not rhetoric." Letter to *Chicago Tribune*.
- "All that other stuff is rhetoric and bull. I don't think about it." Athletic coach.
- "[What I've just said] is not rhetoric or metaphor. It's only truth." Columnist attacking race prejudice.
- "President Bush's speech was long on rhetoric and short on substance." *New York Times Editorial*.

Even many dictionaries concentrate on the pejorative. Here is how one of them puts it:

> *rhetoric*: n. the theory and practice of eloquence, whether spoken or written, the whole art of using language to persuade others; false, showy, artificial, or declamatory expression; *rhetorical*: oratorical; inflated, over-decorated, or insincere in style; *rhetorical question*: a question in form, for rhetorical effect, not calling for an answer.

Thus we rhetoricians are not surprised – just scandalized again – when a literary critic says, as I heard recently in a discussion after a fine lecture: "Let's cut the rhetoric and get down to some serious talk." We have encountered that dismissal ever since Socrates, quarreling with the Sophists in Plato's *Phaedrus*, summarized his attack: "He who would be a skillful rhetorician has no need of truth." Serious talk deals with realities, rhetoric is fluff, or, when it is inescapable, it is merely the necessary art we have for dealing with probabilities rather than certainties.

My effort here to expand the recent flowering will not be a denial of how much shoddy rhetoric we face – much of it deserving to be called mere rhetrickery. A great proportion of rhetoric, however we define it, is in fact dangerously, often deliberately, deceptive: just plain cheating that deserves to be exposed. Is it not then naive to hope that rhetorical terms and their study can be restored to full respectability? Can the condemners be woken up to see that "rhetoric" covers, not just rhetrickery – the art of *producing* misunderstanding – but what I. A. Richards calls "the art of *removing* misunderstanding"?[3] Can we hope that more and more will see rhetorical training as essential in learning not only how to protect against deception, but also how to conduct argument that achieves trustworthy agreement and thus avoids the disasters of violence?

Two readers of a draft here have objected: "Of course we need to improve our search for effective communication, but why must we label that search rhetorical?" If you share that objection, perhaps you can invent some term that covers territory as broad as what we rhetoricians see covered by our terms. The territory is, after all, undefinable, since it includes almost every corner of our lives. Rhetoric is employed at every moment when one human being intends to produce, through the use of signs or symbols, some effect on another – by words, or facial expressions, or gestures, or any symbolic skill of any kind. Are you not seeking rhetorical effect when you either smile or scowl or shout back at someone who has just insulted you? As Longaville puts the claim about the rhetorical power of physical gesture, in *Love's Labour's Lost*:

> Did not the heavenly rhetoric of thine eye,
> 'Gainst whom the world cannot hold argument,
> Persuade my heart to this false perjury?

Is not an artist aiming at rhetorical effect when she asks herself, "Will this stroke make the painting seem a better one, to the viewer?" (The point is more obvious when the stroke is deliberately shocking, as in the use of actual elephant dung in a painting.) Wasn't Shelley justified in celebrating poets as the unacknowledged legislators of mankind? Are not those rhetoricians who study music as rhetorical justified? Nothing produces more effect on others than a well-composed and performed song or symphony. Even a deliberate murder can be considered as rhetoric if the intent is to change the minds of the survivors. (That extreme form of rhetoric will be mostly ignored here, as I celebrate rhetoric as our primary alternative to violence.)

In short, rhetoric will be seen as *the entire range of resources that human beings share for producing effects on one another:* effects ethical (including everything about character), practical (including political), emotional (including aesthetic), and intellectual (including every academic field). It is the entire range of our use of "signs" for communicating, effectively or sloppily, ethically or immorally. At its worst, it is our most harmful miseducator – except for violence. But at its best – when we learn to listen to the "other," then listen to ourselves and thus manage to respond in a way that produces genuine dialogue – it is our primary resource for *avoiding* violence and building community.

True enough, defining any term so broadly risks making it seem useless. If we call every effort at communication rhetorical, and every effort to study it "rhetorical studies," what happens to all of our other general terms – to "philosophy," "sociology," "literary criticism," "political science," "theology," or even "scientific discourse"? Well, as is shown by the astonishing explosion of books and articles entitled "The Rhetoric of . . . " (see appendix to chapter 2), we are now invited to think hard about the rhetoric of *everything*; "the rhetoric of philosophy," "the rhetoric of sociology," "the rhetoric of religion," even "the rhetoric of science." Though these rhetorics are not all of the same kind, we should recognize that all of these fields depend on rhetoric in their arguments. Most of them are in fact grappling with rhetorical issues, as they debate their professional claims. Thus we find the old rhetorical question, "What makes effective persuasion?" now expanded to, "How can we distinguish, in every human domain, the good from the bad forms of persuasion or discussion or communication?"

Unfortunately, my "universalizing" definition dramatizes the impossibility of covering the subject in a short book. The breadth forces me into many claims that will seem questionable and unsubstantiated with full evidence. But one solid central claim unites them: the quality of our lives, especially the ethical and communal quality, depends to an astonishing degree on the quality of our rhetoric. And since the pursuit of genuine rhetorical quality is still sadly neglected except by us professional rhetoricians, it is time for a reinforcement of the flowering of rhetorical studies that has occurred in the last six or eight decades, not just in the United States but in many European countries. Unless we pay more attention to improving our communication at all levels of life, unless we study more carefully the rhetorical strategies we all depend on, consciously, unconsciously, or subconsciously, we will continue to succumb to unnecessary violence, to loss of potential friends, and to the decay of community.

A Brief Outline of the Chapters

Chapter 1 addresses the threatening morass of rival definitions of rhetoric, ancient and modern. As I rely on the broader definitions, I do not claim that rhetorical studies can cover the whole of life, or that all academics should drop their rival titles and call themselves rhetoricians. Though I wish they all would acknowledge their kinship with rhetorical studies, the main point is simply that the reduction of rhetorical terms to the pejorative is not just absurd; it is harmful to our thinking.

Chapter 2 traces briefly the rise and fall and rise again of inquiry that has employed rhetorical terminology, from ancient times through the Renaissance to the present. Why was there such a huge decline until mid-twentieth century and then an astonishing embrace of explicit usage and profound study?

Chapter 3 addresses the problem of distinguishing defensible and indefensible rhetoric, tracing the diverse goals of rhetors, from deliberate harm, through winning-at-all-cost, and on to harmonious understanding and even the discovery of new truths. The key test is whether genuine *listening* has been granted opponents. As my colleague Joe Williams has put it, the really defensible rhetor listens to the opponent so well that she can answer his questions before they're even asked. But even listening-rhetoric, which I label LR throughout, raises ethical distinctions: Am I listening with the hope for a kind of ethical understanding, a true joining of inquiry, or am I listening merely in order to trick you – or at least win by defeating you?

Chapter 4 first illustrates the obvious point that all thinkers, even "hard" scientists, cannot escape rhetoric. Then it celebrates a selection of first-class thinkers who have revived rhetorical inquiry, in the wake of the decline produced by various forms of "scientific positivism." The serious probing by what I call the "rescuers" – some using rhetorical terms, some not – could almost be described as "the history of modern, and *post*modern, thought."

Chapter 5 laments the widespread neglect of rhetoric in education. What are the consequences of our current failure to educate young-sters in how to protect themselves from the floods of rhetrickery, and in how to practice the good kinds of rhetoric? What *is* good rhetorical education, and what bad?

Chapter 6 turns to politics. Nobody questions that awful rhetoric is found everywhere in politics – not just rhetoric that fails with this or that audience but rhetoric that *deserves* to fail. Risking the charge "What's new about *that*?" I trace some of the ways in which political failure to practice LR harms both those of us subjected to it and ultimately the rhetors themselves.

Chapter 7 pursues the closely related problems in our media, especially the floods of rhetrickery that could be blamed for the predominantly pejorative definitions of rhetoric we live with. Too often we ignore how all of us – even those who think of ourselves as thinkers – get swept by the media into erroneous choices. Though a small number of journalists try to combat the trash, few among them move beyond mere outbursts of contempt to a genuine search for cures.

Chapter 8 turns to the toughest question of all: How can the deepest form of LR, which I awkwardly label "rhetorology," yield not just diplomatic truce but discovery of new shared truths? How can we push LR to the point of finding common ground, shared assumptions, on which opponents can not just stand together but move forward together, as they probe their differences?

The chapter pursues ways in which the neglect of rhetorology often corrupts our lives. Using the warfare between science and religion as the central example, I explore how opponents might labor – probing their rival rhetorics – to discover the undisputed, firm platforms both sides stand on, as they pursue their arguments. The point is not that our disputes will go away, but that thinking about our rival rhetorics can often rescue us from meaningless conflict.

I hope it is clear by now that despite the academic emphasis in some parts of this book, especially chapter 4, it is not addressed only to academics. Though I try to wake up a few professors in every field to rhetoric's relevance to everything they do, both in teaching and in research, my fusion of celebration and lamentation is addressed to all readers who care about misunderstanding and the skills required to achieve understanding. No matter who we *think* we are, no matter where we now stand, triumphant or trembling, we are – to repeat again – in constant need of further thought about how we address our friends or enemies, in speech, in writing, in live performance, in the arts.

None of our problems with rhetoric will ever be completely solved, even by studying those geniuses I mention in chapter 4, or by reading regularly in any of the many new journals that concentrate on rhetoric (see chapter 2, n. 1). But if you and I are to avoid disastrous choices we must work even harder than I have done, through my five decades of probing, to recognize when we should cool down and really listen, and when one or another rhetorical version of reality offers us good reasons for changing our minds – and our ways of "talking back."

Every professional rhetorician will feel some exasperation here about my neglect of this or that major rhetorical issue. "You have almost nothing about the vast range of choices among figures of speech that every rhetor depends on." "You say nothing about the decline of attention to stylistic and formal clarity, as dramatized by linguist John McWhorter in his book *Doing Our Own Thing: The Degradation of Language and Music and Why We Should, Like, Care* (2003)." "You haven't a single section on any of the great classical rhetoricians." I can only answer: "Sorry, but did your last short book cover *everything*?"

Acknowledgments

Because of the flowering through my lifetime, no thank-you list can be adequate. If you do not find yourself here or in the appendices to chapters 2 and 4, or in my endnotes, please forgive me.

For advice about the status of rhetoric today in classical studies, thanks to Danielle Allen and Shadi Bartsch. For a lifetime of criticism of my rhetorical blunders, and for editing here, my wife Phyllis. For other editorial suggestions, chapter by chapter, thanks to Brandon Hopkins, Adam Kissel, James Phelan, and Ambika Seshadri. For the title, "Rhetoric of RHETORIC," Judith Segal.[1] For other editing of selected chapters, a small selection: Frederick Antczak, Tom Conley, Robert Denham, Eugene Garver, Homer Goldberg, Marshall Gregory, Walter Jost, Haskel Levi, Richard Levin, and Peter Rabinowitz.

Part I

Rhetoric's Status: Up, Down, and – Up?

It's hard to think of any academic subject with a history more confusing than that of rhetorical studies. Not only is the story longer than that of any besides philosophy. Rhetoric's reputation has risen and fallen probably more times, and more drastically, than that of any other subject. It's true that most subjects – even philosophy and science – have received some blind attacks along the way. But rhetoric and the study of its good and bad features have been uniquely controversial. Or so I claim, without even a hint of empirical proof of the kind lacking in most rhetorical studies. It is that lack that has sparked many of the dismissals, especially since the Enlightenment.

In these four chapters, after further tracing of the confused history of rival definitions (chapter 1), and a brief dramatization of rhetoric's disasters and triumphs (chapter 2), I address the complex evaluation problems that have led so many critics to see *all* rhetoric as contemptible (chapter 3). Finally, I celebrate a variety of thinkers who have revived serious rhetorical inquiry after the assassination attempts by positivists. Many of these rescuers have used almost no rhetorical terms, as they have fought to revive serious inquiry into emotion (pathos) and character (ethos) and other neglected topics. The concluding rescuers, those who receive most space, are – not surprisingly – those who openly revived rhetorical terms and concepts. They are the ones who have practiced a rhetoric of *rhetoric*.

1

How Many "Rhetorics"?

*Words! Mere words! How terrible they were! How clear, and vivid, and cruel!
One could not escape from them. And yet what a subtle magic there was in
them! They seemed to be able to give a plastic form to formless things, and to
have a music of their own as sweet as that of viol or of lute. Mere words! Was
there anything so real as words?*
Oscar Wilde, *The Picture of Dorian Gray*, chapter 2

Rhetoric, that powerful instrument of error and deceit.
John Locke, *Essay Concerning Human Understanding*

*The new rhetoric covers the whole range of discourse that aims at persuasion and
conviction, whatever the audience addressed and whatever the subject matter.*
Chaim Perelman

Any confident claim about the importance of rhetorical studies
requires as a first step some sorting of diverse definitions. No one
definition will ever pin rhetoric down. As Aristotle insisted, in the
first major work about it – *The Art of Rhetoric* – rhetoric has no
specific territory or subject matter of its own, since it is found
everywhere. But it is important to escape the reductions of rhetoric
to the non-truth or even anti-truth kinds. The term must always
include both the verbal and visual garbage flooding our lives and the
tools for cleaning things up.[1]

Contrasting definitions of rhetoric, both as the art of discourse and as
a study of its resources and consequences, have filled our literature,

from the Sophists, Plato, Aristotle, Cicero, Quintilian, and other classicists, on through the Middle Ages and Renaissance, until today. In its beginning, rhetoric was often confined to the oratory of males; usually it was the range of resources for winning in politics. By now everyone rejects the male emphasis and many agree to extend the terms, as I have already done here, to cover more than all verbal exchange; it includes all forms of communication short of physical violence, even such gestures as raising an eyebrow or giving the finger.[2]

From the pre-Socratics through about two millennia, most definitions, even when warning against rhetoric's powers of destruction, saw it as at least one of the indispensable human arts. Nobody questioned the importance of *studying* it systematically. Even Plato, perhaps the most negative critic of rhetoric before the seventeenth century, saw its study as essential. Though he often scoffed at it as only the Sophistic "art of degrading men's souls while pretending to make them better" (from the *Gorgias*), he always at least implied that it had to be central to any inquiry about thinking.

Thus for millennia scholars and teachers assumed that every student should have extensive training in rhetoric's complexities. Sometimes it was even placed at the top of the arts, as a monarch supervising all or most inquiry (See p. 5). The queen was of course often dethroned, becoming for many at best a mere courtier, or even a mere servant assisting the other three primary arts: logic, grammar, and dialectic. Even the most favorable critics recognized that in its worst forms it was one of the most dangerous of human tools, while at its best it was what made civilized life possible. Here are a few of the best-known premodern definitions:

- "Rhetoric is the counterpart of dialectic. It is the faculty of discovering in any particular case all of the available means of persuasion." (Aristotle)
- "Rhetoric is one great art comprised of five lesser arts: *inventio* [usually translated as invention but I prefer discovery], *dispositio, elocutio, memoria*, and *pronunciatio*. It is speech designed to persuade." (Cicero)

4

Rhetorica waving her sword over other sciences and arts.

- "Rhetoric is the science of speaking well, the education of the Roman gentleman, both useful and a virtue." (Quintilian)
- "Rhetoric is the art of expressing clearly, ornately (where necessary), persuasively, and fully the truths which thought has discovered acutely." (St. Augustine)
- "Rhetoric is the application of reason to imagination for the better moving of the will. It is not solid reasoning of the kind science exhibits." (Francis Bacon)

With the explosion of passionate "scientific rationality" in the Enlightenment, more and more authors, while continuing to study and teach rhetoric, followed Bacon in placing it down the scale of genuine pursuit of truth. The key topic, *inventio* (the discovery of solid argument), was shoved down the ladder, while *elocutio* (style, eloquence) climbed to the top rung. By the eighteenth century almost everyone, even those producing full textbooks for the study of rhetoric, saw it as at best a useful appendage to what hard thinking could yield, as in the Augustine definition above. As scholars embraced the firm distinction between fact and value, with knowledge confined to the domain of fact, rhetoric was confined to sharpening or decorating either unprovable values or factual knowledge derived elsewhere. Even celebrators of rhetorical study tended to equivocate about rhetoric's claim as a source of knowledge or truth – a tool of genuine reasoning.[3] Here is George Campbell's slightly equivocal praise, in mid-eighteenth century: "Rhetoric is that art or talent by which discourse is adapted to its end. All the ends of speaking are reducible to four; every speech being intended to enlighten the understanding, to please the imagination, to move the passions, and to influence the will."[4]

Many others, even among those trained in classical rhetoric, became much more negative. Perhaps the best summary of the negative view of rhetoric is that of John Locke, who wrote, in his immensely influential *Essay Concerning Human Understanding* (1690):

[If] we would speak of *things as they are*, we must allow that all the arts of rhetoric, besides order and clearness, all the artificial and figurative

6

application of words eloquence hath invented, are for nothing else but *to insinuate wrong ideas*, move the passions, and thereby mislead the judgment; and so indeed *are perfect cheats*: and therefore, however laudable or allowable oratory may render them in harangues and popular addresses, they are certainly, in all discourses that pretend to inform or instruct, *wholly to be avoided; and where truth and knowledge are concerned, cannot but be thought a great fault,* either of the language or person that makes use of them. . . . It is evident how much men love to deceive and be deceived, since *rhetoric, that powerful instrument of error and deceit,* has its established professors, is publicly taught, and has always been had in great reputation: and I doubt not but it will be thought great boldness, if not brutality, in me to have said this much against it. Eloquence, like the fair sex, has too prevailing beauties in it to suffer itself ever to be spoken against. And it is in vain to find fault with those arts of deceiving, wherein men find pleasure to be deceived. (Book 3, chapter 10, conclusion; my italics)

As such rhetoric-laden mistreatments flourished (note Locke's use of "the fair sex"!), Aristotle's description of rhetoric as the counterpart or sibling (*antistrophos*) of dialectic became reinterpreted as a reinforcement of the view that even at best it is no more than our resource for jazzing up or bolstering ideas derived elsewhere. And more and more thinkers reduced it to rhetrickery, sometimes even today simply called "mere rhetoric."

It was only with the twentieth-century revival that the term again began to receive more favorable definitions. Aristotle's claim that it was the *antistrophos* of dialectic became again interpreted to mean that rhetoric and dialectic overlap, as equal companions, each of them able to cover everything.[5] By now, many of us rhetoricians have decided – to repeat – that all hard thought, even what Aristotle called dialectic, either depends on rhetoric or can actually be described as a version of it. Here are some modern additions to the expanded definitions:

- "Rhetoric is the study of misunderstandings and their remedies." (I. A. Richards, 1936)

- "Rhetoric is that which creates an informed appetite for the good." (Richard Weaver, 1948)
- "Rhetoric is rooted in an essential function of language itself, a function that is wholly realistic and continually born anew: the use of language as a symbolic means of inducing cooperation in beings that by nature respond to symbols." (Kenneth Burke, 1950)
- "Rhetoric is the art of discovering warrantable beliefs and improving those beliefs in shared discourse . . . the art of probing what we believe we *ought* to believe, rather than proving what is true according to abstract methods." (Wayne Booth, 1964)
- "Rhetoric is a mode of altering reality, not by the direct application of energy to objects, but by the creation of discourse which changes reality through the mediation of thought and action." (Lloyd Bitzer, 1968)
- "We should not neglect rhetoric's importance, as if it were simply a formal superstructure or technique exterior to the essential activity. Rhetoric is something decisive in society. . . . [T]here are no politics, there is no society without rhetoric, without the force of rhetoric." (Jacques Derrida, 1990)
- "Rhetoric is the art, practice, and study of [all] human communication." (Andrea Lunsford, 1995)
- "Rhetoric appears as the connective tissue peculiar to civil society and to its proper finalities, happiness and political peace *hic et nunc*." (Marc Fumaroli, 1999)

Though many rhetoricians today still reserve some intellectual corners for other modes of thought about communication, all of us view rhetoric as not reducible to the mere cosmetics of real truth or solid argument: it can in itself be a mode of genuine inquiry. As Umberto Eco puts it, though rhetoric is often "degenerated" discourse, it is often "creative."[6]

The painful fact remains that despite the flowering of interest that we come to in the next chapter, rhetoricians still represent a tiny minority on the academic scene. Most serious books in most fields

8

still have no reference to rhetoric at all, and those that refer to it usually do so dismissively. Even works by professional rhetoricians are often deliberately mislabeled. A colleague recently informed me that his last three books, all of them originally employing "rhetoric" in their titles, had been retitled by the publishers, since rhetorical terms would downgrade the text and reduce sales!

Imagine how those commerce-driven publishers would react to my celebration of rhetoric here: "If you expand the term to cover all attempts at effective communication, good and bad – the entire range of resources we rely on, whenever we try to communicate *anything* effectively – doesn't it become meaningless, pointless? Surely you cannot claim that the shoddy rhetoric people object to shouldn't be called *rhetoric*."

As I said earlier, that objection is partly justified: "rhetoric" must include not only "the art of *removing* misunderstanding" but also the symbolic arts of *producing* misunderstanding. Employing the term rhetrickery for the worst forms can't disguise the fact that much of what we find repulsive is a form of rhetoric.

Another major ambiguity in expanding "rhetoric" to cover all efforts at communication is that it muddies the distinction between the *art* of rhetoric and the *study* of the art. The practice of rhetoric is not the same as the systematic effort to study and improve that practice. When I say "My field is rhetoric," what will my colleague in the philosophy department hear? "So you are a preacher of the arts that have nothing to do with truth, only persuasion? Do you deserve a professorship here for doing *that*?"

I see no escape from that ambiguity. But we can at least distinguish the *rhetor* – each of us, in and out of the academy, saying or writing this or that to produce some effect on some audience – from the *rhetorician*, the would-be scholar who studies the most effective forms of communication. To study the rhetoric of rhetoric is one thing; to work as a rhetor, as I am doing most of the time here – arguing for, sometimes even preaching about, the importance of that kind of study – is quite different. Yet we all often travel under the same term: "My field is rhetoric."

I thus hope that it will be useful to introduce a third term, covering those rhetors and rhetoricians who see their center as not just how to persuade effectively but how to practice listening-rhetoric (LR) at the deepest possible level. When LR is pushed to its fullest possibilities, opponents in any controversy listen to each other not only to persuade better but also to find the common ground behind the conflict. They pursue the shared assumptions (beliefs, faiths, warrants, commonplaces) that both sides depend on as they pursue their attacks and disagreements. So we need a new term, *rhetorology*, for this deepest practice of LR: not just distinguishing defensible and indefensible forms of rhetoric but attempting to lead both sides in any dispute to discover the ground they share — thus reducing pointless dispute.[7] This point becomes the center of the final chapter.

The term may seem to you a bit silly, but before you reject it, just think about the history of other -logies: socio-logy, theo-logy, anthropo-logy, bio-logy, psycho-logy, neuro-logy, musico-logy, gastroentero-logy, ideo-logy, and so on. If you can think of a better term for the deepest rhetorical probing, pass it along. There are indeed other terms in many fields that are intended to overlap with my rhetorology: hermeneutics, dialogics, problematology, social knowledge, even "philosophy of discourse."[8] As I explore further in chapter 4, the best thinkers in most fields have often concentrated on rhetorical and rhetorological territory, with or without acknowledging their kinship.

Since rhetorical terms are so ambiguous, it will be useful to rely throughout on the following summary of the distinctions I've suggested:

Rhetoric: The whole range of arts not only of persuasion but also of producing or reducing misunderstanding.
Listening-rhetoric (LR): The whole range of communicative arts for reducing misunderstanding by paying full attention to opposing views.[9]

Rhetrickery: The whole range of shoddy, dishonest communicative arts producing misunderstanding – along with other harmful results. The arts of making the worse seem the better cause.

Rhetorology: The deepest form of LR: the systematic probing for
"common ground."

Rhetor: The communicator, the persuader or understander.

Rhetorician: The student of such communication.

Rhetorologist: The rhetorician who practices rhetorology, pursuing common ground on the assumption – often disappointed
– that disputants can be led into mutual understanding.

Obvious Synonyms

Much of the annoyance with rhetorical studies springs from the fact
that rhetoricians can be said to steal subjects from various other
"fields." Most obviously, rhetoric covers what others call "English
Studies," "Composition Studies," "Communication Studies," or
"Speech and Communication." In a work celebrating the achieve-
ment of a major British thinker about how to teach writing skills in
English,[10] most of the essays could be described as about how to
teach good rhetoric rather than bad. But the word "rhetoric" is
hardly mentioned. The journal *College Composition and Communication* was for decades the center of education in rhetorical studies in
America; but only rarely did a paper appear in it with a title like my
"The Rhetorical Stance" (1963).

What about non-academic synonyms? Everyday language includes
many synonyms for defensible rhetoric: *sound point, cogent argument,
forceful language, valid proof* – and on through terms for style: *graceful,
subtle, supple, elegant, polished, felicitous, deeply moving, beautiful.* Some
even praise an outburst as *eloquent* without meaning to suggest exces-
siveness or the dodging of rationality.

We have an even longer list for the bad stuff: *propaganda, bombast,
jargon, gibberish, rant, guff, twaddle, grandiloquence, purple prose, sleaze,*

11

crud, bullshit, crap, ranting, gutsy gambit, palaver, fluff, prattle, scrabble, harangue, tirade, verbiage, balderdash, rodomontade, flapdoodle, nonsense: "*full of sound and fury, signifying nothing.*"

These synonyms dramatize once again why rhetoric has no single territory but covers almost everything, including the ethical judgments we come to in chapter 3.

How Do Different Rhetorics Not Only Reflect Realities but Make Them, Whether Ethically or Unethically?

Even among the new celebrators of rhetorical studies, many still treat it as only reflecting realities or truths derived by other methods. But we universalists insist that if we think of reality as consisting of any "fact" about "the world," including how we feel about it and how we react to it, it is clear that rhetoric *makes* a vast part of our realities.[11] Reality was changed not just by the fact that your roof leaked in the rainstorm last night but by the way you and your spouse discussed what to do about it and whether you are now cheerful or gloomy. This point must be stressed at some length here, because it is essential to my central thesis: when we neglect the study of how to improve rhetorical *makings*, we are in trouble.

To clarify that point we must distinguish sharply among three realities.

Reality One: Permanent, Unchangeable, Non-Contingent Truth

We embrace many realities that were not made by rhetoric, only reflected by it and too often distorted by it. Is the earth really a sphere and not flat? Will it ever turn out to have been true that it was flat? Obviously not, even if the sphere gets shattered or everyone decides that the flat-earthists were right after all. Are the truths about the universe's origins that cosmologists are seeking temporary? No, only this or that version is temporary: the actual truth that is sought has been "there" from "the beginning," awaiting our discovery, and will

12

be there whether we find it or not. If I drop a teacup on the floor, its splintering was not made by anything but the non-contingent truths about ceramics and gravity. Only explanations offered about my carelessness or anger in dropping the cup depend on rhetoric.

The history of philosophy has been full of debates about whether some value judgments deserve to be added to this category of hard, unchangeable fact. Saving that issue for chapter 4, I must confess here, as much of my previous work reveals, that I am strongly on the "Platonic" side: torturing a child to death for the sheer pleasure of it is *always* wrong, and that *fact* will never be changed by any form of rhetoric. Slavery will *always* be wrong, no matter how many cultures practice it. Though rhetoric is needed to change minds about such truths – they're only in effect discovered through centuries of catastrophe and discussion about it – they are for me still part of unchangeable reality. I hope that you would join me in automatically ruling out any defense of a pleasure-motivated child-murder that depended on an effort to prove that such infanticide is simply acceptable, in some circumstances, since we can't prove our moral case scientifically. Can you join me in claiming that no amount of future rhetoric will justify slavery, even if this or that culture becomes convinced that it is needed and thus justified?[12]

My case here will of course be rejected by skeptics and utter relativists, and by some social constructionists who argue that even our deepest values are totally contingent. But even if one of them were so clever as to change your mind or mine, that would not change the ethical facts about child-abuse or slavery.

To defend such joining with most Platonists and many theologians – "many truths, even ethical judgments, preexist before any discovery or 'making' of them" – would require a book-long philosophical/ rhetorical treatise. But it is important to repeat that current critics of rhetoric are wrong when they tie it to the claim that everything is totally contingent.[13] Rhetoric did make the reality of our discovery, but it did not make the ethical truth itself.

Thus while rhetoric has created many *temporary* realities – hard but temporary facts of the times: this war, that truce – it finally sometimes discovers innumerable *unconditional* truths. It then, with its diverse forms of making, converts more and more into believing them.

In short, rhetoric does not *make* Reality One, Unchangeable Truths. It aids us in discovering them, as it makes and remakes our circumstances and beliefs – our temporary realities – along the way.

Reality Two: Realities Changeable but Still Not Created by Rhetoric: The History of How Nature Moves from Contingency to Contingency

The cosmos changes its contingent facts every moment: it was a hard reality yesterday that Mountain X had a peak of 10,303 feet above sea level; but this morning the reality is that its peak has been nipped off by a volcano blast, reducing the elevation to 9,702 feet, while the facts about the valley below are being transformed as the lava flows. The tornado that struck last night changed the reality of the village it destroyed, though the hard truths (Reality One) about what makes a tornado were overseeing the whole shifting show. (The fact that scientists' convictions about those truths shift from "paradigm" to "paradigm," generation by generation, does not change this point; the full actualities of Nature being studied do not change simply because scientific rhetoric changes.)

Reality Three: Contingent Realities about Our Lives: Created Realities that are then Subject to Further Change

To be sure, many of our daily changes do qualify as realities not made by rhetoric. The gravity and slippery ice that pulled me down and broke my rib produced radical changes in the way I slept and walked, for months. But the way my wife and doctor talked with me about it changed the reality of how I felt and acted. Our lives are often overwhelmed by such rhetorical changes of reality:

- Hitler's rhetoric – along with the rhetoric of many others – *made*, or *created*, World War II. The rhetoric of President Bush, Prime

Minister Blair, and Saddam Hussein *made* the Iraq war of spring 2003, with each side blaming the rhetoric of the other side.

- Churchill's rhetoric *created* a radically different World War II than would have been created if Chamberlain had remained prime minister.
- President Kennedy's rhetoric (and that of his opponents) *created* our escape from the Cuban missile crisis.
- Persuading your husband two years ago to accept the advice of architect X rather than the advice of architect Y *created* the reality of your living room and bathroom right now.
- A speaker's blurting out a forbidden epithet or misunderstood word can change the reality not only of the audience's view of that speaker – he's now a villain – but the reality of how he and others will be treated in the future. Most writers in America now avoid the word "niggardly," because of widespread protests identifying it with "nigger." Sooner or later dictionaries – reflectors of vocabulary reality – will warn against it. Our speech codes are changed daily by how we obey or violate them.
- A speaker's playful or ironic speculation can create awful realities. On November 20, 2002, a journalist, writing about the controversy in Nigeria over whether the Miss World contest should be held there, playfully speculated that if Mohammed were alive he might choose Miss World as an additional wife. Reports said that the protest riots had killed at least 220 and injured another 500. A sentence or two changed the reality not just of those killed or injured but of thousands of others.
- The rhetoric of legislators (and of those who lobby them, and of those who pay the lobbyists) creates the votes that recreate society.
- Controversy about whether the huge Millennium Dome south of the Thames was a good or bad idea will probably long continue, but that invention and the claims about its failure are now part of a new reality that would not be here without the role of rhetoric. This is not to deny that the actual construction – the interlocking of steel beams and painting of walls – was usually not rhetorical

but mainly dependent on the unchanging rules of mechanics. But even in choices about what to hammer or how to pour the cement, we can be sure that rhetorical exchanges among workers figured at every moment, changing Reality Three.

Offering such obvious examples from our factual world is not to claim that rhetoric was the only factor in those creations. The point is to call for more open acknowledgment of how rhetoric is to be praised, or blamed, for the makings.

One central question of this chapter – how do we decide whether such creations are defensible or indefensible? – leads to many problems, including debates about objectivity and subjectivity.

We may not want to call the realities made by rhetoric "objective," because we always have only our "subjective" pictures of them: this point has been stressed by many postmodernist social constructionists. The constructions can be encountered and tested only in our experience, and our experience always relies on subjective assumptions. Precisely what realities were created by World War II, rhetorically or militarily, can never be fully pinned down in any one account. But even though our descriptions will vary, the realities made by war-rhetoric then and now are – to repeat – *real*, as is the existence of your present domicile and the Millennium Dome. That their reality might be destroyed by further rhetoric in the future does not in any way undermine the key point here: *rhetoric makes realities, however temporary*. And meanwhile it creates a multiplicity of judgments about what the realities *really* are. After every election or every war, there is never full agreement about what new reality has been created.

In short, it is not just that rhetoric makes many realities: study of rhetorical issues is our best resource for distinguishing the good makings from the bad. As postmodernist Marxists like Louis Althusser have claimed that "ideology" makes, or changes, realities, and linguists and philosophers have increasingly emphasized how "language-games" make realities, they have dramatized (sometimes unwittingly) our need for effective ways to distinguish the good makings from the bad.

16

How Rhetoric Relates to Three Sub-Kinds of Rhetoric-Made Realities

Contingent realities made by rhetoric have been variously classified by all rhetoricians, most often following Aristotle's distinction of three kinds:

- *Deliberative* – attempts to make the future. Politicians or committee members debate about how to act or vote; husbands and wives and architects debate about house remodeling.
- *Forensic* – attempts to change what we see as truth about the past (attempts which may of course also affect the future). A lawyer skillful in rhetoric can sometimes make it clear that a death penalty decision for murder was false, thus creating a new reality – for defendants, prosecutors, victims, and their families. Historians can debate about how much blame to give Presidents Kennedy, Johnson, and Nixon for the Vietnam fiasco.
- *Epideictic* – attempts to reshape views of the present. An orator or birthday-party friend can change the reality of how we value people and their creations. A hero can be revealed as a con artist, or a CEO turned from hero to villain. A widely mocked art movement can be turned into a celebrated artistic revolution.

Obviously all three of these can have effects on the other two, but the distinction can be quite useful, both as the rhetor tries to decide what to say and as the critic of rhetoric tries to decide whether a given rhetorical stroke deserves praise. An epideictic stroke useful *now* in changing a vote can prove contemptible if judged as deliberative.

What has been too often overlooked or understated in rhetorical studies is that when our words and images remake our past, present, or future, they also remake the personae of those of us who accept the new realities. You and I are remade as we encounter the remakings. And that remaking can be either beneficial or disastrous. In short, rhetoric of all three traditional kinds creates a fourth kind: the character, the *ethos*, of those who engage with it. This is why the quality of our citizenry depends on whether their education has concentrated on the productive forms of rhetorical engagement.

Distinction of Domains

Adding to the problem of defining these three different kinds – whole books have been written on the differences – is the fact that rhetorical standards and methods contrast sharply, depending on differences in what Kenneth Burke called the "scene" and others have called the "culture" or "discourse community." Everyone lives in a different version of what I choose to call the "rhetorical domain," narrow or broad: the community that preaches and practices rhetorical standards that contrast sharply with the standards embraced by those in other domains.[14]

All successful communication within any given domain will depend on tacit shared assumptions about standards and methods, including what Stephen Toulmin taught us to call "warrants." Some domains are huge, some tiny. Almost everyone in American journalism, for example, abides by the rule, "Never report it if a political leader uses the word 'cunt.'" A somewhat smaller group – the most "respectable" journals – cannot even use "fuck" or "shit." Meanwhile the standards in some journals, like the *New Yorker,* and in most British journalistic domains, are much looser. But the differences are far broader than about mere obscenities. Everybody obeys different standards depending on audience differences. Do I write "it's" or "it is"? Do I begin the sentence with "But" or reserve "however" to follow the first phrase? Reporters all claim that the persona of a president, chatting on a plane trip, is totally different from the one he presents before a microphone. Secular newspapers assume readers who assume that when a "scientific study" releases a report, the report must be reported, not just as newsworthy but as probably valid. News addressed to this or that fundamentalist group will assume, in contrast, that if a "scientific study" contradicts religious belief, it should be either ignored or attacked. Members of a Buddhist community in Tibet will depend on standards sharply different from those in an Amish community in Iowa. Members of a street gang will reject as bullshit the language that a prosecutor uses in charges made against them before a judge, while the judge considers much of their language (if recorded on a tape behind their backs) unintelligible — not just in pronunciation but in vocabulary.

Thus every society shares some rhetorical standards, while actually possessing a variety of sub-domains with different standards. A hard-nosed scientist appearing before a judge or a government committee will face entirely different argument standards from those she faces when writing her research paper. And standards will differ even in different sections of the same journal. What makes good rhetoric on the front page of your local newspaper will differ sharply from the style of the sports section or business section or editorial page.

A prime example of how wide the differences can be even among those who think of themselves as dwelling in the same domain is the contrast among academic disciplines. Critics outside the academy tend to assume that academese is one thing, public discourse another. But in fact there are major differences of standards ranging from field to field: what constitutes evidence or valid argument, what questions are worth asking, what choices of style will work or even be understood, which authorities can be trusted, how much eloquence is permitted. Even in large loosely defined fields like English, where people quarrel about discourse norms, there are underlying "warrants" or "commonplaces" that are taken for granted as not requiring discussion; in some other fields those "unquestionable" warrants will not only be questioned but sometimes openly rejected as totally unreliable. Most authors in the hard sciences assume, without bothering to argue about it, that hard data are required to make a case. They will be suspicious of historians' assumption that quotation and citations provide adequate evidence for any conclusion. Authors in this or that branch of sociology will assume different standards for what is self-evident and needs no proof.[15] The rhetoric effective in a journal called *Deconstruction* or *Culture Studies* will differ greatly from what is effective in the *Journal of Economics*, the *Chronicle of Higher Education*, or even something as broad as *The Economist*.

The borderline between some domains within a given culture can be extremely hazy. It can often invite clever satire, when those committed to one domain express contempt for another by parodying its style. Perhaps the most effective rhetorical stroke of this kind in recent years was that of the physicist Alan D. Sokal, in an ironic article that became known as the "Sokal Hoax." Annoyed by what he saw as a radical decline in argument standards in some branches of the humanities, he submitted to the journal *Social Text* an elaborate "demonstration" that all truths, even the "hardest" scientific truths, are not objective but just socially constructed. The careless editors overlooked his hundreds of obvious clues to his satirical point, printed the article, and Sokal quickly became famous for exposing the contemptible standards in that domain.[16] He later described his spoof this way:

> To test the prevailing intellectual standards [in that domain], I decided to try a modest...experiment. Would a leading North American journal of cultural studies...publish an article liberally salted with nonsense if (a) it sounded good and (b) flattered the editors' ideological preconceptions?...Why did I do it? While my method was satirical, my motivation is utterly serious. What concerns me is the proliferation, not just of nonsense and sloppy thinking *per se*, but of a particular kind of nonsense and sloppy thinking.[17]

Sokal thus dramatizes his contempt for the argument standards of those connected with a journal like *Social Text*; for him much of what they publish is no more than rhetrickery. In my view, however, his attack struck home not because that opposing domain has no validity whatever but because the editors of the journal were *for that moment* carelessly failing to employ their own real standards. Because the essay seemed to validate their convictions, they failed to study the rhetoric carefully. They later apologized – not very persuasively, as I see it.

The point about contrasting domains can be illustrated even within the community of those of us who actively study rhetoric. We too often think and write as if we communicate in a domain self-evidently superior to all those other domains "out there" – as if to say:

> By studying rhetoric decade by decade, we have developed standards of argument superior to everyone else's. What is really good rhetoric, according to our heroic teachers, might just puzzle those ignorant of the tradition.

But that domain is not as clearly defined as we might wish, or claim. History reveals endless quarrels among rhetoricians who embrace rival superior domains: "Unlike the rest of you, we have found the one true set of rhetorical standards." I'm sure that some of what I say later about "rhetorology" will inevitably appear to some as foolishly elitist, or just plain puzzling.

What is inescapable is that underlying all our differences about what makes good communication there is one deep standard: agreement that whatever the dispute, whatever the language standards, communication can be improved by *listening to the other side, and then listening even harder to one's own responses.*

Obviously, saying that does imply a judgment of domains: whenever we manage to listen first and continue listening, we are far superior as rhetors than when we aim our words at targets that don't exist. The thesis of this book might thus be reduced to: Let us all attempt to enlarge the "domain" of those who work to avoid misunderstanding. (In chapter 7 we will face the major "domain revolution": the expansion of the TV audience to include the whole world.) Even though rhetoric will never have a single definition, and even though conflicting domains will always frustrate our efforts to communicate, there are ways to escape, in every corner of our lives, the popular degradations of rhetoric. Practice LR!

Will that practice remove the problems of rhetoric? Obviously not. Even the most skillful pursuers of LR, considering it the supreme rhetorical art, encounter nasty problems – especially when what is *heard* is an unwavering threat, explicit or implicit: an implacable demand for caving in or self-censorship. We will face some of those problems throughout, especially when dealing with political rhetoric. Again and again I catch myself with the question, "Have you really listened hard enough, deeply enough, to your target here?" And the answer is too often, "No."

2

A Condensed History of Rhetorical Studies

Writing the history of rhetoric is impossible. To do it properly the historian would have to discuss everything. To do it fairly, the author would have to give credit to 10,597 authors who contributed to the history. To make it interesting, the author would have to make it even shorter than this chapter. Any rhetorician who is not a fool will choose to write about one or two small rhetorical domains: fiction, irony, teaching, modernism, the craft of research . . . and so on.

Anon

As I've suggested already, rhetorical studies today can be said to be either dying or flourishing, depending on where we look and how we define rhetoric. In America, in the field of "English," those new postgraduates who are trained in "rhetoric and composition" are at least as likely to get hired as those who have focused on other studies within the amorphous discipline of "English." Because most colleges still require all students to take a beginning course called "Composition," or "Writing," or "Rhetoric and Communication," or – rarely – just "Rhetoric," there is a strong demand for those who know something about the subject. While participants may quarrel about how rhetoric's role fits in the required course, and about why the teachers are still so often treated as if they were mere servants of the real scholars found under other titles, nobody can doubt that as compared with last century, rhetorical studies are surging forward – at least in America and some European countries.

In contrast to the academic world at it was when I encountered that scoffing don in Oxford, there are now many journals and professional associations featuring rhetoric.[1] Doctoral degrees concentrating on it are flourishing. Though there are hardly any full departments with the label, the challenges of how to study and improve rhetoric are without question faced by more and more scholars every year.[2]

On the negative side, when you scan through the major journals in "literature," "criticism," "the humanities," "the social sciences," or any of the other fields, you find relatively few explicit references to rhetoric. Though most authors are inevitably engaged in some corner of what traditionally would have been considered rhetorical study, there is little open acknowledgment of the connection. And as I have already stressed, when the term "rhetoric" does appear, it is far too often employed as a label for the bad reasoning of some critical opponent.

I encountered a strong illustration of the neglect when I recently was asked to judge which "special issue" of fifty-one "humanities" journals should be awarded the prize as "the best." There were hardly any rhetorical terms in any of the journals, even when authors were obviously grappling with problems of "persuasion" or "effective discourse" or "cultural formation" or "how to reduce pointless controversy." "Rhetoric" was simply off the chart. It was almost as if nobody had ever heard of the rhetorical tradition. And of course that near-total neglect of references would have been found even more dramatically if the journals had been from outside the humanities.

Such neglect by so many academics is a bit surprising when one considers the amazing outburst of serious rhetorical inquiry since the mid-twentieth century. I'm tempted to call it an "explosion" – it was so dramatic – but that might imply that it destroyed rather than enhanced other studies. Besides, from the perspective of a typical quantum physicist, say, the outburst would seem about as insignificant as a small firecracker going off in a distant forest. And so,

24

deliberating about a minor rhetorical choice here, I will continue to label what happened a *flowering*. (One colleague has urged, "Drop the metaphor 'flowering,' because all flowers *wilt*.")

If you call up books and articles about rhetoric, in the British Library or US Library of Congress catalogues or the *PMLA* bibliographies, you find an amazing rise in the past five or six decades. If you search for books with the title *The Rhetoric of_____*, filling in your favorite subject, you are almost certain to find at least one book probing your area under such a title. I find more than 600 works with the title *The Rhetoric of_____*, almost all of them published since 1950. I find only nineteen before 1950 – most of them on Aristotle or other individual authors. Only two or three of those earlier works sound as interesting as Mortimer Wilson's *The Rhetoric of Music: Harmony, Counterpoint, Musical Form* (1907) or George Winfred Hervey's *The Rhetoric of Conversation: Or Bridles and Spurs for the Management of the Tongue* (1845).

If you add books with titles like "Rhetoric *and* X, Y, or Z," the contrast before and after 1950 is even more striking. And if you call up works with rhetoric *somewhere* in the title, in World Cat, you find, in the millennia before 1960, 2,205, and in the single decade 1990–9, 3,196.

Anyone who doubts the extent of the flowering should take a quick look now at the appendix to this chapter, where I illustrate the spread of open rhetorical inquiry to almost every conceivable topic, starting with Kenneth Burke's *The Rhetoric of Motives*, in 1950. The flowering can be dramatized by counting books entitled *The Rhetoric of [This or That]* according to date.

Before 1950:	19
1950–9	8
1960–9:	18
1970–9:	41
1980–9:	155
1990–9:	296

(No doubt the annual numbers will decrease, once every conceivable field is thought to have been sufficiently covered. If we multiply the 57 in the years 2000–2 by 5, making a decade, we already see a slight decline from the 1990s: 285.)

Another bit of revealing evidence of the flowering is that though the number of books with "rhetoric" in the titles is still slightly behind "anthropology" and "sociology" (with both of them far behind "psychology" and further behind "theology"), it is clear that open rhetorical language is catching up. (One reader has said, "Cut that sentence; it sounds foolishly competitive. Who cares who's on top?" Well, foolish or not, we who have been sidelined do care, and we do take comfort in any sign of increased attention to what really matters.)

Histories of the rise and fall of rhetoric have been attempted by many – usually limited, as in this chapter, to the open use of rhetorical terminology. (In chapter 4 we will turn to the different history that emerges when we consider the issues studied, regardless of contrasting terms for them.) Some histories, like George Kennedy's or Marc Fumaroli's, are immensely long, while Terry Eagleton's is only twelve pages.[3] There are many intriguing moments in rhetoric's history when it triumphed, or crashed, or produced anguished conflict. St. Augustine, for example, having been originally trained as a rhetorician, became troubled, after his conversion to Christianity, with the conflict between unquestioned faith and rhetoric's seeming reduction of *everything* to contingency. Should a believer in the one divine truth continue to work with persuasive devices that depend so much on shaky evidence – and often on downright deception? Augustine in the end decided that, since the devil has in his hands the resources of rhetoric, we on God's side must feel free to use it in defense.[4]

By the time of Aquinas, rhetoric was still a prime subject for every student, though it stepped down a bit from the position granted by Cicero, Quintilian, and others. It was now reduced to being only one of seven arts: the trivium (grammar, rhetoric, and dialectic) and the quadrivium (geometry, arithmetic, astronomy, and music). Because

26

the trivium was studied mainly by beginning students, who only later went on to deal with the quadrivium, the term "trivial" later became pejorative, with rhetoric often dropped even below grammar and dialectic.

Some scholars, however, tended to put rhetoric toward the top of the seven. For many, by the Renaissance, rhetoric became not just how we conduct persuasion, not just a prominent rival of science and logic and arithmetic, not just *one* rival source of knowledge, but the *queen* of the sciences and arts, as we saw on page 5. That woodcut, published in 1507, portrays Rhetorica as worshipped by the other sciences and their prophets: in philosophy, in history, in poetry, in law, etc. Such imagery dramatizes the fact that every schoolboy in most Western countries was then receiving a serious, steady "drilling" in rhetorical terminology, evaluation, and construction.

Colorful illustration of the consequences of such education is provided in most literature of the time, especially in Shakespeare's works. Like all the other authors of the period, Shakespeare had been trained in rhetorical studies, and all of his plays and poems reveal the results of that training. As David Bevington puts it in his *Shakespeare* (2002), after explaining that all would-be poets studied the "arts of rhetoric" to "perfect their craft":

> Poetry was seen as a branch of rhetoric; one learned to make one's ideas more persuasive and affective [*sic*] by adorning those ideas with images, extended metaphors, and "conceits." . . . The art of *Venus and Adonis* is the art of rhetoric, being practiced by an eager apprentice. (p. 14)

The effect of rhetoric's pedagogical centering is even more evident in the dramatist's portrayals of political debate, as in the quarrel between Cassius and Brutus about whether they should kill Caesar. (We meet some of Shakespeare's war-rhetoric in chapter 6.)

Like Shakespeare, all who were formally educated, on through the seventeenth century and most of the eighteenth, were taught to pursue rhetorical mastery. This is not to say that they were all trained well, or that they were all trained in the same version of rhetoric, or that their rhetoric was always used in justified causes; the definitions are as diverse as the broad range we met in chapter 1. But "everybody who was anybody" studied texts like Erasmus's *De Copia* (first published in Paris in 1512). As a required text ostensibly offering a summary of the whole range of rhetorical topics, while concentrating on the use of "copiousness" ("abundance," "eloquence"), it survived through many editions in many countries (always in Latin, I believe). From my perspective the book is somewhat misleading, as it celebrates eloquence while relegating Aristotle's key term, *inventio* (invention or discovery or making of arguments and thus of realities), to a very late chapter. But it is still a splendid example of how Rhetorica dominated education. Though often not quite the Queen of *all* the Sciences, she was always up there among the pedagogical royalty.

The dethroning quickly ensued, especially as those joining the "Enlightenment" sought "hard truth" or "certainty." But whatever the perspective – whether rhetoric was queen or servant or slave of the truth-seeker – it was still clear that every student should be trained rigorously in rhetorical matters.[5] Even by the time Locke issued his powerful pejoratives (pp. 6–7 above), rhetoric was still present in every educational setting.

But the decline of status continued throughout the eighteenth century. A most intriguing example is the work of Adam Smith. With his reputation today as the author of *The Wealth of Nations* (1776),[6] almost nobody would think of him as having had anything to do with rhetoric. But with the discovery in 1958 of his student's extensive lecture notes from Smith's course on rhetoric, published now as *Lectures on Rhetoric and Belles Lettres*,[7] our understanding of him and his writing should be radically revised. He actually began his career, after giving up medicine, as a teacher of rhetoric in Glasgow, and made his living that way for a long time. His lectures reveal an astonishingly rich knowledge of every traditional issue. He has full sections on the rhetoric of poetry and fiction and the visual arts and music – approaches seen only rarely until our time. (See especially his Lecture 13, and p. 6.)

Most revealing as illustration of the decline in rhetoric's status, even among its teachers, is Smith's strong distinction between "two Sorts of Discourse: the Didactick and the Rhetoricall":

> The former proposes to put before us the arguments on both sides of the question *in their true light*, giving each its proper degree of influence, and has it in view to perswade no farther than *the arguments themselves appear convincing.* [A good summary of listening-rhetoric, but for him the opposite of rhetoric.] The Rhetoricall again endeavours by all means to perswade us; and for this purpose it *magnifies all the arguments on the one side and diminishes or conceals those that might be brought on the side conterary* [*sic*] *to that which it is designed that we should favour. Persuasion which is the primary design in the Rhetoricall is but the secondary design in the Didactick.* (p. 62) . . . When we propose to persuade at all events, and for this purpose adduce those arguments that make for the side we have espoused, and magnify these to the utmost of our power; and on the other hand *make light of and extenuate all those which may be brought on the other side*, then we make use of the Rhetoricall Stile. (p. 89; my italics)

Thus the young man, whose lectures reveal an amazing knowledge of every conceivable rhetorical move, echoes all the other scholars who saw it as serving other ends than the search for truth, even while being indispensable.

A similar example of a major professional rhetorician downplaying rhetorical terminology is Giambattista Vico. Earning his living as a teacher of rhetoric, and writing a good deal about it, he made his justified fame with *Scienza Nuova* (1725). Working to establish a new science that escapes the trap of Descartes's quest for certainty, Vico sees the revival as centered in poetry and aesthetics. Though his work is loaded with speculation obviously derived from his rhetorical training, rhetorical terms are again seen as largely irrelevant.[8]

It is hardly surprising, then, that by the end of that century, the requirement that all students study rhetoric had almost disappeared, both in England and America, except in some departments of Speech and Classics and some preparatory courses in writing and speaking. Attention to it did continue to flourish for a while in Scotland and on the continent, and textbooks for introductory courses continued to sell for a long time. And some scholars, like Richard Whately and Richard Claverhouse Jebb, continued to do serious scholarly inquiry into the nature and value of rhetoric.[9]

In musical studies, especially in Germany, rhetoric survived a bit longer.[10] Nevertheless, although inquiry into rhetorical issues was still alive almost everywhere under other terms, it soon came to be seen as what my opening anecdote (p. vii) revealed: a "field" to be automatically dismissed.[11]

We will never have a full picture of the forces that wiped out official rhetorical studies. Historians have speculated about widely different causes, and as I now list some of them, I warn you to be skeptical; only the first three seem to me unquestionable. (Some of them may actually have been more the *effects* than the causes. Cultural trends that develop simultaneously can never be distinguished clearly as cause or effect.)[12]

Scientism

The genuine triumphs of science inevitably raised hopes that the path to *all* truth had now been found. Of course nobody denied that even brilliant scientists had to have training in how to write well, to promote their discoveries. And some scientists still pursued the possibility of reconciliation between scientific methods of thought and rhetorical methods, especially in theological inquiry. But reductive positivists persuaded more and more followers to believe that scientific proof was the *only* form of genuine reasoning. Scientists were on *the* path to genuine knowledge, while all other pursuers of knowledge depended on flimsy decorations.[13]

Secularist Humanism

As science invaded more and more of life's territories, religion found itself on the defensive, employing arguments and methods that scientists had proved did not yield real knowledge. (I address the current significance of this conflict in chapter 8.) Though no secularist ever escaped reliance on rhetorical resources, many came to hope for a time when that escape would be possible.

Reductionism

A powerful reinforcement of that hope was the "scientistic" reduction of truth from generalities or universals to particularities: facts, data. Instead of trying to "reason down" from the top, like Plato and other naive philosophers, we must "reason up" inductively. Occam's razor – the law of parsimony – became for some almost a divine commandment. Since the principle of simplifying had indeed accomplished wonders when applied rigorously to some parts of the natural world, it should be applied everywhere. There are still many scientists who claim – openly using the term reduction – that all genuine truth will finally be found to depend on how physical particles interrelate. What role could rhetoric possibly play in that quest – except in arguing for its superiority?

Logicism

Some notions of solid argument erected logic, *logos*, as the only method for pursuing truth, whether in science or philosophy. The word "proof" was granted narrower and narrower scope. Philosophers increasingly sought conclusions totally, independently demonstrable; their task was to promulgate truth that even a logician as rigorous as Gottlob Frege could not question. So logicians joined physical scientists in tossing pathos and ethos and even dialogue (*dia-logos*) into the garbage can.

Individualism

Following authors like Rousseau, increasing numbers saw the goal of life as the discovery of one's true, "natural" self; "To hell with all those other 'others' who simply complicate my search. What counts is me, my motives, my soul." Some forms of romanticism – though by no means all – reinforced forms of individualism that simply dismissed the importance of building trustful *communication communities*.[14] Stop attempting to listen to those "others": learn how to listen to your own deepest, truest, inner Self. What can rhetorical studies teach you about that?

Historical Determinism

Many historians, influenced by these other causes, became more and more addicted to deterministic views: what happens now, or next, is totally dependent on everything that has happened before, not on any rhetoric that happens to emerge about it now. The way this doctrine was promulgated reveals – paradoxically – the power of human expression. Notions of determinism were embraced in the face of everyone's everyday experience of its falsity. We *all* know from daily experience that what is said right now *does* help to create the conditions – the reality – of right now; an apology can defuse social tension *right now*, while an insult can create more tension. A coach who restores an athlete's self-confidence with one timely word of praise can change the athlete's behavior right now. Yet the idea of historical determinism became for many far more credible than the notion that what they say *changes* reality. (Any determinist would reply to my point here: "What that coach said was determined by history up to that moment. You are caught in your own trap!")

32

Though many thinkers these days recognize, following Karl Popper's lead, that historical determinism is "poverty-stricken," until recently many of them have offered, as their escape, some form of "logic of investigation" pushing in the direction of scientism.

Rhetoric is of course totally unable to supply anything approaching a history-free form of inquiry: every step of any rhetorician is embedded in questions like "Just who is speaking? Who is in the audience? What are the norms of discourse in that discourse community?" But various forms of "prosopography" or "cliometrics" have assumed a kind of "implanted motivism" that would render pointless the study of what rhetors said or wrote; they were determined by forces already there. Thus they move toward joining the branch of scientism embraced by some cultural materialists and the more extreme evolutionists. Though no responsible evolutionist says these days that "it's *all* nature; no nurture," a surprising number still write as if they believe it can all be reduced to the history of the genes.

We could add the following to these superficial speculations about the causes (or effects):

- Some forms of aestheticism – art for art's sake, "poetry makes nothing happen" and it therefore makes rhetorical study irrelevant.
- What might be called "psychologism" (tied closely to individualism) probably contributed to the fall. Over the years some have argued that psychoanalysis should seek the causes of human behavior only in internal subconscious forces, so rhetoric has no role in producing internal change. (This position ignores the way in which my internal dialogues among my diverse selves depend on rhetorical resources.)
- Excessive versions of economic determinism: rhetoric has nothing to do with the vast daily changes produced by commerce and the stock market.
- Perhaps most powerfully, the routine pedantic teaching of rhetorical codes and terms – memorizing textbooks while

33

ignoring the excitement of listening-rhetoric (LR). Compagnon sees this as a major cause of the decline in France.

- Some have seen democracy itself as one cause of the fall. If the future depends on the sheer number of voters, voting out of self-interest, what's the point of cultivating elitist rhetorical reasoning?

What is rhetoric's status now? Even after our recent flowering very few would paint Rhetorica again as a king or queen waving a sword of power, surrounded by mostly unconscious worshippers like Darwin, Wittgenstein, and Einstein; by T. S. Eliot and W. H. Auden and Emily Dickinson; by Virginia Woolf and Tolstoy; by Winston Churchill and Eleanor Roosevelt and more recent leaders; by every philosopher and sociologist and political scientist. Most academics today will no doubt scoff at the portrayal of Rhetorica. Yet if we take the flowering seriously, and the broader definitions I have suggested, could we not imagine a revival of that metaphor of royal dominance? Rhetoric, when defined as our daily communication, dominates almost every moment of our lives (as I have already said perhaps too many times), and thus rhetorical *studies*, traveling with diverse passports, are essential in all fields.

Should the undeniable flowering lead to optimism about the future? I hope so, but most references to rhetoric that I meet, in and out of the academy, still echo the recent charge against the president and his opponents: "That talk was all rhetoric, with no substance."

Appendix

The following titles openly addressing rhetoric are still a gross reduction from the thousands in the flowering of the past half century. To save space I've offered only one title in each field, though in some there could be dozens. The University of Wisconsin Press has published, in its "Rhetoric of the Human Science" series, more than a score of books concentrating on rhetoric – but with fewer than half of the titles actually mentioning rhetoric.

Most on the list are explicitly labeled "The Rhetoric OF X." You will probably find your field of interest in capitals, down through the alphabetical list.

The Rhetoric of ABOLITION, ed. Ernest G. Bormann, 1971.

The Rhetoric of Struggle: Public Address by AFRICAN-AMERICAN WOMEN, ed. Robbie Jean Walker, 1992.

The Social Use of Metaphor: Essays on the ANTHROPOLOGY of Rhetoric, ed. J. David Sapir and J. Christopher Crocker, 1977.

Rhetoric of ART, Jorge Glusberg, 1986.

BIBLE. See NEW TESTAMENT.

Rhetoric of [the] BLACK REVOLUTION, Arthur L. Smith, 1969.

Blindness and Insight: Essays in the Rhetoric of CONTEMPORARY CRITICISM, Paul De Man, 1971. (I resist the strong temptation to list my own works.)

The Rhetoric of COURTSHIP in Elizabethan Language and Literature, Catherine Bates, 1992.

Oral History and Delinquency: The Rhetoric of CRIMINOLOGY, James Bennett, 1981.

DEAF EMPOWERMENT: Emergence, Struggle, and Rhetoric, Katherine A. Jankowski, 1997.

Thought and Character: The Rhetoric of DEMOCRATIC EDUCATION, Frederick J. Antczak, 1979. (See PEDAGOGY.)

Rhetoric and the Arts of DESIGN, David S. Kaufer, 1996.

Selling the Free Market: The Rhetoric of ECONOMIC CORRECTNESS, James Arnt Aune, 2001.

The Rhetoric of ECONOMICS, Deirdre (Don) McCloskey, 2nd ed., 1998.

Contesting Cultural Rhetorics: Public Discourse and EDUCATION, Margaret J. Marshall, 1995. (If we think of all the synonyms for education, this category would probably have the largest number of recent works.)

The Rhetoric of ELECTRONIC COMMUNITIES, Tharon W. Howard, 1997.

ETHICS and Rhetoric: Classical Essays for Donald Russell on His Seventy-Fifth Birthday, ed. Doreen Innes, Harry Hine, and Christopher Pelling, 1995.

The Rhetoric of EXISTENCE, Miguel de Unamuno, 1967.

FEMINIST Rhetorical Theories, Karen A. Foss, 1999.

The Rhetoric of FICTION in Defoe's "Robinson Crusoe" (and other texts), Colloquium of Toulouse, 1992.

The Rhetoric of FILM, John Harrington, 1973.

Seduction and Theory: Readings of GENDER, REPRESENTATION and Rhetoric, ed. Dianne Hunter, 1989.

Rhetoric and HERMENEUTICS in Our Time, ed. Walter Jost and Michael Hyde, 1997.

The Rhetoric of HISTORY and the History of Rhetoric: On Hayden White's Tropes, Arnaldo Momigliano, 1987.

The Rhetoric of IMAGISM, In the Arresting Eye, John T. Gage, 1981.

INFORMATION TECHNOLOGY and Organizational Transformation: History, Rhetoric, and Practice, ed. Joanne Yates and John Van Maanen, 2001.

(Where is JOURNALISM? There are many "rhetorics of journalism," but I'm surprised to find none with that title. Journalists still avoid the word except when referring to cheap persuasion tactics. See MEDIA below.)

The Rhetoric of LAW, ed. Austin Sarat and Thomas R. Kearns, 1994.

Legal Discourse: Studies in LINGUISTICS, Rhetoric, and Legal Analysis, Peter Goodrich, 1987.

LITERATURE as Revolt and Revolt as Literature: Three Studies in the Rhetoric of NON-ORATORICAL FORMS, Edwin Black, 1970.

Landmark Essays in Rhetoric and LITERATURE, ed. Craig Kallendorf, 1999.

The Rhetoric of LOVE in the Collected Poems of William Carlos Williams, ed. Cristina Giorcelli and Maria Anita Stefanelli, 1993.

The Rhetoric of the Contemporary LYRIC, Jonathan Holden, 1980.

Ragged Dicks: MASCULINITY, Steel, and the Rhetoric of the Self-Made Man, James V. Catano, 2001.

MEDIA Rhetoric as Social Drama, Thomas Farrell, 1984.

Theophrastean Studies: On Natural Science, Physics, and METAPHYSICS, ETHICS, RELIGION, and Rhetoric, ed. William W. Fortenbaugh and Robert W. Sharples, 1986.

Richard Selzer and the Rhetoric of SURGERY [MEDICINE], Charles M. Anderson, 1989.

Rethinking the History of Rhetoric: MULTIDISCIPLINARY Essays on the Rhetorical Tradition, ed. Takis Poulakos, 1993.

Phrasing and Articulation: A Contribution to a Rhetoric of MUSIC, with 152 musical examples, Hans Keller, 1965.

NATIVE AMERICAN DISCOURSE: Poetics and Rhetoric, ed. Joel Sherzer and Anthony C. Woodbury, 1987.

The Rhetoric of the NEW TESTAMENT, Burton L. Mack, 1990.

Rhetoric of Purity: Essentialist Theory and the Advent of Abstract PAINTING, Mark A. Cheetham, 1991.

Reclaiming PEDAGOGY: The Rhetoric of the Classroom, ed. Patricia Donahue and Ellen Quandahl, 1989.

The Critical Turn: Rhetoric and PHILOSOPHY IN POSTMODERN DISCOURSE, ed. Ian Angus and Lenore Langsdorf, 1993.

(Note: No title found in the form, The Rhetoric *of* Philosophy, except for I. A. Richards's *The Rhetoric of Philosophy*, clear back in 1936!)

Rhetoric and POETICS, Jeffrey Walker, 2000. (And there are of course many works that deal with the interrelationship, such as Kenneth Burke's *Language as Symbolic Action*, 1966.)

Conflict and Rhetoric in French POLICYMAKING, Frank R. Baumgartner, 1989.

POLITICAL PHILOSOPHY and Rhetoric: A Study of the Origins of American PARTY POLITICS, John Zvesper, 1977.

Macbeth and the Rhetoric of the Unconscious: An Experiment in PSYCHOANA- LYTIC CRITICISM, Lynda Bundtzen, 1972.

American Dissent from Thomas Jefferson to César Chavez: The Rhetoric of REFORM AND REVOLUTION, ed. Thomas E. Hachey and Ralph E. Weber, 1981.

Reasoning and Rhetoric in RELIGION, Nancy Murphy, 1994.

Reading Empirical Research Studies: The Rhetoric of RESEARCH, ed. John R. Hayes et al., 1992.

The Rhetoric of ROMANTICISM, Paul de Man, 1984.

Landmark Essays on the Rhetoric of SCIENCE: Case Studies, ed. RandyAllen Harris, 1997.

Loyola's Acts: The Rhetoric of the SELF, Marjorie Boyle, 1997.

Visual Rhetoric and SEMIOTICS, Edward Trigg, 1992.

The Rhetoric of SEXUALITY and the Literature of the Renaissance, Lawrence Kritzman, 1991.

A Rhetoric of SILENCE, and Other Selected Writings, Lisa Block de Behar, 1995.

Readings on the Rhetoric of SOCIAL PROTEST, ed. Charles E. Morris III and Stephen H. Browne, 2001.

Rhetoric in SOCIOLOGY, Ricca Edmondson, 1984.

Philosophy, Rhetoric, and the End of Knowledge: The Coming of Science and TECHNOLOGY Studies, Steve Fuller, 1993.

The Rhetoric of TELEVISION, Ronald Primeau, 1979.

The Rhetoric of TERRORISM and COUNTERTERRORISM, Richard W. Leeman, 1991.

Modern Drama and the Rhetoric of THEATER, William B. Worthen, 1986, 1992.

Rhetoric and THEOLOGY: The Hermeneutic of Erasmus, Manfred Hoffmann, 1994.

Control and Consolation in American Culture and Politics: Rhetoric of THERAPY, Dana L. Cloud, 1998.

The Rhetoric of TRAGEDY: Form in Stuart Drama, Charles O. McDonald, 1966.

Rhetoric of WAR: Language, Argument, and Policy During the Vietnam War, Harvey A. Averch, 2002.

3

Judging Rhetoric

Rhetoric is the science of speaking well, the education of the Roman gentleman, both useful and a virtue.

Quintilian

Knowing what is good does not by itself tell us what to do. . . . Aristotle's Rhetoric points to a complexity in the diversity of goods [leading to] incommensurability. Because of the difference between what is good and what I should do, a given rhetorical argument and plea within one kind cannot be translated automatically into another genre. Overall, what is just, noble, and useful coincide, but each has its own kind of surplus that resists translation.

Eugene Garver

No critical judgments can be more complicated than trying to distinguish good rhetoric from bad. We all make those judgments daily, hourly; you may be at this very moment criticizing my use of "complicated," since you prefer "threatening" or "hopeless" or "puzzling." I am (or rather, I was, a long time before you encountered these word-choices) wrestling with what makes the best rhetorical maneuver in opening this chapter. One rhetorician-friend labeled a previous opening "lousy, uninviting." And so I scrapped that one, along with three other possible openings.

Most such judgments seem, on first thought, to have nothing to do with ethics. In what sense, if any, are my choices here related to ethics? Since I obviously want to keep you engaged, are not your judgments about my choices simply judgments of method and skill, not of ethics?

As I say "no" to that tough question, I land us into territory too often avoided even by committed students of rhetoric. And that landing is what has led many positivists to rule out rhetoric from genuine inquiry: whenever ethics intrudes, objectivity disappears.

My claim that ethical judgments inevitably intrude even on our judgments of technique applies to all three of the traditional rhetorical kinds – deliberative, forensic, and epideictic. It also applies to every rhetorical domain, broad or narrow. (Some prefer the term "moral"; that term can be misleading, because many see it as referring only to some narrow fixed code. "Ethical" explodes outward into the whole domain of effects on ethos, on character or personality.)

If you look closely at attacks on rhetoric, you will frequently find explicit ethical judgments, sometimes with explicit use of moral terms. "This rhetoric is just plain immoral: the speaker is cheating, lying, manipulating, deliberately distorting." Such judgments of rhetrickery are implicit in the definitions of *good* rhetoric we've encountered so far; defensible rhetoric both depends on and builds justified trust. It portrays or implies admirable ethos in the rhetor, and thus it helps to create it in the audience.[1] Indeed all of the favorable definitions, including mine, could almost be reduced to a flat commandment:

> It is ethically wrong to pursue or rely on or deliberately produce misunderstanding, while it is right to pursue understanding. To pursue deception creates non-communities in which winner-takes-all. To pursue mutual understanding creates communities in which everyone needs and deserves attention.

Like all "commandments" claiming to cover every corner of our lives, this one clearly presents choices that are as complex as the whole of life. Those who subscribe to it will encounter what all commandment-obeyers encounter: disagreement about how to interpret it. What constitutes understanding? Which roads for pursuing it are effective and which threaten to victimize those who are understood? And so on.

Even for some rhetoricians, especially in recent decades, ethical distinctions are irrelevant: quality is judged solely according to technical skill. For them, if a slave-owner and an abolitionist are arguing, in 1850, the quality of their rhetoric has nothing to do with whether slavery is *really* a vile human practice. It is just a question of whether the rhetoric is performed well. "Even if we think Harriet Beecher Stowe's *Uncle Tom's Cabin* is just or unjust in its treatment of slavery," they would say, "we can't praise or blame her narrative rhetoric because of that. Surely we should not say to any rhetor: 'Because I agree with your cause, and know that you *know* that your cause is just, you are a fine rhetorician.'"

In such a view, even if we know the rhetor is insincere, that knowledge has nothing to do with the quality of the rhetoric. Even if we are sure — as most are by now (mid-year 2004) — that President Bush and his advisers knew that the evidence for Iraq's weapons of mass destruction (WMD) was shoddy, why should their cheating affect our judgment of the *rhetorical* skill they exhibited as they brilliantly succeeded in persuading Americans that preemptive attack was essential to national security?

This neutralist argument is by no means stupid, if we mistakenly think of rhetoric not as a path to truth but as mere decorator of truth or lies. Most who argue for any one cause believe in it as firmly as I believe that slavery is an evil, and their rhetoric reveals their convictions. At this moment when you are reading here, millions of quarrelers (we can confidently predict) are shouting slanderous, self-righteous rhetrickery at their enemies, convinced in their hearts that their cause is uniquely just, or even holy. If I find myself on their side, should that shift my judgment about whether their rhetorical strokes are praiseworthy?

The problem is thus that in judging rhetoric we can never fully escape our own deepest convictions. As we examine any rhetorical move, it will probably seem better or worse according to our own judgment about the case being made. Of course we will often find people on "our side" employing rhetorical moves that we deplore, and people on the opposite side employing rhetorical moves that we consider clever. But the fact remains that in criticizing rhetoric, in advising about it, in trying to educate about its good and bad forms, we cannot ignore the influence of our beliefs about what is ethical. The speaker's presumed basic intention must have some effect on our judgment of the good or bad *in that domain*. A practice that is absolutely justified in one situation may prove contemptible in another. And this requires that all of our judgments be considered in the light of the particular rhetorical domain.

Does that claim mean that ethical judgments are irrelevant or inevitably untrustworthy? Are you surprised to hear me answer, "Absolutely not!"? My claim is that the worst consequences of the widespread neglect of rhetorical studies are our failures to detect deliberate deception. Is the rhetor being honest, fair, forthright? Or dishonest, self-seeking, or even intending harm?

Every critic's attempt to answer such a question is complicated by the fact that – to repeat – he or she is influenced by ethical convictions. Most readers from America, for example, will believe, as they study Thomas Jefferson's draft of our Declaration of Independence, that it exhibits not just brilliant technical rhetoric, but methods and purposes totally defensible on ethical grounds: it is a presentation of all the *good* reasons why we should break free from the "wicked" British. Jefferson was totally sincere, we can assume. On the other hand, most British readers, especially back in 1776, would surely find many of his arguments not just shaky but scandalous, making unfair, even dishonest claims against the enemy. Yet if two thoughtful rhetoricians today, one from America and one from England, analyze the speech together, they can easily agree in their judgment of the quality of *most* of Jefferson's moves: he is honestly pursuing a cause he believes in, and he makes many defensible charges. But even now they will find points of strong disagreement about this or that rhetorical move. Then, if the two practice a bit of rhetorology, they will surely find a good deal of common ground underlying the differences. At the end, however, they will not be able to divorce

42

completely their judgment of the entire rhetorical endeavor from whether they think the American Revolution was a splendid reality created by that honest rhetoric.

Underlying such complexities lies one useful distinction in that word "honest": is the rhetor attempting to achieve an end she believes will be harmful to her listeners, or one she honestly believes will prove beneficial? *Skillful* rhetoric works either way, often with the tragic consequences that have given rhetoric such a bad name. Fully *defensible* rather than deceptive rhetoric is what we mainly depend on for daily survival.

As you trace the following three kinds of rhetoric – actually broken into ten sub-kinds and distinguished according to both skill and intentions – keep in mind the ways in which awareness of the distinctions is important, for both the rhetor and the audience. It is not just that defensible rhetors practice the good kinds; effective listeners know how to protect themselves from skillful but unethical rhetrickery.

1 "Win-Rhetoric" (WR)

What the Greeks labeled *eristic*: the intent to win at all costs, whether honorable or dishonorable. As in war, victory is essential, regardless of what must be sacrificed.

WR-a – the honest kind: My goal is to win because I know that my cause, my case, my convictions are, like Jefferson's, right, my opponent's cause absolutely wrong, and my methods will be totally sincere and honest.

Skillful win-rhetoric will obviously be judged good whenever the critic considers the cause unquestionably defensible, or at least sincerely embraced. We judge Winston Churchill's famous war speeches as great both because of their skill and because we share his cause. We "know" that winning support for the fight against

Hitler was a noble cause, and we can thus add to Churchill's skill in rhetorical moves the rightness of his cause and his sincerity as he pursued it. Only if we found hard evidence that his only true motive was to become known as the greatest of all prime ministers would we have reason to change our judgment from "top prize" to "both brilliant and dubious."

WR-b: Since my cause is absolutely justified I will win at all costs, including the cost of integrity, if necessary.

The rhetor is willing to employ false evidence or misleading arguments to make his or her case. The critic here must again distinguish between two judgments: about the skill and about the ethics. Here we move toward the kind of rhetrickery that a columnist recently attributed to President George W. Bush: "The Bush rhetoric technique – of implying one thing while doing quite another." Bush had made up his mind long ago that he would attack Iraq, but he persistently said he was still deciding. And he persistently joined those on his staff determined to exaggerate the evidence about Saddam's threat.

WR-c: I know that my cause is unjust, but winning will be profitable to me, and I'm so skillful that nobody will realize my deceptions: I will employ rhetrickery that appears to be honest.

The critic here can judge whether the rhetorical methods are brilliant or skillful or clumsy, while condemning the moves entirely on ethical grounds. Rhetorically skillful defense lawyers often find themselves practicing WR-c, sometimes feeling miserable about it. A lawyer friend of mine, after some years defending criminals whom she knew were guilty, finally shifted to the prosecution side. When I asked her if on that side she again found herself often arguing for a case she thought false, she blushed and refused to answer.

It is the identification of all rhetoric with the last two versions of win-rhetoric that contributes to the dominance of pejorative labels for it. The prominence of WR-c is especially worrisome. When the tobacco companies' ads conceal the *known* disastrous harm, both the cause and the methods are indefensible, even when the techniques are extraordinarily clever.

2   Bargain-Rhetoric (BR)

Here the intent is to pursue diplomacy, mediate, find a truce.

BR-a: I want to avoid violence by achieving productive compromise. (Sometimes called "dialogic" in contrast to "agonistic.")

Most critics will offer the judgment "good rhetoric" if the result pursued is an "accord" considered genuinely good by both sides, not merely a sell-out. When Nelson Mandela managed to avoid open warfare in South Africa, most of us saw it as a stupendous triumph of bargain-rhetoric, though of course only rhetoricians even mentioned any such term. Whenever a seller and buyer finally agree on a price that satisfies both, bargain-rhetoric has worked.[2] At its best, this is sometimes labeled "win-win rhetoric." Business advisers like Stephen Covey have made fortunes with their advice about how to "succeed" by employing win-win rhetoric.

BR-b: I will compromise even if I know that the result is evil. I won't stand up to the enemy.

Bargain-rhetoric will be judged bad when the accord or truce leaves the opponent triumphing. Most of us would judge Prime Minister Chamberlain's rhetoric highly questionable as he "achieved" the Munich Accord. We now know, as only a minority knew then, that almost everything Chamberlain said was misleading, whether he was employing sincere arguments or was consciously relying on rhetrickery.

BR-c: I want to bargain but I don't know how to do it; I'll simply say yes, while concealing my actual hopes.

Bargain-rhetoric will be judged bad, whether the cause is right or wrong, if the methods, the arguments, the style, are weak and the true purpose concealed or abandoned. Back in March of 2003, the bargain-rhetoric – or lack of it – of both the American administration and Saddam Hussein and his ministers was extremely clumsy, and would be judged so by any perceptive critic, whether for or against the US attack. Neither side was willing to settle down to genuine bargaining based on genuine listening. Even the efforts of some of Hussein's minions to bargain, as revealed in November 2003, were in a form totally unpersuasive to the "enemy." Though in my view the US leaders should have listened to the offer to back down long enough to decide whether it was authentic, there is no doubt that the surreptitious offer from Hussein's side was a clumsy one.

3   Listening–Rhetoric (LR)

I am not just seeking a truce; I want to pursue the truth behind our differences.

LR-a: I have reason to hope that my opponent here will respond to my invitation for both of us to engage in genuine listening.

The critic here should celebrate both disputants when both sides have genuinely addressed the opposing arguments, one or both moving – or trying to move – beyond original beliefs to some new version of the truth. They have *studied* the rhetoric intensively, on both sides, while practicing it. As will be clear throughout here, LR-a is what I most long to celebrate and practice – the kind that is sadly rare. At its deepest levels it deserves my coinage "rhetorology" – an even deeper probing for common ground. Here both sides join in a trusting dispute, determined to listen to the opponent's arguments, while persuading the opponent to listen in exchange. Each side attempts to *think* about the arguments presented by the other side. Neither side surrenders merely to be tactful or friendly. "If I finally embrace your cause, having been convinced that mine is wrong, it is only because your arguments, including your implied character and emotional demonstrations, have convinced me." Both sides are pursuing not just victory but a new reality, a new agreement about what is real.

LR-b: Though I am quite sure that my opponent is determined to ignore my case, I will listen to his, hoping to discover some way to engage him in genuine dialogue.

Our lives are plagued with rhetorical assaults from dogmatists who seem to be unshakably committed to an absolutely unquestionable cause. Encountering them, even the most passionate devotee of LR-a has only dim hope of discovering any common ground. But history shows that sometimes the effort to listen can pay off.

We turn now to forms of listening that raise deep ethical questions.

LR-c (a shoddy version of win-rhetoric): I know that only by listening closely to my opponent can I hope to outsmart her – and thus gain what I want, no matter what it costs her.

Every successful advertiser or salesman has learned to listen to the desires of the audience while too often ignoring their true interests. Obviously if the listener listens only in order to perform more effective rhetrickery – "Oh, yes, of course, I see now that this is the kind of guy who can be sucked in with an AD for SUVs that proves SUV owners to be superior to Toyota drivers" – listening becomes unethical intrusion. The victim has every right to respond, "You listened closely to my arguments and character only in order to manipulate me." The advertiser who conducts a poll of potential customers, determining how many are vulnerable to this or that deceptive appeal, lying about rival prices, about health effects, and so on, may raise sales by such "listening." The victim, once he discovers the fraud, has a right to sue. Under various terms – projection, intervention, empathy, sympathy, co-option – there has been endless debate about which forms of intrusion on the minds or souls of others are defensible: What right have I to claim that I have understood you better than you have understood me?

LR-d (what might be called "surrender-rhetoric" or "self-censorship"):
Unless I give in, and pretend to have been persuaded, I will suffer this or
that bad consequence – loss of job, of money, or even of life.

Every writer or speaker who has lived in a totalitarian society has faced the need to say only what the powers want to be said, totally violating one's own beliefs. (More about this below, and again in chapter 7.)

Perhaps the most troublesome problem is that on too many occasions listening is impossible – I'm too late, my case will be ignored, no matter how admirable. Facing a fundamentalist Mormon convinced that God has explicitly ordered a murder, my chances of calming him down by listening to his case are almost nil.[3] Nobody who happened to learn that Samson was planning his suicide "bombing" could have persuaded him, with LR, to listen to arguments against pulling down the pillars. Like present-day suicide terrorists, Samson knew that he was headed for the sanctification that followed his attack. In World War II, could any pilot ordered to perform a kamikaze attack have been talked out of it?[4] Only the most "dogmatic" LR devotee would at least make a stab at it. We might call that form

LR-e: I'll be so committed to my listening dogma that I will insist on it
even when I can see that the results will be disastrous, both for me and
for others.

In other words, when there is an immediate threat of violent destruction, one must choose either to surrender or practice violence. LR of productive kinds becomes hopeless; force or the threat of force or humble surrender must take over. (Total pacifists will, I assume, cringe at this notion of responding with violence.) Would I try to practice LR-a if I were on an airplane and encountered a terrorist with a box-cutter threatening me or the pilot? I would naturally *want* to be able to get him to listen to my case against his action. I might be tempted to *try* to get him to listen for a moment (if we spoke the same language) – perhaps to shout at him that he is harming his own cause. But would I attempt to listen to his defense for his own case, in the name of good rhetoric? Obviously not. Should Churchill and Roosevelt have said to Hitler, "Let's talk about it," just after Hitler took over Paris?

As I first drafted this section, in early March 2003, many were using this point as praise for President Bush's force-threatening rhetoric against Iraq; for them any form of LR with that devil, Hussein, would be stupid. As I tried to listen closely to such arguments, fearing the certainty of war, I could see why their case was not totally unreasonable, given their mistaken conviction that Saddam was threatening with WMD. "Saddam is obviously a cruel, world-threatening madman. Just look at his record. We've tried to reason with him, but he never listens. Our only alternative, with those who will not listen, is the threat of force, and then actual violence." But as I revise, in late 2003 and on through 2004, I wonder daily what kind of LR could have averted all this, and what kind might now be productive in addressing the increasing numbers of those who claim to hate us.

One of the saddest forms of LR-d comes when it is obviously impossible to fight back: either surrender and engage in self-censorship or die. "I must say what those with the power over me want me to say." J. M. Coetzee addresses this problem in *Giving Offense: Essays on Censorship* (1996).

> The Greek writer George Mangakis . . . records the experience of writing in prison under the eyes of his guards. Every few days the guards searched his cell, taking away his writings and returning those which the prison authorities – his censors – considered "permissible."

49

Mangakis recalls suddenly "loathing" his papers . . . : "The system is a diabolical device for annihilating your own soul. They want to make you see your thoughts through their eyes and control them yourself, from their point of view." (Quoted from p. 33 of *They Shoot Writers, Don't They?*[1984])

Coetzee rightly sees many forms of self-censorship as paranoia, "a pathology for which there may be no cure" (p. 36). Self-censorship in a concentration camp is one thing; it is much more questionable when the threat from above is not immediate annihilation but a lost job or accusation of disloyalty. Anyone attending to political rhetoric these days, as arriving through the media, knows that while on the one hand too many are *not* listening to the other side, on the other hand too many are simply listening and then practicing self-censorship that will echo what has been heard.

Facing all such "incurable" problems, what can we say about totally defensible, attentive LR-a? At its best it is the quest by the listener for some topics, *topoi*, warrants, to be shared with his or her opponent – agreements from which they can move as they probe their disagreements. It is the rhetor practicing rhetorology in the effort to discover, in the "other," some ground or platform where, as a community, they can move from *some* understanding toward *some* new territory. When both sides listen not just as rhetors but as *students* of the rhetoric on both sides, they can hope for a kind of diplomacy that goes further than a mere bargain or truce.

Self-Censorship vs. "Accommodation to Audience"

Perhaps the most challenging problem faced by anyone embracing LR and pursuing ethical distinctions is the fact that all effective rhetors must alter their rhetoric, at least to some degree, in order to "hit" the audience they *think* is there – whether or not they have actually "listened." Isn't that immoral? Shouldn't one say that the only honest rhetoric is the kind uttered in total sincerity by the rhetor, with no tricky self-censorship altering techniques or emotional appeals?

If we answer yes to that we are in trouble. No rhetorical effort can succeed if it fails to join in the beliefs and passions of the audience addressed, and that almost always requires some "accommodation," "adjustment," or "adaptation" to the audience's needs and expectations. Listening will be useless unless you let it change your rhetoric. From the Sophists and Aristotle on, all rhetoricians have stressed the necessity of accommodation to the audience: attention to the biases, beliefs, hopes and fears, emotional habits, and levels of comprehension about the subject. As Vico put it, "the end sought by eloquence always depends on the speaker's audience, and he must govern his speech in accordance with their opinions." Baltasar Gracian says that effective speech is "like a feast, at which the dishes are made to please the guests, and not the cooks."[5]

It is true that the methods used for different audiences will often overlap. If Winston Churchill had found himself addressing an American audience in 1940, urging us to join England against the Nazis, some of his strokes would have resembled those he employed in his "blood, sweat, and tears" talk in England. The actual talk, however, would have had to be surprisingly different, taking into account his picture of who "we" might be. Back home, as he talked to Parliament and to the French, he played up, perhaps even a bit dishonestly, his expectations that America was ready to join in the cause, even though he had serious doubts about our joining. Would such dishonest accommodation have to be judged as unjustified? Is that kind of accommodation ethical or unethical?[6]

The answer obviously depends on just how much is accommodated and in what way the spinning or self-censorship is performed. If everyone assumed that to be sincere a speaker must sound exactly the same for all audiences on all occasions, our social world would collapse. We depend, in all of our exchanges, on what might be called "putting on masks": enacting, for *this* audience, a projected ethos that would never work on *that* audience. Every rhetor must choose from among the diverse "personae" that might be projected.

A speaker who feels today so angry about her opponent that she is tempted to violence may find, in addressing that opponent tomorrow, an absolute "command" to suppress the anger in order to win her point. A husband who hated a judge deciding his divorce case would be foolish to reveal that hatred honestly in the courtroom.

So the boundary between defensible accommodation and waffling, catering, sucking-up, shoddy spinning, or plain unforgivable lying is always hard to draw. But all major rhetoricians have argued that what is clearly unethical is to repudiate your main points or deepest beliefs solely for the purpose of winning an audience. Speaker and listener may thus in a sense join, and this looks like success. But when the cause won violates the speaker's own deepest convictions, the listener becomes a dupe and the speaker becomes a winning hypocrite.

On the other side, the speaker who thinks only of his or her true beliefs and proclaims them, without thinking about how to accommodate to a given audience, will usually fail. Such totally *un*accommodating "sincerity," supporting your one true cause at all costs, can certainly be defended in some circumstances. "Speaking out," "blurting out," rejecting self-censorship may even be considered noble if the speaker is, say, about to be executed by a Nazi. In our fictions, honest blurting is one of the most widely employed signs of true "character": heroes and heroines are created by portraying total sincerity. Whistle-blowers, revealing the misbehavior of their superiors, are heroes of the media – in my view rightly so, at least when they are telling the truth. But if any nation's leaders refused to "accommodate" to particular audiences on particular occasions, they would soon fail, and they would often harm the nation.

None of this should make us doubt that the distinction between justified and unjustified accommodation, though fuzzy, is real. My favorite example of totally defensible rhetoric was Edmund Burke's effort to persuade Parliament and the king to pursue conciliation with the American colonies. He knew that to oppose what England was doing in America was likely to harm him, politically. But he chose to speak out. His unsuccessful but soon famous speeches "On American Taxation" (1774) and "On Conciliation with the

Colonies" (March 22, 1775) were wonderfully skillful and defensible according to any standard I can imagine. The second speech, much more passionate in urging conciliation than the first, is one of the most ethically admirable political speeches in history. Accommodating to his audience as much as honesty allowed, he urged Parliament to consider diverse ways of listening to the colonists' case, to think themselves into the colonial situation, and thus to cancel absurd tax laws and pursue conciliation. He thus presented a case that later became famous, not just in America where it seemed to support our case, but also in England. It was considered by almost every critic as first-class rhetoric, partly because readers knew that Burke knew that he was risking personal harm.

If his rhetoric had been fully attended to and his advice followed, it might even have reversed America's fight for independence – with consequences we can never pin down. But his pleas were easily rejected, not by excellent opposing rhetoric but by the unshakable biases of the king and the Tories. As E. J. Payne put the case for Burke's greatness,[7] "Nowhere else . . . is there to be found so admirable a view of the causes which produced the American Revolution as in these two speeches. They both deserve to be studied with the utmost diligence by every American scholar."[8]

And they should be studied by everyone who thinks that good rhetoric is mere winning, even when the victory requires violating your deepest beliefs. Burke knew that he was treading on dangerous territory, but his passion for the good of the nation and for the truth of the current situation drove him to a great rhetorical moment. His effort to win not just immediate success but success for a just and true cause was in one sense a grotesque failure. Winning our admiration over the centuries was an unquestionable rhetorical victory.

Unethical accommodation – betraying one's basic convictions or the welfare of the audience – can often yield impressive political victory. But it becomes disastrous whenever an audience discovers that the rhetor has violated what he said yesterday before a rival audience. Such embarrassing discoveries of shoddy accommodation

53

were much less likely centuries ago than they are today, with our elaborate media recording.

But the increased likelihood of being caught doesn't seem to reduce the practice. Excessive accommodation plagues almost every political scene, almost every commercial decision, and far too many judgments by academic administrators. The rhetors openly violate their true beliefs, in order to gain support from this or that voting group or authority or donor or Board of Trustees. Whether or not they are *technically* skillful orators, they argue for conclusions that they think the audience wants, not for what they personally believe. Unlike Burke, they want to win at *all* costs, including loss of personal integrity, or predictable harm to the city or nation or world. (Am I suggesting that if I had been in the situation of Osip Mandelstam, in a Soviet prison, commanded to write a poem honoring Stalin, I would have flatly refused, choosing death? I doubt it; I would have given in and "composed an adulatory ode.")[9]

None of this widespread cheating contradicts the basic rhetorical principle: all good rhetoric depends on the rhetor's *listening to and thinking about the character and welfare of the audience*, and moderating what is said to meet what has been heard. To repeat again: the good rhetor answers the audience's questions before they're asked.

Such rhetorology may sound like a purely academic practice of LR, but I hope that non-academic readers here will see its universal relevance. In a world where win-rhetoric of the thoughtless or vicious kind seems to triumph more and more, from top politicians and CEOs down to the talk shows, and where too much LR produces nothing better than self-censorship, the training of everyone to pursue critically the defensible kinds of rhetoric is one of our best hopes for saving the world – or at least this or that corner of it.

4

Some Major Rescuers

While in the presence of others, the individual typically infuses his activity with signs which dramatically highlight and portray confirmatory facts that might otherwise remain unapparent or obscure.

Erving Goffman, *The Presentation of Self in Everyday Life*

All argumentation aims at gaining the adherence of minds, and, by this very fact, assumes the existence of an intellectual contact.

Chaim Perelman

We need a new architectonic, productive art. Rhetoric exercised such functions in the Roman republic and in the Renaissance. Rhetoric provides the devices by which to determine the characteristics and problems of our times and to form the art by which to guide actions for the solution of our problems and the improvement of our circumstances.

Richard McKeon

Traditionally, the key term for rhetoric is not "identification" but "persuasion." . . . [But that] classical notion of clear persuasive intent is not an accurate fit for describing the ways in which the members of a group promote social cohesion by acting rhetorically upon themselves and one another.

Kenneth Burke

This chapter celebrates a small selection from the host of thinkers, mainly in the twentieth century, who have labored to rescue the study of rhetorical issues and methods. Many of them do not employ rhetorical terms. All of them, however, are in my view "rhetoricians" deserving much closer attention. Though none of them would reject the achievements produced by the scientific revolution over the centuries, all of them have attempted serious criticism of various positivisms which that revolution produced: the separation of know-ledge/rationality/proof from the resources of argument that rhetoric (and life) provide.

Before tracing the topics that were downgraded or totally cast out by the positivists, and then at least partially rescued, I must further dramatize the still neglected question of why even the most "hard-proof" thinkers can never escape rhetoric.

The most obvious reason is their everyday dependence on it. From birth onward, even the most dogmatic positivists had learned hour by hour a great deal about their dependence on rhetoric. When they were first learning to listen and speak, their parents and siblings and friends were in effect nagging them daily about how to do it all better – often without *explicit* advice. Their daily successes and failures to get the responses they wanted from others had taught them moment by moment some fundamentals about just which efforts to communi-cate work and which do not. Then in their school years, they were all taught, as you and I were, at least a few more of the essentials. Unlike most students these days, most of the older generations even had teachers who actually used rhetorical terms. Thus even the most rigorous of the converts to scientific methods and positivistic theories had from the beginning learned how to employ rhetoric day by day, while sharing the need to do it better and better. Even as they learned indubitable facts early, such as $2 + 2 = 4$, the earth is not flat, the sun does not rotate the earth, they also learned that there are better and worse ways to present and dwell on those facts, depending on one's audience.

The strongest claims about the irrelevance to *genuine* knowledge of all that rhetorical learning came from various domains of science. Soon labeled "positivism," by Saint-Simon and Auguste Comte, positivism in diverse contrasting forms rapidly took over more and more of the intellectual world, with many believing that "science is

56

the only valid knowledge and facts the only possible objects of knowledge."[1] Some, like Comte, did acknowledge that we cannot escape thinking about emotions, ethics, and religion. But for most, pursuing truth leaves all that behind.

If you are at all tempted by such a claim, just pick up any book in the science section of your bookstore and read any paragraph, flagging words or phrases that offer no empirically testable facts and instead rely on rhetorical resources. Does it employ, or at least hint at, emotional engagement in the cause (*pathos*)?[2] How does the prose imply the author's trustworthy character (*ethos*)? Does the text rely on trusted authorities, named or unnamed? Does it depend on taken-for-granted commonplaces (shared unprovable *topoi* or "warrants")? Does it employ *enthymemes* rather than full syllogisms? Does it employ some metaphor or analogy or other figure of speech or technical resource? Perhaps you should just read a bit of Einstein and ask, "Why did he use so many analogies, and then place the train analogy *here* and the elevator analogy *there*?"

The dependence is most obvious when scientists are addressing readers not in their own narrow research domain. When the distinguished biologist Ernst Mayr addressed a broad audience, including many of us non-biologists, with the book *This is Biology: The Science of the Living World* (1997), almost every paragraph was full of such expressions as "One of the most wonderful aspects of development is . . ." and sentences like "Nor do I know of a single reputable living biologist who supports straightforward vitalism." Science? No. That is effective rhetoric.

The impossibility of escape is much more striking when we look at "strictly scientific" papers addressed to fellow scientists. Consider the famous essay on the double helix by James D. Watson and Francis Crick: two pages that transformed biological studies. In that report what do we find? Actually scores of *rhetorical* choices that they made to strengthen the appeal of their scientific claim. (Biographies and autobiographies have by now revealed that they did a lot of conscientious revising, not of the data but of the mode of presentation; and their lives were filled, before and after the triumph, with a great deal of rhetoric-charged conflict.[3]) We could easily compose a dozen different versions of their report, all proclaiming the same scientific results. But most alternatives would prove less engaging to the intended audience.

They open, for example, with

> "*We wish to suggest* a structure" that has "*novel* features which are of *considerable* biological *interest*." (My italics, of course)

Why didn't they say, instead: "We shall here *demonstrate* a *startling, totally new* structure that will *shatter* everyone's conception of the biological world"? Well, obviously their rhetorical choice presents an ethos much more attractive to most cautious readers than does my exaggerated alternative. A bit later they say

> "We have made the *usual chemical assumptions*, namely . . . "

Why didn't they say, "*As we all know . . .* "? Both expressions acknowledge reliance on warrants, commonplaces within a given rhetorical domain. But their version sounds more thoughtful and authoritative, especially with the word "chemical."

Referring to Pauling and Corey, they say,

> "They *kindly* have made their manuscript available."

Ok, guys, drop the rhetoric and just cut that word "kindly." What has that got to do with your scientific case? Well, it obviously strengthens the authors' ethos: we are nice guys dealing trustfully with other nice guys, in a rhetorical community.

And on they go, with

- "*In our opinion*" (rather than "We proclaim" or "We insist" or "We have miraculously discovered": again ethos – we're not dogmatic);

- Fraser's "*suggested*" structure is "*rather ill-defined*" (rather than "his structure is stupid" or "obviously faulty" – we *are* nice guys, right?).

And on to scores of other such choices.

Do I mean to suggest that they might have done an even better job if some college teacher had required them to study this or that major rhetorician? Probably not: their paper is brilliant as it stands, so they must have been trained early on in how to write well. But the point here remains: no matter how "pure" their scientific thinking, they cannot get it across even to an audience of scientists without relying on rhetorical choices.

A bit less obvious and much more important to us here is the second main reason why even the profoundest, most rigorous thinkers cannot escape rhetorical territory: every corner of life invites not just the *use of* but *thought about* how the language in that corner both changes realities and depends on indemonstrable beliefs about what is real. The pursuit of knowledge cannot be divorced from rhetorical issues. That is why in most fields most genuine thinkers address the rhetorical questions openly, though usually in non-rhetorical terms. They probe questions about the reliability of the assumptions and methods on which all of them depend – often with no "scientific" proof.

Once we ask questions like:

- When should I change my mind?
- How can I really get you to change yours?
- How has this or that "ideology" or "communication system" or "mode of linguistics" or "philosophical system" changed our realities?
- Where do "unprovable" factors like emotion, moral convictions, and faith in human trust fit into our convictions?

then we find that even the professed enemies of rhetorical studies were actually conducting them.

Were rhetorical studies really dying when John Locke wrote his diatribes against rhetoric (pp. 6–7 above), or when David Hume wrote *A Treatise of Human Nature* (1738), never mentioning rhetoric but providing sections with titles like these?

Of the Origin of Our Ideas
Of Probability
Of the Impressions of the Senses and Memory
Of the Causes of Belief
Of Unphilosophical Probability
Of Compassion
Moral Distinctions Not Derived from Reason
Moral Distinctions Derived from a Moral Sense

Most of Hume's points could be read – and were for generations read – as attacking traditional rhetorical ideas about belief and persuasion. He does engage in implicit attacks on rhetoric throughout, often under the explicit term "eloquence." Here's one of his attacks from his Introduction to the *Treatise* (par. 2). Deploring the "present imperfect condition of the sciences," he says:

> Disputes are multiplied, as if every thing was uncertain; and these disputes are managed with the greatest warmth, as if every thing was certain. Amidst all this bustle *'tis not reason* which carries the prize, *but eloquence*; and no man need ever despair of gaining proselytes to the most extravagant hypothesis, who has *art enough to represent it in any favourable colours.* The *victory is not gained* by the men at arms, who manage the pike and the sword; but by the trumpeters, drummers, and musicians of the army. (My italics)

Leaving aside the clever flourish of his own rhetorical trumpet, and his other rhetorical strokes, is it not clear that central to his claim will be the contrast between good rhetoric, based on his kind of reasoning – good argument – and bad rhetoric, based on mere "eloquence"?

Scores of other examples could be used to show that the "decline of rhetoric" did not occur as any single line: there were innumerable ups and downs, depending on definitions. The weird fall and recent rise that I traced in chapter 2 was mainly of rhetorical terminology, not of the actual range of inquiries. Scholars in most other fields – philosophers, theologians, political theorists, etc. – felt as much threatened by positivism as did professional rhetoricians. The need for rhetorical rescue was being faced in almost every academic field. Everyone knew that if the extreme positivists won, every corner of knowledge-pursuit, except for science itself, would be tossed aside.

How were they to face the unquestionable *fact* that most of our efforts at communication, most of our debates, are about judgments that entail values? How were they to demonstrate that feelings (*pathos*), and reliance on character (*ethos*), and non-empirical forms of demonstration (*logos*) are not totally separable from *rational* persuasion? What have our emotions got to do with truth? Nothing. What influence on our judgment of truth should our judgment of character exercise? None whatever. What forms of proof should be listened to, other than rigorous syllogisms or hard data? None. "The world up to now previously wrestled hopelessly with contingency and incomprehensibility, landing in totally unreliable theological and philosophical dogmas and rhetorical non-proofs; now we can pursue certainty." (There you have my summary of the Descartes "movement.")

The conflict between a quest for certainty and the growing awareness of how little territory that quest can cover produced in some inquirers, such as R. G. Collingwood, a lifetime of struggle: we want certainty, we need it, we pursue it, and it escapes us. We could spend almost this whole chapter on his *Essay on Metaphysics* (1940), or especially *The New Leviathan: Or Man, Society, Civilization, and Barbarism* (1942), as he both pursues certainty and dramatizes the hopelessness of the pursuit. In his chapter on "Reason" he summarizes the problem like this:

14.23. Men reflecting on the knowledge they possess soon realize that it is fallible. However much they try to drug themselves by reiterating the fact that they are convinced of a given proposition, the thought of its fallibility teases them. (pp. 99–100)

As far as I can discover, no one has ever traced the full history of the diverse attempts to rescue the issues that the passion for scientific certainty threatened: the efforts to reverse what I think of as "intellectual losses." Historical attempts have in fact usually limited it all to how this or that philosopher responded. Various "empiricists" followed Hume and Kant in bringing sense-data back into the genuine-knowledge picture. Various "*logical* positivists" rightly insisted that knowledge produced by logic and mathematics could be as unquestionable as results in a laboratory. Meanwhile other philosophers – and sociologists, psychologists, anthropologists, political scientists, and so on – saw both of these moves as merely versions of positivism, equally threatening to full inquiry about valid rationality. So this chapter might be taken as an invitation to some historian of modern thought to expand the history into a three-volume effort, tracing the hundreds of attempts to recover what is lost when reductionists turn all "genuine thought" into a quest for certainty.

Different would-be rescuers concentrated, of course, on different potential losses. I can discuss here under each loss only a crude selection from those who engaged in rescue attempts. Obviously in each category there are many others who deserve our attention (see appendix to this chapter). Another problem with my listing is that each of the rescuers actually wrestled, as did Collingwood, with many other challenges besides the ones he or she is listed under here. In their shoes, I would object: "Why confine my *broad* interests to that single threatened loss?" Answer? Well, we do need that trilogy covering each of the challenges that my invented quotations summarize.

"Why bother about ethos, since the character of an inquirer provides no genuine support for Truth, and since moral judgments can never be proved?"

To me the clearest case of a scientifically trained rescuer of ethos was Michael Polanyi, a scientist in his own right but more famous for his philosophical pursuits *about* science, especially in *Personal Knowledge: Towards a Post-Critical Philosophy* (1958).[4] As I read his book back then, hoping to find a defense against positivist excesses, I was almost overwhelmed by the richness of his project. Especially revealing is Polanyi's persistent demonstration of how all scientific research depends on ethos – undemonstrable but justified reliance on author-ities. Here is how he introduces his project (I insert a few rhetorical synonyms and italics to make my point).

> Upon examining the *grounds on which science is pursued*, I found that it is determined at every stage by *undefinable powers of thought*. No rules can account for the ways a good idea is produced for starting an enquiry [*inventio*]; and there are no rules either for the verification or the refutation of a proposed solution of a problem. Rules widely current may be plausible enough [warrants, shared by all in the presumed audience], but scientific enquiry often proceeds and triumphs by contradicting them. . . . Theories start from *assumptions* which scientists accept on the *authority* of scientific *opinion* [ethos] . . .
>
> In the present volume . . . I faced the task of justifying the holding of *unproven* traditional beliefs [*topoi*]. I made an extensive survey of current *fiduciary* commitments – intrinsic to the intellectual and *social life* of modern man. . . . *[T]he ideal of strict objectivism is absurd* . . . . [O]ur growing familiarity with ubiquitous indwelling brings about the unquestioning acceptance of the paradox that *all knowledge is ultimately personal.* (pp. ix–xi, 2nd ed.)

Much of his table of contents could be quoted as if introducing a rhetoric text. Indeed, some of his 123 chapter headings could almost serve as the title for this manifesto. Here are the ones most relevant to ethos:

Grading of confidence
Forms of tacit assent (A later book was entitled *The Tacit Dimension*.)
Communication

Conviviality (This is a section of sixteen chapters. Avoiding the current popular usage of "convivial" – having a drinking party together – he stresses the root meaning of *con* and *viv*: "together-life." Science can be practiced only through living and communicating together, trustingly.)

Emphasizing throughout the fact that our convictions depend on the authority of those who have taught us – on our trust of them – Polanyi again and again makes clear that he is hoping to find genuine grounds for his personal beliefs, while often acknowledging that they depend on good rhetoric – in my definition. "Throughout this book I am affirming my own beliefs, and more particularly so when I insist . . . that such personal affirmations and choices are inescapable, and when I argue . . . that this is all that can be required of me" (p. 209, 2nd ed.).

In short, Polanyi expresses throughout what could be called a *faith* in ethos, what he calls the "fiduciary" commitment. Every scientist depends on *conviviality*.

His pursuit of ethos has been echoed in many fields, especially as lawyers, anthropologists, social scientists, and political theorists have defended the importance of *trust*.[5] But the point is still far too often ignored, as Susan Haack reminds us in her recent book *Defending Science – Within Reason* (2003). As she defends the rational achievements of science, residing between the absurd excesses of "scientism" on the positivist side and "cynicism" on the relativist side, Haack relies on Polanyi again and again in reminding reasoners how much they depend on ethos: "[S]cientific inquiry is advanced by *complementary* talents . . . [by] a delicate mesh of reasonable confidence in others' competence and honesty" (p. 25).

For many would-be rescuers, the major threat was not so much loss of attention to rhetors' character as the loss of serious, rational debate about moral questions. As skeptical, positivistic claims against moral thinking persisted through the centuries, rescue attempts multiplied (too often merely as superficial sentimentality about fear of hell). In addition to major rescuers who appear later here, and the many pre-positivist profound thinkers, the three most influential in my own narrow perspective have been Alasdair MacIntyre, Bernard Williams, and novelist-philosopher Iris Murdoch.[6]

"Discard pathos! Emotional appeal has nothing to do with Truth."

Many of the pursuers of *positive* knowledge would accuse me of being unfair with that summary of their dogma; like Collingwood, they were themselves troubled by the loss of serious thought about emotion. Any close reading of the Hume quotation above (p. 60) shows that he was aware of the threats produced by that loss. Many so-called romanticists were attempting to rescue emotion as a key element in all thought. But it was only well into the twentieth century that thinkers in many fields pursued aggressively and in depth a revival of *pathos* as essential to rational inquiry.

Consider the once famous but by now somewhat neglected works of Susanne Langer: *Philosophy in a New Key* (1942) and her less well-known thousand-page trilogy, *Mind: An Essay on Human Feeling* (1967–82). Her works might be unfairly reduced to: a lifetime rhetorical effort to restore our awareness of the powers of emotion (and resulting moral commitment) in all thinking.

Here is how she puts her case toward the end of *Philosophy in a New Key* – her passionate appeal for attention to "symbolic transformation."

A philosophy that knows only deductive or inductive logic as reason, and classes all other human functions as "emotive," irrational, and animalism, can see only regression to a pre-logical state in the present passionate and unscientific ideologies. . . . All other things our minds do are dismissed as irrelevant to intellectual progress; they are residues, emotional disturbances, or throwbacks to animal estate.

But a theory of mind whose keynote is the symbolific [*sic*] function, whose problem is the morphology of significance, is not obliged to draw that bifurcating line between science and folly. It can see these ructions and upheavals of the modern mind not as lapses of rational interest, caused by animal impulse, but as the exact contrary − as a new phase of savagedom, indeed, but inspired by the rational need of envisagement and understanding. . . . It is the sane, efficient, work-a-day business of free minds − discursive reasoning about well-conceived problems − that is disturbed or actually suspended in this apparent age of unreason; but the force which governs that age is still the force of mind, the impulse toward symbolic formulations, expression, and understanding of experience.

Those few who read her now, some of them rhetoricians, keep hoping for her revival. The hope is dim, because so many other thinkers have taken up her cause − often without even knowing about her work.

"Throw religion into the trashcan, since science will ultimately cover the whole of Truth."

That positivist extreme has been opposed by many devoted scientists through more than three centuries. As we'll see in chapter 8, even physical scientists have often attempted many varieties of religion-rescue. And many in the social sciences (sometimes labeled as the "softer" sciences) have tried to show how religion − at least in some forms − could be *studied* rationally, or even rationally defended. (See for example Max Weber's *The Sociology of Religion*, 1922).[7] But it seems clear that religious inquiry has suffered even more than rhetorical studies from positivist triumphs.

Since chapter 8 concentrates on the warfare between science and religion, I put it to one side here.

"Ordinary language, everyday language, simply corrupts Truth, and is not worth deep study."

Since so much of rhetorical skill and rhetrickery occurs in everyday informal exchanges, it was hardly surprising that ordinary language was for centuries cast aside as having nothing to do with genuine intellectual matters. Though many empiricists acknowledged that our sensations are in themselves facts, our language about those sensations did not, for most of them, produce knowledge. (Indeed, that charge could also in a sense be made against classical rhetoricians; they tended to concentrate on political oratory, leaving ordinary language to one side.) Positivists like Fritz Mauthner were absolutely explicit in their claim that ordinary language could have nothing to do with the pursuit of truth, and thinkers should thus concentrate only on positivist projects.

Ludwig Wittgenstein would probably be cited by most as the major influence on revival of ordinary language studies, but there were many other rescuers before, and especially after, his *Tractatus Logico-Philosophicus* (1921): for example, Norman Malcolm, W. V. Quine, and F. H. Bradley.

Consider briefly J. L. Austin's *How to Do Things with Words* (1962; paperback, 1971). Would that not be a good title for a book about rhetoric? Austin's main point is that ordinary language does not merely describe (and often distort) surroundings but actually performs actions, changing the world – or, in my terms, it remakes reality, rather than merely reflecting or distorting it. Here is how he introduces Lecture VIII.

> [T]o say something is to *do* something, or *in* saying something we do something, and even *by* saying something we do something. . . . [T]o say something is in the full normal sense to do something. . . . The act of "saying something" in this full normal sense I call, i.e., dub, the performance of a locutionary *act*, and the study of utterances thus far and in these respects the study of locutions. (p. 94; my italics)

He then claims the relevance of his case to all "grammarians and phoneticians," with no hint about how he is rescuing rhetorical studies.

In many other fields scholars have pursued the powerful effects of the way we address one another in the everyday world. One key example deserving full treatment is the popular work of sociologist

Erving Goffman, especially his *Presentation of Self in Everyday Life* (1959). Relying quite heavily on the works of Kenneth Burke (whom we meet below), Goffman grapples with how, in our everyday rhetoric, we "accommodate to the audience" (not his language) by putting on this or that mask, "performing roles" (his language) that are needed for social success and even for the pursuit of genuine knowledge. (See postscript, p. 83.)

"Practical consequences of argument have no relevance to Truth; 'what works' is irrelevant to genuine inquiry."

Until the positivist revolution, almost everyone – including the most dogmatic theologians – had acknowledged that whatever "works" successfully in the world does have relevance to our decisions about truth. Even the most ardent positivists could not deny that words and ideas do have consequences. But they pushed hard against the claim that because an idea produces satisfying practical effects you can use that result to prove a bit of truth.

It is hardly surprising, in retrospect, that such claims should have produced a flood of counter-arguments, culminating in the so-called pragmatists; while everyone acknowledged that relying on practical effects can lead to error, the truth value of practice should not be ignored in sound reasoning.

Though Charles Sanders Peirce, a primary founder of the pragmatist movement, did comparatively little publishing, he impressed all who studied him, especially by his covering every practical dimension, including the toughest logical inquiry.[8] (See especially his essays "The Fixation of Belief" (1877) and "How to Make Our Ideas Clear" (1878)).

In his footsteps, William James spent a lifetime rescuing pragmatic convictions from the dustbin. Often defending a pluralistic version of religion, sometimes concentrating on attacking "radical empiricism," his mission was to attack those who claim that "no argument for what *ought to be* to what *is* is valid."[9] His plurality of thought-systems – those revived once positivism surrendered – naturally included religion, especially in *The Will to Believe* (1897) and *The Varieties of Religious Experience* (1902).

John Dewey was equally passionate in his defense of practical effect as a source of truth, as in *The Quest for Certainty: A Study of the Relation of Knowledge and Action* (1929). Attempting to "interpret the conclusions of science with respect to their consequences for our beliefs about purposes and values in all phases of life," he rightly claims that the pursuit "can proceed only slowly and through cooperative effort" (p. 313). In other words, when we abandon the foolishly excessive pursuit of certainty and study *consequences*, we enter Polanyi's domain of the "convivial."

Will I anger current (excessively relativistic) pursuers of pragmatic questions and methods, like Richard Rorty or Stanley Fish, by claiming that the movement might be renamed as "The Rhetoric of Practical Choice"?[10]

"The undeniable powers of art (and especially metaphor) are irrelevant to either Truth or the study of behavior; judgment of those powers is irrelevant to inquiry."

For positivists, one of the most self-evident truths was that art – whether poetry or painting or music – makes no contribution to truth; it is divorced from reality, and it contributes nothing to truth about reality – especially ethical reality. Many positivists simply ignored the subtle argument of Hume, in "Of the Standard of Taste," that there are genuine, though subtle and elusive, aesthetic standards.

The threat to artistic judgment produced a flood of arguments proclaiming art's transformative powers.[11] Perhaps the most influential was I. A. Richards, the hero you have encountered here already. Though rhetorical terms were not featured in many of his works, he revolutionized the rhetoric of literary criticism. He was persistently wrestling with how our language changes the world – both how bad rhetoric, including bad poetry, and careless reading, produces misunderstanding, and how good rhetoric can reduce it.

Unlike many other would-be rescuers, he did have his moment of fame. The explosion of interest in "formalism" and "close reading" in the 1930s and 1940s was partly triggered by his *Practical Criticism: A Study of Literary Judgment* (1929) – a work still worth reading. It was a brilliant demonstration of how close reading is essential in grasping a poem's significance: what he chose not to call its rhetorical powers. The book was embraced especially by a group who soon became known as the "New Critics" – Cleanth Brooks, John Crowe Ransom, Robert Heilman, William Empson, William Wimsatt, Robert Penn Warren, Monroe Beardsley, and others. As they tackled individual poems to discover their true (and usually ironic) center, and as they joined Richards in openly rejecting the *flesh-and-blood* author's intentions, they were always emphasizing – without the terms – the *implied* author's rhetorical intention. (Some of them would cringe at that summary, asserting the "fallacy" of intentionality; but they would be again downplaying the difference between the implied author, as finally realized in the text, and the flesh-and-blood author's stated intentions throughout the act of composition.)

Richards's influence is now largely ignored – though not quite as regrettably as Langer's. As Ann E. Berthoff says, introducing her anthology of his contributions, "he is virtually unread today, even by critics who pretend to be assessing his status and evaluating his critical ideas."[12] *The Philosophy of Rhetoric* (1936), like his other books, has been out of print for a long time. Only recently have his works been revived by Berthoff and John Constable. My hope is that they may awaken young students of literature to the persuasive vitality implanted in every successful poetic invention, and discovered only by devoted close readers.

Except for the explosion of close reading, the most influential part of Richards's work was his celebration of metaphor as the supreme communication device. Quoting Aristotle, "The greatest thing by far is to have a command of metaphor," Richards spends most of his last two chapters almost summarizing this book: by studying the "command of metaphor" we "can go deeper still into the *control of the world that we make for ourselves* to live in" (my italics). Both in our daily lives and in our literary studies, we depend for our "healthy growth" on our capacity to achieve the rhetorical bindings produced "with a small-scale instance – the right understanding of a figure of speech – or with a large-scale instance – the conduct of a friendship."

> [W]ith enough improvement in Rhetoric we may in time learn so much about words that they will tell us how our minds work. It seems modest and reasonable to . . . hope that a patient persistence with the problems of Rhetoric may, while exposing the causes and modes of the misinterpretation of words, also throw light upon and suggest a remedial discipline for deeper and more grievous disorders; that, as the small and local errors in our everyday misunderstandings with language are models in miniature of the greater errors which disturb the development of our personalities, their study may also show us more about how these large-scale disasters may be avoided. (pp. 91–2)

He then closes with a long citation from Plato's *Timaeus*, ignoring the master's occasional downgradings of rhetoric and implying that Plato, by celebrating God's gift to us of myth and metaphor, is entirely on the side of those who passionately pursue a revival of serious study of how literature re-creates us.

"All genuine inquiry into economics and commercial matters must be quantitative; ethos and pathos and technical eloquence have nothing to do with the Truth about how business or the market work."

Scores of economists overlooked Adam Smith's ethical concerns, emphasizing only his celebration of competition.[13] Even by the time Deirdre McCloskey, then Don, published *The Rhetoric of Economics* (1985), many economists were deeply offended by the book's argument for the relevance of rhetoric to economic studies.

A much more widespread repudiation of quantitative reductionism has come from those who think hard about how businesses are to be conducted effectively. Though some guidebooks still reduce training to "getting ahead of the others," mere win-rhetoric, many by now openly acknowledge that all business depends, day by day, on listening-rhetoric. Bookstore shelves are laden with works advising business leaders on how to improve daily communication, and some of them by now stress the importance of genuine dialogue: Polanyi's "conviviality." Though the books almost never use rhetorical terms, they are at every point teaching executives how to achieve more effective communication, by *thinking* about ethos and pathos: listen to each other so that both sides can win. (This is not to deny that many seem to favor a form of listening performed in order to dominate or cheat.)

Among the most popular are the works by Steven Covey. Here is how he comes close to summarizing my plea for better listening:

Habit 5
SEEK FIRST TO UNDERSTAND, THEN TO BE UNDER-
STOOD . . .
Communication is the most important skill in life. We spend most of our waking hours communicating. But consider this: You've spent years learning how to read and write, years learning how to speak. But what about listening? What training or education have you had that enables you to listen so that you really, deeply understand another human being from that individual's own frame of reference? . . . If you want to interact effectively with me, to influence me . . . you first need to understand me. And you can't do that with technique alone. . . . The real key to your influence with me is your example, your actual conduct.

That is to say: "the rhetoric you use on me." Could I dream that if I met Covey I could persuade him, using LR, to call his next book "The Rhetoric of Effective Business Management"?

"Forget about the study of the tools of classical rhetoric. Who cares about petty technical matters like metonymy, synecdoche, or any of those other weird terms?"

Only fairly late in the manifold attempts to combat positivism did scholars begin labeling the losses as rhetorical. And very few of the rescuers actually dwelt on the loss of study of technical resources. So a major revolution occurred when Chaim Perelman and Lucie Olbrechts-Tyteca celebrated the full range of traditional rhetorical resources, in a "new" way: *The New Rhetoric* (1958, translated 1969).[14]

Perhaps the most influential of all those discussed here, Perelman is by now sadly neglected. His was the most complex effort to explore all rhetorical resources for combating the "absolutist," "Cartesian" view of truth. Paralleling but deepening the previous efforts to combat the certainty-quest, he establishes, with hundreds of examples, an irrefutable case for the existence of genuine truth-claims that do not rely on mere hard facts about facts. In effect almost summarizing this whole chapter, he says that his book

> constitutes a *break with a concept of reason and reasoning due to Descartes* which has set its mark on Western philosophy for the last three centuries. . . . Descartes' concept . . . was to "take well nigh for false everything which was only plausible." It was this philosopher who made the self-evident the mark of reason, and considered rational only those demonstrations which, starting from clear and distinct ideas, extended, by means of apodictic proofs, the self-evidence of the axioms to the derived theorems. . . . The result is that reasonings extraneous to the domain of the purely formal elude logic altogether, and, as a consequence, they also elude reason. (pp. 1–2)

Then, after tracing briefly how Descartes's error took over, he summarizes his assault:

> We feel . . . that just here lies a *perfectly unjustified and unwarranted limitation of the domain of action of our faculty of reasoning and proving.* (p. 3)

Thus he launches an amazingly deep, rich, all-inclusive exploration of rhetorical resources, both from classical giants, especially Aristotle, Cicero, and Quintilian, and from Renaissance anti-Cartesians on to 1969. Here is a selection from his challenging 105 chapter headings:

73

1   Demonstration and Argumentation
2   The Contact of Minds
3   The Speaker and His Audience
4   The Audience as a Construction of the Speaker
5   Adaptation of the Speaker to the Audience
7   The Universal Audience
13   Argumentation and Violence
16   Facts and Truths
18   Values
41   Rhetorical Figures and Argumentation
45   The Characteristics of Quasi-Logical Argumentation
II   Arguments Based on the Structure of Reality
64   Ends and Means
75   The Symbolic Relation
III   The Relations Establishing the Structure of Reality
86   The Status of Analogy
IV   The Dissociation of Concepts
91   Philosophical Pairs and Their Justification
104 The Order of the Speech and Conditioning of the Audiences
105 Order and Method

Does a list like that invite you to do some serious studying of your own rhetorical practice? Or does it simply drive you away from the whole project? The answer will depend more on who you are, and your rhetorical domain, than on Perelman or me.

"There is only one True domain of truth, and our method pursues the one True path to it; those who oppose us turn the pursuit of Truth into crass relativism."

The rescuers who in my view are the most profound are those who, like some of the pragmatists mentioned above, acknowledge the inescapable multiplicity of truth domains. As I said at the beginning, the positivists were not wrong when they insisted that one *branch* of truth can best be pursued with rigorous scientific methods or hard, indisputable logic. They were only wrong in dismissing all other methods as yielding nothing but falsehood. Unfortunately, too many of those who combated positivist excesses were themselves dogmatically committed to some one version of truth: "My thought mode may not have it all yet," philosophers like Bertrand Russell would admit, but they would go on to imply, "ultimately this will prove to be the one right way – relying on science but employing philosophy to go even deeper." Even some pragmatists who thought of themselves as anti-positivist still felt that they were on the one right path.

To trace the full complexities of pluralistic claims is obviously not possible here. But three major pluralists call for our attention.

Kenneth Burke is perhaps the most influential among the rescuers who explicitly employed rhetorical language. Burke offers floods of ideas, some of them turning out to be profoundly connected, while others are hard to harmonize with any one thesis. This anti-syntactic style produces a "system" that can in no way be adequately summarized; it respects many systems. I once published an adulatory essay about him, proud that I was the first reader in the world who had really probed to his wonderfully important core. His reply, called "Dancing with Tears in My Eyes," was the justified claim that I hadn't succeeded at all; I had "pinned him down" in the wrong corner.

The fact was that no one corner existed. Though Burke sometimes wrote as if he thought he had it all "pinned down," his range of interests has led to his being influential in an incredible range of disciplines.

Perhaps the best evidence of his contribution is a brief quotation from his key work, *A Rhetoric of Motives* (1950). His central term is "identification" – which might be taken as a synonym for Richards's "understanding" and my "listening-rhetoric."

> ... we [that is, KB; he almost never used "I" in publications] think that the relation between "truth" and the kind of opinion with which rhetoric operates is often misunderstood. ... The kind of opinion with

which rhetoric deals ... is not opinion *as contrasted with truth*. There is the invitation to look at the matter thus antithetically, once we have put the two terms (opinion and truth) together as a dialectical pair.

This leads him to several pages on how we rhetors and listeners *identify*:

> You persuade a man only insofar as you can talk his language by speech, gesture, tonality, order, image, attitude, idea, *identifying* your ways with his. Persuasion by flattery is but a special case of persuasion in general. But flattery can safely serve as our paradigm if we systematically widen its meaning, to see behind it the conditions of identification or consubstantiality in general. ... True, the rhetorician may have to change an audience's opinion in one respect; but *he can succeed only insofar as he yields to that audience's opinions in other respects.* (pp. 54–6; my italics)

As he pursues at length the path of identification through the study of motives, he naturally expands his views over the years, finally celebrating such concepts as "all language is symbolic action," and literature provides our "equipment for living" – which is what both he and I claim for what rhetoric does. Stressing the communal effects of the right kind of rhetoric, Burke puts it this way: "I never think of 'communication' without thinking of its ultimate perfection, named in such words as 'community' and 'communion.'"[15]

To me, though not to many of his admirers, the most important of his works was his *Rhetoric of Religion* (1961). In it he pursues the question of what we can say about our perfectionist *language*, and particularly about our God-talk, whether or not there *is* a God. And he finds, tracing a path roughly similar to the steps of the traditional ontological proof for the existence of God, that in the very nature of our human language, even the most scientific, there is an irresistible, hierarchical drive toward God-*terms*, terms that "perfect" the scale of values implicit in all language. In other words, a serious study of rhetoric, of the whole range of uses to which we put language, cannot for Burke be undertaken without doing what he calls a "logology," a study of the hierarchies that leads to identifying linguistic capstones confirming or supporting those hierarchies. In every dimension of our lives we are pursuing perfections – often with synonyms for God and always finding the perfection unattainable. He steadily reveals the qualities, productive and harmful, that are embodied in those hierarchies and pursuits of perfection.[16]

The effect of the book is not just to get theologians to think harder about their rhetoric but to get everyone to see how much of our rhetoric about "perfecting" – or even mere "improving" – parallels religious language. Practicing logology, he falls into my tiny collection of really great pluralists.

Jacques Derrida, by now much more widely known than Burke, has seldom been given the label "rhetorician." He is almost always called a "deconstructionist," and most readers fail to catch the many signs of his dependence on and passion for rhetorical inquiry. But any full attention to his life and work cannot ignore how powerfully and openly the rhetorical pursuit of plurality has dominated his thinking.[17]

As even most of his followers have not realized, Derrida was educated intensively in classical rhetoric, and he has often expressed openly his devotion to and dependence on rhetorical questions. Everything he has written, he says, including his questioning of classical norms,

> has not only been made possible by but is constantly in contact with very [*sic*] classical, rigorous, demanding discipline in writing, in "demonstrating," in rhetoric. . . . The fact that I've been trained in and that I am at some level true to this classical teaching in rhetoric is essential . . . whether in the sense of the art of persuasion or in the sense of logical demonstration.[18]

At the same time he has been rightly determined not to let rhetorical studies take over everything. "Rhetoricism" for him would be the naive claim that rhetorical effects are entirely uninfluenced by anything but rhetorical structure – totally unaffected by the circumstances in which the rhetorical encounter occurs: a claim denying my Reality One on pp. 12–13 above. Though rhetoric is essential in every corner of our lives, "this doesn't mean that everything depends on verbal statements or formal techniques of speech acts. . . . [T]he possibility of speech acts . . . depends on conditions and conventions which are not simply verbal . . . political situations, economical situations, the libidinal situation" (p. 16). And those situations are so diverse that diverse thought modes are required for dealing with them.

His deepest commitment – it is as risky to try to pin him down as it is with Burke – might be put this way: Philosophy, as Plato argues, is more important than rhetoric, but it depends on it. If the Sophists were what Plato portrayed them as, Derrida might well join Plato in opposing them. But his position is to reconstruct the Sophists sympathetically and employ their techniques, while still seeing himself as ultimately "on the side of philosophy, logic, truth, reference, etc."

> When I question philosophy and the philosophical project as such, it's not in the name of sophistics of rhetoric as just a playful technique. I'm interested in the rhetoric hidden in philosophy itself because within, let's say, the typical Platonic discourse there is a rhetoric – a rhetoric against rhetoric, against Sophists. . . . I'm not saying that all concepts are essentially metaphors and therefore everything is rhetoric. No, I try to deconstruct the opposition between concept and metaphor and to rebuild, to restructure this field. . . . I try to understand what has happened since Plato and in a recurrent way until now in this opposition between philosophy and rhetoric. (pp. 16–17)

What has happened, as he laments, is that too many of his readers, favorable or opposed, have seen him as a totally relativistic "rhetoricist" claiming that *everything* is reducible to shaky rhetoric (usually under other terms) – and thus to the annihilation of knowledge and truth. Some of his statements are indeed easily misread as such an annihilation, for example his famous: "There is no outside-text" (*il n'y a pas de hors texte*). Whole professional associations have been organized by those eager to defend "traditional" values by attacking versions of deconstruction. One, the ALSC (Association of Literary Scholars and Critics), has concentrated on literature, which was seen as threatened by the rise of "ideological" studies. As one announcement puts it, the mission is to do genuine literary study, "without recourse to the exclusionary argot of academic coteries," as exemplified in the Modern Language Association. The other, NAS (National Association of Scholars), has embraced all academic fields, attacking from an even more radically "conservative" stance.

Some of their targets have deserved the attacks – those who transform Derrida's inquiry into a flat rejection of all truth. But too few have recognized the way in which the shrewder deconstructionists were actually reviving the necessity of pluralistic rhetorical inquiry: truths are multiple, and most truths are uncovered only by methods available when we give up the quest for absolute certainty. The attackers too often sound as if they are certain that they have the one true method of dealing with texts.

My anti-deconstructionist colleagues are sure to be annoyed with this defense of Derrida as a heroic rescuer. I can only ask them to reread Derrida, especially his later works like *The Gift of Death*, and acknowledge how he is probing our rhetoric in a quest for the grounds, however shaky, for our deepest human values. After one of his lectures, I asked whether he would object to my labeling him as a "disguised theologian." He accepted my label. Was he being ironic?

Richard McKeon, a sadly neglected rescuer, was in my view the most profound of those who tried to escape such dogmatism without falling into destructive forms of relativism. Like most philosophers, he began his career in the hope of finding the one true path to truth, and he later confessed that as a young man he had often believed that he'd found it: in Spinoza (his first book); in Aristotle (article after article); in a decisive original philosophy of his own. But soon he concluded that different methods, purposes, and assumptions could yield valid rival truth-systems, each of which appeared inadequate and refutable to dogmatic pursuers of the others. Close analysis of the rhetoric of those systems revealed both why they clashed and how they might be reconciled. Any passionate Platonist working from the top (Ideas and Forms) down, could "prove" the fallacies of any passionate Humeian working from the bottom (empirical fact) up. And vice versa. Yet both approaches were in fact irrefutable.

Though his pluralistic development began with that twofold system – what he called "holoscopic" vs. "meroscopic" – it expanded over the years, becoming threefold, then fourfold, and finally sixteen-fold. Pursuing what he sometimes labeled "architectonic rhetoric," sometimes "philosophical semantics," and sometimes "systematic philosophizing," he worked to construct a kind of architecture inhabitable by all valid truth-pursuits. He was inevitably forced to acknowledge that his umbrella, devised to cover all diverse rhetorics, was only one of many possible umbrellas; even an architectonic rhetoric must acknowledge the inescapable need for other architec-tonics. But what he provided was a rhetorical tool for escaping meaningless controversy among the rivals. (Unfortunately the complexity of his lifetime project encouraged a writing style that put off many readers – it is even denser than Burke's or Derrida's.)

When he became a crucial member of the United Nations Educa-tional, Scientific, and Cultural Organization (UNESCO), McKeon contributed a good deal to UNESCO's 1947 Declaration of Human Rights, in effect teaching other members, as he put it, "to examine certain fundamental terms, such as human rights, democracy, free-dom, law, and equality" across not just diverse cultures but diverse philosophical approaches.

His project might be described as the opposite of what some philosophical skeptics pursued – for example, the by now almost forgotten Pierre Bayle. Bayle, author of the first great philosophical encyclopedia, set out to demonstrate that every philosophical effort had failed; only "faith" could finally be relied on. While McKeon also enjoyed exposing others' failures, his major effort was to show that despite minor failures, many contrasting thought modes had uncovered truths that other modes had mistakenly rejected.[19]

Because his defenses of diverse modes were so persuasive, his defenders have often disagreed about where on his elaborate charts his own thinking might be placed. Inexperienced students would sometimes accuse him of being a dogmatic Platonist, or Aristotelian, or Spinozist, or Humeian, or Deweyite. But he was in fact a passionate defender of all of the greats.

This pluralistic mission naturally led many to conclude that he was a relativist, a skeptic like Bayle, denying the existence of genuine truth. Not at all. It is true that he can be considered a neglected pre-deconstructionist, with his insistence that all claims, even of the factual, rely for their validation on the modes of thought in which the claims occur. Believers in "hard facts" that can be described with no dependence on cultural influence have often attacked him, ignoring his frequent assertions that truth is real, or rather that *truths* are real, even though they will always remain inescapably multiple, often seemingly contradictory. His influence, even on philosophers, has been relatively slight, and he is seldom cited in rhetorical works. I hope that some readers here, those who care about what to do when a brilliant philosopher like Bertrand Russell "refutes" all philosophies except his own, will go courageously to McKeon's works and learn how absurd the rhetoric of philosophical refutation can often be. Truths are real, but they are multiple, and their pursuers too often hope for one single truth, as they practice complex forms of win-rhetoric – without listening.

Conclusion

My unfair allocation of more space here to open rhetoricians than to those working in other languages may seem to suggest that disguised rhetoricians might have done even more important work if they had incorporated the rhetorical tradition explicitly. For those who had in fact been educated in rhetorical studies but abandoned the terms, the essential arguments would not have been changed much just by relapsing into rhetorical language. The good effect would have been only that their readers would not have been misled into thinking that the particular field had nothing to do with daily rhetorical efforts to understand. I resist listing those who needed better rhetorical education.

I cannot resist, however, the biased claim that almost all of them would have done an even better job of rescuing us from destructive dogmatic positivism if they had dug into what a full rhetorologist like Richard McKeon might have taught them. Too many of them end up, as they passionately pursue their brilliant defenses, proclaiming their mode of thought as the only legitimate kind. McKeon's way of employing architectonic rhetoric – listening to and interrelating major thought modes, pluralism rather than monism – could have led most of them into even more skillful use of their rescue tools. And practicing his form of aggressive cross-disciplinary listening could produce an academic world in which more and more of us acknowledged our kinship with, and reliance on, the others.

Appendix

To reduce my anguish about having omitted many rescuers who themselves deserve to be rescued, I offer here a list of those who have taught me a lot about rhetoric, even when I have sometimes disagreed with them, or have even silently cursed them for neglecting my work. Some on the list may feel offended that I have included one or another of their enemies.

The list does not include those acknowledged in the Preface, or many mentioned in footnotes. Any full encounter with any one of them would help reverse our current neglect – and ignorance.

They are again not in order of importance, or even chronology – just alphabetical. To me the list exhibits Polanyi's conviviality – a cross-generational family, dead and alive.

Frederick Antzcak, Hannah Arendt, Janet Atwell, Jerzy Axer, Michael Bakhtin, Charles Bazerman, James Berlin, Don Bialostosky, Lloyd Bitzer, Patricia Bizzell, Vivian Bradford, James Britton, Gregory Clark, Gregory Colomb, Paul de Man, Rosa Eberly, Peter Elbow, Steve Fuller, Marc Fumaroli, John Gage, Howard Gardner, Gerald Graff, Ernesto Grassi, Marshall Gregory, Jürgen Habermas, Rom Harré, Gerald Hauser, Paul

Hernadi, Winifred Horner, Samuel Howell, Kathleen Hall-Jamieson, Jay Kastely, George Kennedy, James Kinneavy, Thomas Kuhn, Janice Lauer, Michael Leff, Andrea Lunsford, Alastair MacIntyre, Steven Mailloux, James Murphy, C. K. Ogden, Richard Ohmann, Gary Olson, Walter Ong, Richard Poirier, Takis Poulakos, Arthur Quinn, David Richter, Paul Ricoeur, Amélie Oksenberg Rorty, Richard Rorty, Harold Rosen, Jacqueline Royster, Sheldon Sacks, George Saintsbury, James Sledd, Thomas Sloane, Martin Steinmann, C. Jan Swearingen, Charles Taylor, Stephen Toulmin, Brian Vickers, Karl Wallace, Richard Weaver, Hayden White, James Boyd White, Reed Whittemore, Bernard Williams, Joseph Williams, George Williamson, Ross Winterowd...

And on to the thousands more now studying rhetoric professionally – unknown or forgotten by Booth, or even known about but unread.

Postscript

Another sociological contribution, much more up-to-date than the work of Goffman, concentrates on "accommodation" in the form of genuinely sympathetic listening-rhetoric among academic disciplines: *The Dialogical Turn: New Roles for Sociology in the Postdisciplinary Age*, ed. Charles Camic and Hans Joas (2004). The book is an anthology of essays honoring the lifetime effort of sociologist Donald Levine to pursue intellectual dialogue as "a paramount cognitive and ethical objective in its own right" (p. 5). It could almost be summarized as an argument that sociology, from its founding by Auguste Comte, has been a plea for more serious listening-rhetoric among academics.

Part II

The Need for Rhetorical Studies Today

Our choice of language is a matter of truth or error, of right or wrong — of life or death.

Michael Polanyi

All life therefore comes back to the question of our speech, the medium through which we communicate with each other; for all life comes back to the question of our relations with one another.

Henry James, *The Question of Our Speech*

Since rhetoric, good and bad, makes a great part of our reality, and since at its best it is the art of removing misunderstanding, there is no corner of our lives that would not deserve a full book about the dangers of neglecting its careful study. My choice of three of the largest of those corners – education, politics, and the media – has not been easy. Surely I should include a long section on the rhetoric and rhetrickery of lawyers; of psychologists, including Freudians and their enemies; of self-help books, from destructive to profound; of gerontologists, ecologists, Marxists, postmodernist art critics, and so on. Why not a full chapter on the neglect by economists, celebrating Deirdre McCloskey's two fine books that attempt to awaken fellow economists to their inevitable reliance on rhetoric? Why not a chapter on the appalling rhetrickery by the managers of huge corporations?

85

The universality of rhetoric and its problems should not surprise anyone who thinks a bit about our beginning as human beings, whether traced biologically or as religious myth. Whoever wrote the first draft of Genesis had to decide what rhetorical exchanges to report. "Should I have Satan trick those two new creatures by saying 'God doth know that in the day ye eat thereof, then your eyes shall be opened, and ye shall be as gods, knowing good and evil'? Should I have Cain shout up 'Am I my brother's keeper?' Shouldn't I make it more interesting by having Adam argue more effectively against God's decision to punish?" The whole of Genesis might well have been revised further and entitled "the rhetoric of creation problems." Even literalists who believe that God was responsible for the narration should face the fact that God had to make rhetorical decisions, if His story was to work well.

But long before Genesis was written and revised again and again, "we" all faced the challenge of how to talk effectively with one another, in this complex, not to say messy, not to say shit-bound world. Consciously or unconsciously, from "the beginning," one or another of us paused for a moment, in the relentless hunt for food or sex – the struggle to be "the fittest" – and for the first time took a serious look at a fellow human being, as yet unnamed. Some man or woman experienced not just sexual desire for some available creature but actually *attended to* and then fell in love with an *Other* – a fellow creature who deserved not just to be screwed but to be listened to. At about the same time some father or mother suddenly recognized that a child was more than just the only automatic way to continue the species.[1] The infant finally was seen as a fellow communicator, a partner in dialogue. As neurobiologist Daniel Siegel puts it, they discovered, as all effective parents continue to discover, "contingent communication." Here's a rough summary of some of his points about that discovery of "attachment":

> Children are born with an innate need to be attached to their caretakers. Effective parents perceive and respond to the child's signals, making sense of them in terms of what they mean for the child. They

86

achieve a form of joining, of communion: patterns of communication promoting emotional well-being and a positive sense of self.[2]

At some such moment, our ancestors realized that "we" were not just an isolated "I" but an "I" needing to join a "we," with something superior to mere physical strokes: rhetoric! From that "moment" onward – it was of course innumerable moments preceding the first recorded history – "we" knew, consciously or unconsciously, that we were in constant need to find effective ways of communicating with other "I"s. And we all thus discovered (most often unconsciously, of course) just how rhetoric of the wrong kind lands us in disaster.[3]

5

The Fate of Rhetoric in Education

The Future Depends on Education.
Poster on a railroad overpass in Chicago

Isocrates was famous in his own day, and for many centuries to come, for his program of education (paideia), *which stressed above all the teaching of eloquence. His own works . . . were the vehicles for his notion of the true "philosophy," for him a wisdom in civic affairs emphasizing moral responsibility and equated with mastery of rhetorical technique.*
Thomas Conley

"Take those [gift] books away, M. Paul," I said [to my teacher], "and teach me no more. I never asked to be made learned, and you compel me to feel very profoundly that learning is not happiness."
Heroine of Charlotte Brontë's *Villette*, plagued with pedantry

Moving now to the sorry consequences of poor education in rhetoric, we arrive at a rough center for this whole book: "How neglect of rhetorical education, Rhet-Ed, threatens our lives." Any nation is in trouble if its citizens are not trained for critical response to the flood of misinformation poured over them daily. A citizenry not habituated to thoughtful argument about public affairs, but rather trained to "believe everything supporting my side" and "disbelieve everything supporting the bad side," is no longer a citizenry but a house of gullibles. As Curtis White says in his book *The Middle Minds: Why Americans Don't Think for Themselves* (2003):

Americans are not much in the habit of poking at the dominant realities of our lives. We're delicate. We're used to deferring, though we like to think of ourselves as rebels. What parents, teachers, presidents, and Dan Rather say is usually good enough for us. Even if it is demonstrably false, we submit out of habit and fright over what not submitting might require of us. We sacrifice our lives out of a feeling that there is some sort of comfort in deferring.

White does not mention rhetorical studies as a cure for what he calls "the new censorship" (close to the self-censorship described by Coetzee above, pp. 49–50). But like almost everyone else who thinks about our problem, he knows that our only hope is to find ways to produce a public that both cares about serious, penetrating, courageous, mutually respectful argument and is trained to conduct that argument productively – whether or not calling it rhetorical education.

The worst threat to good education is the increasing blind partisanship of those who do speak out about their beliefs. "Trained" not to listen but to shout, we end up with what Nicholas Kristof calls "snarling from the left and snarling from the right." "Liberals have now become as intemperate as conservatives, and the result – everybody shouting at everybody else – corrodes the body politic."[1] Students learn, from year one, as they observe the public scene, that *that's the way to do it*. And too often they do *not* learn, in the classroom, that there are other, better ways.

Unfortunately, the problems in education are by no means limited to mere neglect of Rhet-Ed. The increasing decline in financial support leads to cutting of music and art programs, reduction in physical education opportunities (except for would-be professional athletes), and grotesque increase in class size. While schools in some affluent regions escape these problems, most schools spend less and less per student, while the government promises to "leave no child behind." Similar problems apparently arise in England. On a visit in April of 2003, I found the British press full of lamentations about a decline in funding for schools.

90

With teachers underpaid and exasperated with routine imposed testing, building repair neglected, class size bloated, and federal and state grants for food and book purchases radically reduced, more and more children find themselves in a daily setting that leads them to consider "education" a meaningless, even hateful imposition of hours in a nasty, overcrowded, pleasure-free environment to be escaped whenever possible. Instead of saying, at the end of each day, "My hours at school were the best of my day," they feel those hours were the worst.[2] It is hardly surprising that dropout rates are increasing rapidly: more than one in five Chicago residents between age 16 and 24 are both out of school and out of work.[3]

The abominable disparity between what is spent on children in wealthy neighborhoods and what is spent in the inner cities or impoverished rural areas ought to incite mass protest. Recent studies have claimed that about 44 million Americans cannot even read – yet almost all of them have been subjected to this or that version of "education" in cheapened public schools.

The main point here, however, will not be the decline of economic support but the widespread neglect of Rhet-Ed, even in well-funded schools: *our democracy depends on better Rhet-Ed than most of our children now receive.* Now is the time for all of us to fight against miseducation in rhetoric.

You may well wonder, "Why offer another jeremiad about bad education, when we are already flooded with studies, from the right, left, and center, proving bad quality?" Well, too often the complaints are not about failure to learn the *arts of Rhet-Ed* but simply about the failure to impart this or that bit of *essential knowledge* that everybody who is anybody must possess – as if to say: "Students who don't recognize the names Mad Anthony Wayne or Oliver Cromwell must be failed. Students who don't recognize the quotation, 'To be or not to be, / That is the question,' or who have not read *Great Expectations*, or cannot diagram a sentence or understand Euclidean geometry, must start over" (or too often, by implication, drop out; a great many "studies" demonstrating a rise in test scores have deliber-ately suppressed the fact that dropout rates have been increased, leaving only the "better" students to be tested and thus raise the faked scores).[4] And schools whose students do badly on this or that idiosyncratic information list are put on probation, while the few students who pass the tests are transferred to a better school or given vouchers for such a transfer.

Surely our efforts at reform should not depend on the claim that this or that fact has been lost or that things were in the old days better. No serious thinker about education in any earlier period in any country could ever have said, "All is well." In 1776, what percentage of American citizens, of *all classes*, had studied *Hamlet*? How large was the minority who could actually read, for themselves, the Declaration of Independence? What proportion of the population in England, the year before that, had actually read, or could have read if they tried, Burke's speech recommending conciliation with the Colonies?

Can we really claim that education in America a hundred years ago, when only 3 percent of the population, most of them males, graduated from high school, was better than it is today, when almost 85 percent graduate from high school and more graduate from college than in any nation except Japan?[5] Was British education better in the early post-war period, when only 7 percent of 19-year-olds went to university, than it is now, when 43 percent of young people attend?[6]

All claims of decline are thus debatable. Even my claim about the increasing neglect of Rhet-Ed could be rejected by many responsible teachers of "Rhetoric and Composition," "Freshman Composition," or "Writing." Some might rightly respond to me with: "How much do you know about it, since you've only taught the elite at the University of Chicago? We're teaching rhetoric in our courses, and teaching it well, with or without the terminology." They could then cite innumerable examples of teachers giving full attention to improvement of communication, to the reduction of misunderstanding, to the creation of students who know how to join a community of mutually trusting inquirers. I have encountered scores of such teachers – at all levels – committed to teaching the benefits and delight of listening-rhetoric.[7] And doesn't the "flowering" that I reported in chapter 2 make my lamentation a bit out of date?

So I must put aside my undemonstrable belief that things are getting worse and turn instead to the consequences of neglect *now*. Whether we think the scene is worse than ever, or getting better all the time, it is still badly in need of a cure.

What Should *Everybody* Learn?

Only slowly over the centuries did the ideal of universal education develop, and these days it is the failure to come even close to such an ideal that produces most of our jeremiads, including mine. Most lamenters, rightwing and leftwing, repeat the truism: "Education is essential for *everyone*." So what must every citizen of a democracy know, if democracy is to function?

One part of the standard answer is correct: every citizen needs to know how to read and write, and to do these well does entail an absorption of huge amounts of information about the world. But hardly ever is that answer put in the form, "to read and write *well* one must learn how to read and listen to rhetoric *critically* and then write or speak *effective* rhetoric in response. And if you learn to do these well, the absorption of necessary information will occur as you read and write." Rarely do the official reformers talk about what the better teachers are meanwhile working on: how to motivate children to pursue learning for the love of communion with others who pursue learning *with you* – including your teachers. The political proposal for improvement is almost always in the form of imposing national or statewide standard tests of factual knowledge.

I now challenge you to get a copy of your state's or country's version of a "standard" (if you're in the UK get a copy of this or that A-level exam), and test yourself. You'll almost certainly be shocked by your "ignorance" – as I was when I had to give myself an "F" on a set of factual questions I found on a State of Texas standardized test. I am sure that if I had a chance to impose a test on those Texas testers,

I could honestly ask a host of questions about knowledge important to me that would land them in failure. Is it not scandalous that those testers don't know what an *isographeme* is, or even the meaning of *phronesis?*

The point, I should again insist, is not that factual knowledge is unimportant; it is that inert memorized knowledge torn out of the human context of issues discussed with others crushes educational motive. Here is how the sad results of dry standard testing are summarized by a former teacher from Texas, Neil J. Liss:

> Students are deprived of the opportunity to think critically and openly. Teachers are locked into curriculums that deny the freedom to create provocative learning environments. Administrators are shackled to a system that reduces them to sycophants toward their leadership. The community is silenced from a progressive dialogue about real quality in education.[8]

It is true that some teachers who are annoyed by the rules respond with an extreme in the opposite direction: careless invitations to ignore "knowledge" and simply pour out feelings or experiences without bothering to think about audience, and without taking in the knowledge needed to enter the minds of a given intended audience. They may succeed in engaging a larger share of their students, but they still fail to teach the better forms of Rhet-Ed.

In short, with teachers being forced to stress regurgitation of daily fact-menus, rather than critical thinking and productive arguing, how are kids to learn that to conduct a productive argument is far more important and rewarding than learning how not to spell *weird* as *wierd*, or when it is legitimate to split an infinitive, or even to end a sentence with a preposition?[9] They are subjected to the kind of deadening drill that in the past was too often taught under the name of classical rhetoric: mere memorization of terms and categories. (That is what I. A. Richards and others were trying to combat a century ago, by reviving serious attention to rhetoric. Too many were by then reducing rhetoric to rule-imposition.)

But the problem is far greater than just the emphasis on accumulating facts. Political biases, as we'll see in chapter 6, seem increasingly to affect just which facts should be learned, or what texts should be read. As Diane Ravitch has dramatized in her popular book *The Language Police: How Pressure Groups Restrict What Students Learn* (2003), textbook publishers and standard-test-composers are surrendering to censorship requests from both the right and left: students must not read a text that mentions any topic or uses any word that might hurt feelings or produce angry response. It is not just that they mustn't read a book like *Huckleberry Finn*, with its use of the word "nigger," or a quotation in a test that challenges their beliefs. They must not encounter texts that express the slightest criticism of any ethnic or social group, or any political view that is suspect. Textbooks must not upset or even challenge students with views or language that this or that group finds offensive – and too often, as Ravitch brilliantly demonstrates, the publishers and examiners surrender, producing a fake-education that is in fact boring – her word. Here is a selection of banned words and phrases and images that Ravitch reports:

blind leading the blind: banned as handicapism
jungle: replace with "rain forest"
senile: banned as demeaning to older people
snowman: replace with "snow person"
women as more nurturing than men
pioneer woman riding in covered wagon while man walks

As Gary M. Galles puts the problem, assailing the leftwing side of it:

Nothing in PC [politically correct] texts is allowed to be negative. Anything that could be construed as evaluative or judgmental must come across as positive. What cannot be made to appear good in other ways must be achieved through verbal contortions. PC language trades in words that have perfectly clear meanings for phrases that

95

enmesh us in ambiguity. It hinders communication, an essential precursor to learning, undermining education.[10]

What Ravitch and Galles underplay, however, is the way in which the censorship destroys Rhet-Ed of the kind learned only in conducting serious argument, practicing LR. If every potentially offensive or troublesome word or concept is removed, how will students ever learn the practice of productive critical debate, facing contrary views, and how to listen to and respond to them? Though Ravitch's book is important in warning against dogmatic "cleaning up," it fails to mention how her targets, especially ideological censors, are destroying the resources of rhetoric, of argument, of productive conversation (none of these terms gets much attention in any of her works; rhetoric is never mentioned). Yet her book does provide further appalling evidence of how justified Gerald Graff is in his book about education, as he laments the failure to cultivate language experience that produces genuine human engagement.[11]

Miseducation Outside the Classroom

A major problem is not inside the educational system but outside: all students, including those who can pass the standard tests at a 100 percent, are threatened with powerful miseducation the moment their teachers disappear. Not trained to think skeptically about the quality of arguments, never having learned the fun of genuine LR, too many students get hourly training from the media in win-rhetoric of the bad kinds. The goal in life is to triumph.

Various studies have shown that the average child spends almost as much time watching TV as attending classes. Many spend additional hours receiving half-baked or utterly false information on the Internet. And even among those who finally get hooked into serious reading, too many are barraged with books and articles and pamphlets proclaiming outrageous doctrines and "confirming" hate-ridden myths, with no internal hint of how the assertions might be challenged. Though examples are plentiful on all sides, left and right, secular and religious, to me the most dreadful are the publications by religious fundamentalists of diverse kinds. Students read claims by organizations like "Christian Identity" that "northern Europeans" are biologically and theologically superior to Jews, who are "Satan's minions." They fall upon book after book proving that arguments for evolution are absurd since the earth was created 6,000 or 10,000 years ago. (Pollsters claim that 58 percent of Americans believe that God created human beings within the last few thousand years.)

But it is not just religious excesses. Large numbers believe in UFOs, in astrology, and in alien abductions. Many believe – because of politicians' assertions – that Iraq sponsored Al Qaeda; evidence that Osama bin Laden included Saddam Hussein among his enemies was simply suppressed by administration reports of Bin Laden's speeches. (President Bush finally rejected this myth in September 2003.) Instead of encountering serious discussion about such claims, students are met with bland, dogmatic assertions. So what they "learn" outside the classroom, about "the world" and how to deal with fact-claims and arguments about them, is outrageously contrary to Rhet-Ed.

They are similarly miseducated by implicit messages about how one should deal with opponents. In popular TV shows they learn not only that violent threats are everywhere but that the only proper response is to shout down, or even threaten violent response, or actually perform it. In news programs and talk shows they observe either shouting down or bland hypocritical cover-ups. How many talk shows have you seen recently in which anyone really listened to and responded to the other side? The more skillful ones do employ the traditional casuistical response: "I see your point. But my claim is . . . " – but with no real encounter with what the point was. Even the "objective" hosts like Jim Lehrer seem deliberately to avoid direct discussion: the guests respond only to questions from the host, without facing each other and arguing productively. Thus viewers too often "learn" only that the business and political world is corrupt, and the way to deal with it is to turn your back on it.[12]

Even if you see my claims as biased exaggerations, I hope you will agree that what people learn about the world and how to deal with it, outside the classroom, is outrageously contrary to Rhet-Ed that stresses LR. The media diet is: stop listening and turn to violence, or at least to shouting down, since your opponents are probably planning violence right now. (We go further into the media problem in chapter 7.)

Back to the Classroom and the Threat of Standard Testing

How can any high school teacher spend time sorting through good and bad rhetoric, when success on the rote tests will determine whether her students graduate, and whether she consequently loses her job or gets a salary hike?

The variety of responses to that threat is dramatized in a recent issue of *Daedalus: The Journal of the American Academy of Arts and Sciences* (Summer 2002). It opens with Diane Ravitch supporting the use of universal "standard tests" – a piece much less admirable than her book mentioned above. The following eleven essays in response illustrate the complexities of judging what is wrong with the "test-score drive." Several of the essays move strongly in our direction here. Psychologist Howard Gardner, after accusing Ravitch of being too often a "mere rhetorician" – can I forgive him the pejorative? – in effect summarizes my case by claiming that the particular bits of knowledge taught "do not matter nearly so much as *the ways of thinking* that are (or are not) taught in those courses" (p. 24, my italics). Catharine Stimpson insists that "what is urgent to address are ongoing changes in our understanding of what it means to 'be human'" (p. 40). Theodore Sizer indicts publishers and administrators for neglecting "the discipline that every teacher faces:...doing what is necessary for *this* group of students to meet *this* standard in a manner that displays not only...[their] grasp of the 'facts' but their ability to apply them in both familiar and unfamiliar

98

situations" (p. 27). Jeffrey Mirel summarizes my case perfectly: "democracy depends on the ability to manage conflict constructively. Learning how to deal with conflict in a civil manner is one of the great lessons that schools in a democracy must teach" (p. 55). Thus most of the indictments are about neglect of Rhet-Ed – brilliant attacks from "non-rhetoricians" who on the whole have listened to the other side.

Some critics these days even more directly turn to moral questions, lamenting the failure of schools to engage in direct teaching of values. But what they too often overlook is that direct nagging about values works no better than nagging about facts – especially when teaching adolescents. Preach a value – "don't smoke" – and many kids see it as a strong motive for smoking. It is only by experiencing the sheer fun and personal profit of genuine listening, followed by really product-ive argument, that students can embrace the highest virtue of all: respect for others, producing trustful exchange.

That word virtue is again important here. How many students are learning to think about why building a community of mutual trust is better than winning this or that material reward? We'll never know, but we do know that too few schools engage students in serious ethical thinking of the kind stimulated by the rescuers we met in chapter 4.

The neglect of ethos, of character, was dramatized for me a few years ago when a "school reform" administrator, Paul Vallas, gave a talk celebrating his goal of raising test scores. In the question period, one of my favorite colleagues raised her hand and asked, "Mr. Vallas, just what kind of *person* do you hope will emerge from your program?" Without a second's hesitation, he almost shouted at her: "The kind who can *pass these tests!*" No doubt today, if confronted with that quotation, now that he is CEO of Philadelphia's public schools, he would either deny it or claim that it was in part ironical: "Of course I care about ethical qualities." But his response drama-tized his indifference to educating ethical *listeners*. And he is still stressing standardized testing, almost as if he believed that hard tests will somehow cure the disasters resulting from the underfunding he strongly opposes.[13]

How to Teach the Remedies

In a longer work I would now take you through a score of pedagogical techniques that implant Rhet-Ed effectively, especially of the LR kind: the whole range of methods, logical, ethical, and emotional, for getting both "sides" to listen. By now we have a rich literature on the relation between good rhetoric and ethical education, and the techniques for pushing that relation.[14] I can now offer only three brief suggestions to teachers, whether in kindergarten or advanced graduate courses. Indeed, versions of them can even be used to turn dinner conversations from disaster into a learning experience, or board meetings into astonishing discovery of new common ground. But I'm thinking here mainly about the classroom.

(1) Don't pontificate; don't slap down students you think are on the wrong side. Even if your group or class is much too large for individual encounters with everyone, *get strong rival opinions on deck.* This first step is the only one taken by some of the TV talk shows that I've excoriated; some of them at least hire opponents willing to shout extreme views. But that's only the beginning.

(2) Once you observe two opponents not listening, intrude authoritatively, shouting (pontificating if necessary):

> *Moderator:* Hey, wait a minute, Sandra. Have you noticed that Sam says you've not understood him? Have you understood what he's arguing for? Can you show him now that you have listened, by putting yourself in his shoes? Pretend that you *are* Sam, and make his case so well that he'll say, "Yes, that's what I'm arguing for."

Sandra then tries.

> *M:* Sam, has she said what you mean to say?
> *Sam* (almost always): Not at all. She's missed X, Y, or Z.
> *M:* Try again, Sandra.

Sandra may by now be furious: "I don't want to make such a silly case." But M. insists, and she tries.

M: Has she got it yet, Sam?
Sam: Not quite, but she's coming closer.

As the discussion goes on, Sandra surprisingly often finds herself shifting ground, saying something like, "Oh, now I see I got him wrong. If what you really mean, Sam, is such and such, now I can see what's really wrong with your position." And as Sam responds to that, M. insists that he attempt to formulate Sandra's position.

Such encounters are risky, of course, especially if M. faces a large number of students, some of whom might be bored with reducing the "performers" to two. But M. can easily expand the dialogue to include everyone in the room. If she has chosen her "targets" carefully, everyone in the room will have become eager to join into the LR.

(3) Once any group has done a half-decent job of articulating rival positions and has made some effort to understand the rivals, it often works to divide the groups physically: those who agree with Sam come over to this corner, those who choose Sandra in that corner, those who prefer what Louise has said over by the door, those who are not sure stand in *that* corner. Then have each corner present its case as persuasively as possible, with the debaters shifting locations whenever they feel persuaded. M. must insist throughout that who-ever joins the argument must address it to someone on the "other side." There is throughout this a potentially dangerous version of win-rhetoric: those in each corner hope that they'll get the most votes by the end. But they know that the others have a full oppor-tunity to present their case, and will not be won over unless they feel they've been listened to.

Sometimes, if the debate in a class is simply about what an author has intended, and if one group has obviously misread an intention, the debate can quickly end in unanimity. When one of my classes was discussing Mill's *On Liberty* years ago, several students and I had taken

101

as Mill's opinion a paragraph – a bit carelessly written – that was in fact his summary of his opponent's views: he was employing *style indirect libre*. Students quarreled about whether it was really Mill's opinion. Within five minutes the more careful readers had won all of us over: Mill's actual words, preceding the paragraph, made his objection clear – though not clear enough.

At other times, the debate can end in productive chaos, with students debating, even quarreling, as they leave the classroom. One of my greatest pleasures as a teacher has come when students ask me to join an after-class discussion, or when they report, the next day, that they went on arguing through the evening, arriving not at full agreement but at fuller understanding. Some even manage to practice what Peter Elbow calls "the believing game" – penetrating the opponent's world so far as really to feel what it would be like to *believe* what before had seemed a totally absurd idea.[15]

If our children encountered teachers, from grade one to the top, who exhibited such LR, Rhet-Ed would – well, I can't quite claim that it would save the world, but it would certainly attract into educational careers many who are now driven away.

Teaching Research

A special area of teaching that is radically dependent on LR is research. In many of the more ambitious high schools and in most colleges, students are required to do research and write up their results, often with no explanation of why the requirement is worthwhile. They seldom learn how essential research is to all of us (indeed, how much they have relied on a kind of research all their lives, whenever they need any information answering an everyday question: "Where can I find the most inexpensive CD store?"). And they too often fail, even in the required courses, to discover how much research can be improved when we practice LR.

Joseph Williams, Gregory Colomb, and I, in *The Craft of Research*, have stressed this view of research as a path to a rewarding rhetorical community. Too much research teaching leaves students bored, wondering why on earth they are being required to do it. They just don't learn the fun of asking and answering questions in a way that entices readers to join in the inquiry. They fail to practice attentive listening to other research reports. They don't learn the importance of asking, at every point, "How will I respond if my reader asks about my work, 'So what? What does it matter?'" They thus lose the fun of it.

What's more, they fail to learn the challenge of facing conflicting hypotheses. Serious researchers (like serious murder investigators) learn the importance of balancing at least two rival solutions, treating each with equal fairness, and deciding whether one or the other is superior. Nothing is more educationally challenging than confronting, in one's own head, two opposing "cases," then listening sympathetically to *all* of the arguments on both sides.

Thus practicing LR can turn research into a capstone of the best Rhet-Ed. Yet every year thousands of students learn to hate research as the ultimate in educational boredom: it is just repeating everything you can find that supports your idea – and who cares whether others share the idea? And too many of those who actually get attracted by research learn to do it not for the fun of learning but "professionally," as the only road to commercial success. The projects they work on are dictated more and more often by money from outside, and their results are measured by how much profit they yield.[16]

Political Cures

As a lifetime aspirer to the role of moderator (and yet in actual practice a frequent authoritarian violator of LR), I am tempted to add here a long list of books and articles that *everyone in all cultures* should study *every day*. Instead, suppose we just think a bit about what any nation might do to combat the neglect of Rhet-Ed.

Obviously some sort of major revolution is required, one that, unlike the British and American and French and Communist and Fascist revolutions, avoids producing more and more vitriolic rhetrickery on all sides. What each society needs – and will never achieve – is a transformation into a Utopia of the kind I accidentally encountered recently when my flight had to take an emergency stop on an island in the South Seas. I found myself in a society I'd never even heard of before, RHETOPIA. Stranded for three days there, I learned that an astonishing prime minister, Sir Rhetrancer, has been supervising educational reform for over three decades, devoting a huge portion of public funds and political energy to improving Rhet-Ed. I was thrilled to see that everyone in Rhetopia works to ensure that *all* students become devoted to building a genuine SOCiety – that is, a SOCial world where SOCial values are at the center. The ability to create genuine LR by removing misunderstanding is now pursued in Rhetopia from kindergarten up through graduate school, in every discipline. Unlike many devoted teachers in the United States who are resigning in order to escape the test-craze, the teachers there are seduced into a permanent vocation, because they have experienced the sheer joy of *connecting*, rhetorically, trustingly, with their students. That transformation has been achieved by Sir Rhetrancer's persuading the legislature – he had to employ first-class rhetoric, of course – to pass thirty-one astonishing laws imposing Rhet-Ed (especially in LR form, of course), from which I select here only the most important ones.

1   Teachers' salaries, in all fields, on all parts of the island, equal the average income of those who have specialized in business education and law. At first there was a great deal of CEO opposition to passing this law, some of it with vast cash donations through lobbyists to legislators, some of it almost violent. But by now, thirty years later, since all of the CEOs and politicians there have themselves passed through genuine Rhet-Ed, they have happily acceded to it, recognizing its benefits. Indeed, many of them are encouraging their own children to become teachers (now that teachers' income equals the average of the most affluent professions).

2   No administrators, whether in schools or universities, are now appointed unless they have specialized in Rhet-Ed, in one field or another. The previous practice of appointing administrators trained primarily in business management, and successful at the bad kinds of win–rhetoric, has been long abandoned.

3   In contrast to earlier practice, the law now requires that precisely the same amount of government cash go to students in impoverished areas as goes to kids in wealthy areas. National inspectors visit all schools to determine that the equipment in all is equal. (The only schools that might receive fewer dollars are those that don't teach Rhet-Ed – and those schools have by now disappeared.)

4   In place of the "standard rote tests" of previous eras, in Rhetopia the test of every school and college is a simple one, though in three parts, graded according to LR performance levels (especially on test "C": do students become committed to continuing education?).

(a)   What percentage of students at the end of each year say they *want* to continue learning, especially learning how to argue better, because they've found it wonderfully fun?

(b)   What percentage of students, after completing their elementary or secondary education, are determined to continue because they love learning about how to correct misunderstandings?

(c)   What percentage of students when facing a powerful assertion of this or that political view respond with, "What are your reasons for believing that?" or even better, "As I understand it, what you are saying is . . ." and then a sympathetic summary?

5   No one is allowed to compete for political office without having spent at least one year as a teacher in public schools or colleges. An original draft of the law required that such teaching be labeled as rhetoric, but citizens rightly insisted that to teach in *any* subject is a good path to appreciating the importance of improving communication, and thus making better political decisions.

6   Every administrator in any university or college or high school –
    even if a top celebrity – is required to teach a first-year rhetoric
    course every year.

7   Every department in every university and college must require a
    "capstone course," preceding graduation, in the special rhetorics
    of that discipline: The Rhetoric of Economics, The Rhetoric of
    Philosophy, The Rhetoric of Mathematics. None is allowed to
    call it merely a "Writing" or "Composition" course.

8   Whenever any journalist or politician uses the word "rhetoric" in
    a way that reduces it to rhetrickery, he or she is instantaneously
    transferred to some job requiring no use of words whatever. This
    law has been one of the most troublesome, because it has proved
    so difficult to find any job that does not depend on successful use
    of rhetoric, and the law thus seems hopelessly elitist. But a large
    part of the Welfare Relief Fund is allocated to feeding hungry
    journalists through a two-year program in rhetorical training.

Well, as I returned from those three days I turned on my old TV and
stumbled on a bit of the program *Crossfire*. Feeling cross, I "fired" by
punching to Public Television and there was the *McLaughlin Hour*,
with almost equally deaf shouting. I flipped again and there was the
Washington Gang on CNN. Horrors. In Rhetopia, not a single one of
those quarrelers now being paid fortunes for never listening would
even exist.

Obviously nothing remotely like Rhetopia will ever be realized.
Who would want to live in a country with so many laws violating our
freedom to choose our own form of miseducation? So the point is not
just to wake up a few professors in every field to see rhetoric's relevance
to what *they* do; it should be clear that if my broadened definition of
rhetoric has any validity, then this celebration (or jeremiad: take your
choice) is addressed to all readers who care about misunderstanding
and the skills required to achieve understanding. The only possible
listeners for whom my point would be irrelevant – those who want to
learn rhetrickery skills in order to win by doing harm in the world –
have of course long since cast this book into the garbage.

6

The Threats of Political Rhetrickery

What shall we do with powers, which we are so rapidly developing, and what will happen to us if we cannot learn to guide them in time?
I. A. Richards, *Principles of Literary Criticism*

In the counsels of government we must guard against the acquisition of unwarranted influence, whether sought or unsought, by the military-industrial complex. The potential for the disastrous rise of misplaced power exists and will persist.
President Dwight Eisenhower, Farewell Address, January 17, 1961

It's not negotiable, and I don't want to debate it.
President George W. Bush, in response to a journalist's question about Iraq policy

In our time, political speech and writing are largely the defense of the indefensible. Things like the continuance of British rule in India . . . [and] the dropping of the atom bombs on Japan, can indeed be defended, but only by arguments which are too brutal for most people to face, and which do not square with the professed aims of the political parties. Thus political language has to consist largely of euphemism, question-begging and sheer cloudy vagueness.
George Orwell, *A Collection of Essays* (1970)

The clearest examples of how rhetoric makes (and destroys) our realities are found in politics, where Aristotle's "deliberative rhetoric" reigns. Changing the present in order to change the future is everyone's political goal. Everybody knows that political argument changes our world day by day, often causing disasters and only sometimes preventing them. Especially in wartime, our lives are flooded with political rhetoric, defensible and indefensible (what I'll label P-Rhet).[1]

Whenever we try to discuss any small stream of such floods, we face three major problems:

- the banality both of the subject itself and of the most dramatic examples of the good and bad kinds. "You deplore our floods of rhetrickery? What's new about political 'spinning' and aggressive lying?" "You praise Churchill's 'blood, sweat, and tears' speech? Surprise!" "You consider it scandalous when President Bush lies about statistics as he pushes his grotesque tax cut plans? What a revelation!" "You think Saddam Hussein was actually lying day in, day out? Just plain boring!"
- the bias of any critic who pronounces P-Rhet "defensible" or "indefensible." No critic of rhetoric can escape bias. Am I among those who are appalled by most of President Bush's self-serving policies and self-touting speeches? Obviously I am. So why should any reader trust my claims that much of his rhetoric is rhetrickery?
- the fantastic complexity of problems, motives, and audiences faced by every sincere political rhetor. Even the most honest among them must do some accommodation to the special interests and emotional commitments of particular audiences.

Feeling threatened by those problems, I wonder how many readers here have been as obsessed as I have been, through many decades, with abominable P-Rhet. In 1963, after the assassination of President John F. Kennedy, I attempted a little book, perhaps to be called "Evil Communication," loaded with lamentations like this:

Whatever the truth about the Kennedy assassination [charges were leveled in every direction, including the claim that Lyndon Johnson

108

engineered it], the truth about its aftermath is that Americans are unable to discuss such matters productively. It may be too strong to say, as some have, that the debate about the assassination is a greater national disgrace than the assassination itself, but no one can read more than a few pages of what has passed for debate to see that there is simply no rational limit on what some Americans will believe. There are no effective limits to what will be said, and no standards for how it will be said. A shout is worth as much as the most carefully reasoned argument.

As I expand that lament here, the center will be the rhetoric of our leaders, with only a short section toward the end about the rhetoric of protesters. Because I am writing and revising throughout 2003 and 2004, and because I was personally appalled when the US invasion of Iraq was first threatened and then carried out (with consequences that, though increasingly troublesome, are still highly unpredictable), many of my examples are by now – whenever "now" is – not just outdated but obviously biased. We can be sure, though, that the cheating and distorting I report, by both leaders and protesters, will go on occurring in future events. Just translate my outdated examples into your current scene. The problems of P-Rhet, and the need for citizens to be alerted to the problem, will never go away.[2]

In chapter 7 I will deal briefly with how our media reinforce political rhetrickery: passionate "proofs" for this or that false belief, left and right, can be found in every morning paper, in every weekly magazine, on every news channel – to say nothing of conversations over dinner. Deceptive P-Rhet is found even in ostensibly objective political science journals. A few of the better journals, like the *Boston Review*, aim for an airing of all sides in a particular quarrel, but even in these one finds the effects of bias in the editing. Thus we need deeper rhetorical education, not just about the media but about political practice.

The Good and the Bad of It

Putting aside judgments of accommodation skills when addressing particular audiences (what some might simply label "technique," the choice of *this* metaphor or cliché or synonym rather than *that* one), what are the differences between justifiable P-Rhet and the stuff we should publicly condemn – or at least personally resist?

The most obvious standard we all apply is that of success. If a speaker wins strong support for a cause that we embrace, we celebrate the rhetoric, even if we spot technical flaws. But if she drives the audience away, we tend to proclaim the speech or article a failure, regardless of the skill exhibited. For many rhetoricians throughout history, this has been the sole, comfortable criterion, especially in time of war. Though P-Rhet that leads to successful diplomacy rather than war is frequently praised – at least when the enemy is not a real threat – most efforts are judged according to their success in uniting those potentially on one side or the other.[3] A leader seeking support for defense feels no impulse to demonstrate that he has really listened to the enemy and is trying to get the enemy to listen – except of course to hear the threat and retreat. Standards of judgments are thus localized: did the speech prove successful in addressing *this* audience, on *this* occasion? Judged by this standard, Edmund Burke's amazing effort to achieve conciliation was poor rhetoric (see pp. 52–4).

Throughout the ages, the most passionate – and thus the most questionable – rhetoric has been about war, from leaders and followers on both sides. Some war-rhetoric can be judged as remarkably skillful, as are most of Shakespeare's inventions of speeches by war leaders. Can we really question the excellence of Henry V's skill in winning his audience, into battle?

> But this lies all within the will of God,
> To whom I do appeal, and in whose name
> Tell you the Dauphin I am coming on
> To venge me as I may, and to put forth
> My rightful hand in a well-hallowed cause. (I, ii. 289–93).

Such speeches are thrilling – to the right local audience: *my country, right or wrong.* Just as Hitler's wild speeches thrilled millions of Germans, war speeches by Franklin Roosevelt and Winston Churchill

110

thrilled me, and President George W. Bush's and Prime Minister Tony Blair's celebration of the Iraq attack have apparently thrilled a majority of Americans (while alienating most of the rest of the world). The very thought of patriotic war violence somehow ignites passionate agreement, often including the belief that God is Himself speaking.[4]

Such stuff works – on those who are ready to receive it and thus already inclined to "join up." Shakespeare knew that Henry V's audience was already on the king's side: he could portray his hero as knowing that the enemy would probably never hear his words; he had no need to think about how those words might inflame his enemies or even attract larger numbers to the enemy's cause. Those on his side would find the passionate rhetoric justifiable, while to me now, considering it "internationally," it seems a dangerous model, one that, like thousands of war songs and memorized war speeches, has "educated" all of us to celebrate the glories of war.

Two Modern Revolutions

Too many political leaders these days seem unaware that rhetorical corners like Henry V's are by now extremely rare. They speak as if oblivious of two major "revolutions" that have complicated every moment of P-Rhet. Everyone is at least dimly aware of these two transformations. Why they are so frequently ignored is a mystery.

(1) The media have by now produced an inescapable expansion and multiplicity of audiences. What a rhetor says to Congress or Parliament will be heard and judged or misjudged not just by those present, or by those in other countries. The words and images will be heard and viewed all over the world, on TV and radio and even on newspaper front pages. What would Shakespeare have had Henry V say if he were writing today, knowing that not only the French but potential friends or enemies in other nations would hear his words?

A major result is that accommodation to specific audiences now becomes much more dangerous than it used to be. Any speaker's enemies can easily check on what was said last week to a different audience, and then declare the speaker dishonest. Democrats have been catching President Bush in these conflicts again and again, and now (revising in March 2004), Republicans are catching probable-candidate Senator John Kerry embracing one position this week to this specific audience, and saying the opposite next week to that specific audience.[5] Thus accommodation to any specific audience, even one as large as "patriotic American" or "anti-Republican," is now easily exposed. A recently released documentary traces how President Bush "accommodated" his claims about weapons of mass destruction (WMD), as his American audience became more and more aware of the shakiness of the evidence for them. At first he was "absolutely certain" that Hussein had "weapons of mass destruction," ready to be released any day now. But by June of 2003 his phrase was "programs of mass destruction." And by the time of his State of the Union address in 2004, the phrasing was "weapons of mass destruction-related program activities."

(2) As a result of the development of weapons of *mass* destruction, and thus the threat of mutual annihilation, war is no longer merely local, promising a clear victory to one "side" or the other. When Henry V attacked France, no other nations bothered much about it. When he spoke about the plan of attack, no leader in Asia or the Near East would have responded, even if they heard his speeches; none of his weapons threatened them. "The world" went its own manifold ways; soldiers fought only other soldiers, with no available planes or rockets to spread the attacks on to civilians.

When President Bush declared war on an "axis of evil" – Iraq, Iran, and North Korea – and then led a preemptive war on Iraq, his words and the technologically advanced attack they supported were overheard – though probably not really *listened* to – by the whole world. Considered militarily, this revolution in what "war" means has been acknowledged in almost everything that leaders like Bush and Blair have said: the "war" on terrorism is a worldwide war, and weapons of mass destruction are a rising threat everywhere. Considered rhetorically, however, their speeches have still been mainly aimed locally, at those already fired up in support of a war. President Bush has occasionally attempted to avert full hatred of all Muslims, as if working to achieve worldwide peace and full democracy everywhere. But most of his words referring to those "out there," the opponents and potential opponents, have been words of threat or hate, employing the military revolution as if the media revolution had not occurred. Whatever the conscious goal inspiring the rhetoric might have been, the effect was generally to increase rather than diminish the number of enemies. When asked about the rise in protest bombings in Iraq, his response was "Bring 'em on."

It is not that the importance of friendly rhetoric has been ignored. When Secretary of State Colin Powell appointed Charlotte Beers as the State Department's undersecretary of state for public diplomacy, the proclaimed goal was to convince the Arab world that we were not what they thought we were: the enemy of Allah and all Arabs. She was to redefine "who America is, not only for ourselves under this kind of attack [September 11], but also for the outside world." Huge sums were spent trying to capture a sympathetic Arab audience, by getting us "branded" as standing for real freedom. But, as Sheldon Rampton and John Stauber put it, in *Weapons of Mass Deception* (2003), "Bombardments of rhetoric can annoy and offend their targets."

The effort had no success: "Attempts to market the United States as 'brand freedom' came into conflict with a U.S. tendency to talk rather than listen" (pp. 11–12). The frightening fact still remains that even if Beers, or the Office of Global Communications (OGC), had been more skillful in their mission of "supervision of America's image abroad," it is extremely unlikely that the targets addressed would have been willing to engage in a discussion based on *listening*.

Thus the two revolutions – they could be dubbed awkwardly as "media globalization" and "globalization of weaponry" – have transformed the narrow audience of classical wartalk into a multiplicity of audiences.[6] By now, some audiences who are not listened to by the speaker will respond as did leaders in North Korea, back in April 2002 after President Bush declared them part of the "axis of evil" and thus implied that they must be destroyed. Under the headline "EMBRACING THE RHETORIC OF ARMAGEDDON," one newspaper reported leaders in North Korea as responding: "We will resolutely wipe out the aggressors and reduce them to a forlorn wandering spirit.... [We will] turn the stronghold of the enemy into a sea of fire" and "take 1,000-fold revenge."[7] Such respondents have been part of Bush's unlistened-to audience, and they answer his careless metaphors with open threats, as frightening as those on our side. As the occupation continues (March 2004), the rhetoric of the Iraqis and other Muslim nations has become increasingly vitriolic against the United States. Would they be talking and acting as they are if President Bush had thought a bit harder about the wide range and deep convictions of his real audience?

In sum, the task of judging P-Rhet, both ethically and technically, has been expanded by the two revolutions to include our having to face not just the effects on any local audience but also the effects on the future of the entire world. If leaders win massive local support, using Henry V's kind of rhetoric, and simultaneously increase enemies around the world, have they truly succeeded? They cannot win the new wars unless their words and images portray effective thinking about how they will be heard globally and how they imply some chance of improving *the world's* future. Only if they have *listened* to the international audience, thinking hard about both the local welfare and the welfare of the world, can their words be judged as not only successful but totally justifiable.

When Prime Minister Blair, for example, addressed the US House of Representatives on July 17, 2003, he revealed a splendid ability to employ arguments and flourishes that would appeal to the strongly pro-war majority – and impress even those of us Americans who oppose his views. He had in effect listened to many Americans, his "local" audience, in advance. Even while opposing his views, I found his talk far superior to anything Bush has said, and must judge it "high-quality win-rhetoric – of the narrow kind." But he had apparently failed to think hard about his British audience, most of whom would hate – or so my guess is – his pandering to US power.

114

(He did incorporate several deep criticisms of Bush's unilateral policies, but so subtly that most of the media didn't even mention them the following morning.) Was Blair not concerned about how America's critics in the UK would respond to his hyped-up praise of the United States as Britain's best friend? Obviously success with the House of Representatives was his primary goal – and he won, in that narrow sense.[8]

Similarly, when President Bush was feeling challenged, in mid-July 2003, about the evidence for WMD in Iraq, his answer was, "*There is no doubt in my mind* that Saddam Hussein was a threat to the world's peace. And *there's no doubt in my mind* that the United States did the right thing in removing him from power" (my italics). In other words, "I don't need to listen to any dissent. You should just listen to me. I will not consider the evidence that may have produced doubt in *your* mind, since there is no doubt in *mine*. And I assume that you'll take my own certainty as hard evidence." When he addressed the UN on September 23, 2002, what was heard was all self-confidence about what would hook Americans; but only a fraction of the media made the point that his words "were aimed more at a domestic audience than the world community" (*New York Times*).

Such examples of non-listening appall me, as does the fact that very little of what we protesters have said has shown any signs of LR. Leaders and protesters on all "sides" are employing mere win-rhetoric, often of the worst kinds.

What the two revolutions require, then, in the face of such P-Rhet, is that we must rethink all of our ideas about accommodation to audiences. Every important bit of P-Rhet is intentionally or unintentionally addressed now to a *worldwide* audience. And our future depends on politicians who can find ways of addressing that larger audience, instead of talking only of "crusades" against "evil" adversaries.

In short, we can no longer depend on clever *localized* P-Rhet. Our leaders must learn to listen to, or imagine, the arguments of all "sides," actually considering global welfare as finally determining the welfare of the speaker and the localized audience.

The consequences of failures to listen are so obvious as hardly to deserve listing. By now (spring 2004) we are already seeing the current consequences of strongly localized P-Rhet, whether from leaders, followers, or protesters. They fall into four main kinds:

- Opponents of even the noblest cause can too often find examples of rhetrickery defending that cause, thus "proving" that the "enemy" is contemptible. "If my enemy's cause is supported by that kind of blind irrationality or immoral accommodation to audience prejudice, what further proof do I need that the cause is both stupid and cruel?" When a protest poster calls President Bush an "asshole" or "evil," all hawks feel confirmed in their support: those doves are blind, cruel idiots. When a leader's defender condemns all critics as "unpatriotic," or even labels them as "traitors," the leader's critics rightly feel that they have strong evidence that their opposition is justified.[9]
- Partisans on all sides become unjustifiably skeptical of *everything* said on the other side. Instead of *listening* and making critical distinctions, everything said is reduced to deception. For many doves, absolutely nothing said by Secretary of Defense Rumsfeld or President Bush can be trusted. The same is true for most non-Americans. A reporter in London's *Financial Times* wrote: "Mr. Rumsfeld is the shock jock of diplomacy, the Howard Stern of American Policy. It is a disgraceful indictment of the Bush administration that this man has become the most identifiable spokesman for the U.S. foreign policy." But that extreme claim is mistaken: even a Rumsfeld should be *listened* to, distinguishing the sound cases from the faked. Meanwhile, in the same way, hawks judge every protest statement as dogmatic, blind anti-patriotism that does not deserve to be listened to. Thus all chances of dialogue are destroyed.
- The mistrust on both sides gets absurdly exaggerated: Instead of merely suspecting some lying or fudging or mild suppression of evidence, the suspicion is extended to charges of criminality. When President Bush rejected Inspector Blix's further pursuit

116

of whether Iraq had weapons of mass destruction (April 23, 2003), thousands of his opponents, in the United States and abroad, assumed that his motive was simply to be able to *plant* those weapons secretly and then tell the world, "At last we've found the evidence proving that we were right in our preemptive strike." None of us who mistrust him has any evidence that he would ever go that far to deceive us, but his less serious deceptions implanted the stronger (and probably absurd) suspicion. When he went on month after month, saying things like "Yes, we have now found the weapons of mass destruction," and, on May 1, 2003, that "In the battle of Iraq, the United States and our allies have prevailed," while "still having work to do in Iraq," more and more "listeners" decided that *nothing* he said could be thoroughly trusted. Many extend the charge to "it's all deliberate lying," overlooking the likelihood that he often believes what he says, only later discovering how he has himself been deceived. So the total suspicion can be misleading and destructive. We thus all risk falling into mistrust of some statement that is actually both true and important. Writing in spring 2004, how can I predict what our future judgment of all this P-Rhet will be?

- Suspicion about deception has always increased in wartime, because wars *require* increased deception. But this time the effect has been one of the strongest ever, as journalists find their own lives depending on victory and their own professional status depending on reports favorable to the White House. As David Bauder put it, on April 22, 2003, "With the reporters quite literally depending on the military for their lives, there was the real possibility it could cost them their objectivity."[10] And some have implicitly followed Rush Limbaugh's open declaration (as reported, reliably?), "objectivity be damned." One congressman has explicitly criticized the US administration for not adequately *censoring* what journalists report from the war. And journalist's spontaneous self-censorship is magnified. The result has been a grotesque increase in mistrust of all media reports, as we'll see in the next chapter.

117

After the dramatic scene of Saddam Hussein's statue crashing down, treated by US media as an unquestionable sign of victory, Hussein or his minions sent out a flood of images and claims that his side was still winning – passionately declaring that Bush, the "sick dog," was talking "garbage" and was losing. The lies issued by Hussein's defender, Mohammed Diab Ahmed, became – understandably – a prominent farcical target for many American journalists, convinced of US victory. US spokesmen exaggerated every such seeming triumph and played down every anxiety in ways that all of our enemies – along with all of us protesters – saw as equally absurd. And at every moment the media were profiting from the daily explosion of vitriolic extremes on all sides and Orwellian double-speak by this or that moderate.

So as the troubles in Iraq mount, rhetoric from the left is full of the word "quagmire," while those on the right claim that using that term proves lack of patriotism. And now that the administrators have been caught in unquestionably dishonest rhetrickery about evidence for weapons of mass destruction, everyone on all sides is heating up and shallowing down the talk about it. We doves are feeling that there is no point in trying to listen to an administration that itself does not listen; all we can do is shout. And the pro-war crowd feels certain that whatever we say is stupid or downright evil. That's what war does to our rhetoric.

As Gunter Grass says, summarizing that degradation: "The rhetoric of the aggressor increasingly resembles that of his enemy. Religious fundamentalism leads both sides to abuse what belongs to all religions, taking the notion of God hostage in accordance with their own fanatical understanding."[11]

What all of this dramatizes are the complex, paradoxical problems faced by any critic attempting to appraise the rhetoric of any intense conflict, any "war" – whether literal or figurative. On the one hand, violence and the threat of violence corrupt rhetoric, producing an explosion of rhetrickery; almost everything anybody says becomes contemptible. On the other hand, critics encounter an increase in their own bias, as violence threatens.

118

All of this is intended to underline the fact that the only real alternative to violence is LR of various kinds, including bargain-rhetoric.[12] We have to choose, when conflict heightens, either to argue or fight. At a given tragic moment, LR disappears, violence takes over, and rhetrickery casts off all thought, on all "sides": except about how to win.

Why Many Judgments Against "Dishonest" P-Rhet are Unfair

What I have said so far underplays the plain fact that leaders on all sides are surely justified in inventing the best possible strokes for defending any cause they consider genuinely noble. In wartime especially, that the cause is just is tacitly "demonstrated" by the "fact" that "our" "noble" lives are being lost to "evil" enemies. And how can anyone say that it is wrong to employ lies, some addressed to the enemy, some to our own side, if those lies will finally save the lives not just of soldiers but of us at home? Lying effectively becomes an honorable weapon of war, rivaling in import-ance even our military strength. If I can save the world by lying effectively, is not the lie more honorable than truth-telling that leads to massive disaster?

That question leads us to really deep problems in any appraisal of P-Rhet. It is not only that you cannot issue judgments about P-Rhet without employing your own rhetoric, which in turn hints at your own political biases. The deeper problem is found in the very nature of political leadership – a problem that has always been with us but that has been heightened by the multiplication of audiences produced in the media and weaponry revolutions that I have mentioned. The troublesome fact is – to repeat what for many is too obvious to need mentioning – that even the most sincere politician faces daily choices among conflicting "goods," choices that require sacrificing or betraying one good on behalf of another. And often that becomes a clear choice between two obvious evils.

Such conflicts have faced all leaders from the beginning – always earning them a bad reputation among moralists. All politicians, whether hoping to be sincere or not, find it necessary to hedge, waffle, dodge, mask, as they practice what we all practice as we choose among rival goods and evils.

As Aristotle put it, we all face the necessity of practicing *phronesis* (practical wisdom): learning how to balance this good against that good and come to some sort of Golden Mean. Such balancing often requires deliberate deception. For Machiavelli, such justified decep-tion is a *virtù* in itself, even when it requires violation of other virtues.[13] What the Jesuits originally labeled *casuistry* – they tend to avoid the term these days – is the balancing of virtues according to the conflicts in a given *case*. Every morning paper reveals moments when politicians and other leaders cannot escape casuistry: Catholic bishops confess their tough choices between protecting children from abuse and protecting the Church from scandal; an American officer openly regrets the choice about whether to release portraits of his ordered killing of two of Saddam Hussein's sons: releasing the photos (which he finally decided to do) will seem like American gloating, yet releasing them might reduce Iraqi fears.

Such practice of "situation ethics" – what T. S. Eliot called a "balance of contrarieties" – is required of us daily, quite aside from politics. I must decide, for example, whether or not to lie to avoid depressing my suffering friend ("You're looking much better this morning") or instead to abide by truth ("I'm sorry, Sam, but you look much worse this morning than you did yesterday"). I often face such hard choices here: surely I should give an honest report of my anger about that cruelly deceptive, already-famous speech given by a leader yesterday, yet surely I must work to create an implied author who meets my own high standards, one who really listens objectively to all sides.

Many modern philosophers have followed earlier efforts to rescue us from guilt over such choices "of the lesser evil." Isaiah Berlin often argued that accepting flatly contradictory "goods" need not lead to relativism: even as the goods conflict, they can both be real, and we must embrace a pluralism that accepts them while living with their regular conflict. Citing Giambattista Vico's *La Scienza Nuova* and Johann Gottfried Herder's works, Berlin says, "there are many different ends that men may seek and still be fully rational, fully men, capable of understanding each other and sympathizing and deriving light from each other."[14]

Aside from such theoretical defenses, actual choices between two or more conflicting "genuine goods," when either choice inflicts harm, are always hard to defend. Like each of us, politicians can never claim (though they often pretend to) that no harm was done by the necessary choice between "evils." The only real defense they can offer is that they have faced the nasty choices by engaging in *genuine listening*, fully honest consideration of the arguments for the conflicting "cases." (I have to confess that I'd hate to be a political leader these days, attempting such honest listening, when we have the multiplication of audiences produced by revolution no. 1, and when the evidence is strong that too many on the other side will never listen.)

Many thinkers in most fields would support the deep-listening alternative as the only protection against the excesses of inescapable deception. A recent book, *Crucial Conversations*,[15] summarizes quite well my argument for LR: "Find a shared goal and you have both a good reason and a healthy climate for talking." If you listen to the targets' words so closely that you discover what they are arguing for, and why, you might then discover a good and a truth superior to the one you felt you possessed when beginning. The "good of the nation" you *thought* you were honestly defending gets transformed. At the same time, by practicing some skillful accommodation to a variety of audiences, you can get them to listen rather than simply increasing their hatred for you.

It should not be overlooked, however, that one form of careful listening can produce one of the worst forms of deception. Really skillful rhetors can invent language that is intended to mean one thing to "insiders" while appeasing "outsiders." As Umberto Eco puts it, the speaker, by speaking in ambiguous terms, is actually sending a message in code that emanates from one power group and [yet] is destined for another. The two [secret] groups, sender and receiver, understand one another perfectly well.... It is clear, moreover, that in order for communication between power groups to carry on undisturbed it must go over the heads of the public, just like the coded message passing between two armed camps in a war situation.... The fact of its not being understood by others is the indispensable condition for the maintenance of private relation-ships between power groups.... Political discourse in this vein, what-ever the aims of the government in question, is anti-democratic because it leapfrogs the citizen and denies him any room to agree or disagree. It is an authoritarian discourse. Unmasking it is the only political activity that is worthwhile...the only real way to exercise rhetoric so as to create convictions rather than to induce subjugation.[16]

So the point of my lament about bad P-Rhet is not that our polit-icians hardly ever speak the plain truth: they wouldn't be where they are, and we would suffer bad consequences, if they were always "sincere." The welfare of any country requires leaders skillful in casuistry. The point is that too often these days P-Rhet is not conducted with a balance of rival *public* goods but simply with a pursuit of this or that personal profit or benefit for some corner of "the world," while harming the larger world: let's have personal triumph, even at the expense of public widespread harm. And – to underline the point of chapter 5 – too few of us have been educated to spot *that* kind of deception in the service of distorted "goods."

What we need most are (1) leaders who can avoid stupidly offending potential enemies, like calling the response to terrorism a "crusade" or labeling those Europeans against us as "old" and weak and those who are for us as "new"; (2) leaders who can balance local triumphs today – such as winning the next election – against the welfare of the world tomorrow; and (3) citizens who can detect the differences between LR and rhetrickery, and conduct their supporting and protesting with rhetoric that can possibly be actually listened to.

How Protesters Violate LR

Saving for the next chapter a look at the motives that corrupt rhetoric, can this protester claim that the rhetoric on his side is less corrupted than that of the leaders? I wish it were so. The future of all nations, and thus of the world, depends very much on the rhetoric of opposition movements, especially as they get strong enough to influence elections. Yet we protesters are, as I have already illustrated, often as guilty of non-listening as our leaders. We forget that democratic resolution of conflict depends not on shouting down those who have the military power but on building up majorities of those who oppose the use of force and, by really listening to our potential friends or "enemies," whether powerful leaders or mere "citizens," finding ways to entice them into hearing our case.

Any careful look at past governmental changes in any nation reveals that when protests reach a certain level – a level considered really dangerous by the leaders – policies do often get changed for the better (though sometimes tyrants take over and destroy the protesters). And many wars have been lost by those who had the military power to win easily, but quickly found that power ineffective in dealing with popular response to the "victory." While it is true that the most powerful military force usually wins, temporarily, history is full of cases in which seeming victory has been turned into defeat not just by guerrilla warfare but by the power of protesters' P-Rhet. Especially since the two revolutions I traced above, preemptive exercise of unquestionable military superiority has become increasingly questionable. Superiority over *what*? More and more military confrontations have turned into what Jonathan Schell labels "People's War" – encounters where democratic protest leads to the triumph of political rather than violent solutions.[17]

As you read here now – no matter when "now" is – massive marches and strikes and email campaigns are occurring around the world, some violent, some not, some successful, some not. Quite often it can be argued that the defeats are caused by the clumsy rhetoric of the protesters, often by misguided violence that alienates those who might have voted for them if they had practiced LR. If the protesters had really listened to their enemies, and modified their own words and actions to meet what they heard, they might have succeeded. Sometimes mass democratic protests, as in the American Revolution, finally work – in a way. The Colonies didn't win through overpowering military victory; they won because of steadily increasing mass democratic support of their cause.

Unfortunately what we usually celebrate about the American Revolution are the *military* triumphs, leading many to see the founding fathers as succeeding only because we fought so well. And this has produced a nation far too often inclined to see violence as the solution to all problems. As we sing "Battle Hymn of the Republic" or even our National Anthem, we are teaching ourselves and our children that engaging in "noble" warfare is the only way to be saved.

It is impossible to demonstrate the implied claim that America and "the world" would be in better shape if America and Britain had sought and found a productive compromise two centuries ago. But the P-Rhet on both sides for the most part simply denied that possibility. While our founders actually practiced some of the best rhetoric ever in winning the support of the people and thus driving the British away, what our textbooks mistakenly teach everyone today is that our tough, courageous fighting was what won. To fight back rather than argue thus became a national standard as the noblest way to go.

Whatever the historical causes, the United States now practices more violence per day, domestically, than most other nations, and some of our leaders talk as if we can finally establish a world in which our military power suppresses all others. It is thus hardly surprising that as we are trained to believe in violence on behalf of noble causes, we protesters too often put our points in terms that threaten blind violence or other forms of irrational excess. Assuming, sometimes justifiably, that the leaders will not listen to any responsible argument about their misdeeds or mistake, and thus that only violent threats will yield change, protesters tend to employ only threats: *without change you will be hurt or killed.*

Fortunately in any democracy, or half-democracy like ours, the threat need not be physical violence but simply lack of votes. As Schell traces so rigorously, open battles have often been averted by the mere accumulation of overwhelming voices in opposition. And that is where *defensible* P-Rhet by protesters comes in. The future of every nation depends absolutely on the quality of argument practiced by those who desire change.

Most of our protests are full of two kinds of shoddy P-Rhet. On the one hand too many who are appalled by leaders' policies simply disguise their true opinions and side with whatever will sell their case and protect them from power punishment, while trying to sneak in some slight objections. On the other hand, many protesters blurt out their protest with no thought about how to earn full attention. Ignoring the arguments and convictions on the other side, and thus with no visible respect for the opponent and with little attention to broadening the grounds for protest, they simply demonize the enemy, thus guaranteeing that no dialogue will ensue. Even when the case is actually, "You must listen to us, because in fact we are far more numerous and powerful than you have recognized," the claims are too often put in terms that seem contemptible to the other side. When anyone, not just a hawk, sees a poster saying "Bush is Satan," is his mind going to be changed? Of course not.

A clear example of risking excess is the movement, begun back in February of 2003 by former Attorney General Ramsey Clark, to lead Congress to impeach President Bush for his Iraq policies. Though many of Clark's claims of constitutional violations seem to me valid, it should have occurred to him that any move of that kind might simply serve to confirm our leaders' view that their opponents are dogmatic, cruel extremists: traitors. I'm fairly sure that it will produce in too many who hear it – not just the hawks – either self-righteous anger or hilarious mockery: it is surely seen as evidence *for* President Bush, not against him.

125

In short, whether protesters are on the left, as is mainly true these days, or on the right, as most of them were when President Clinton was threatened with impeachment, they too often reveal the same flaws as we've seen in leadership rhetoric. I could cite scores of attacks worded in such a way as to ensure non-listening:

- Molly Ivins's column, "Call Me a Bush Hater."[18] No potential critic of Bush will read that column or have her mind changed by it. It's a stupid rhetorical error to head a column with that, when in fact Ivins actually says such things as "It is not necessary to hate George W. Bush to think he's a bad President."
- Gore Vidal's overloaded, shrill attack on Bush's policies, *Perpetual War for Perpetual Peace: How We Got to Be So Hated* (2002). I accept most of Vidal's fundamental points, but too often he falls into a clever rhetrickery that actually provides evidence for the other side. If I were pro-Bush, I would conclude: "lefties don't think, they just shout."[19]

To make my case for a P-Rhet based on real listening would require a long, detailed analysis of at least one major speech – perhaps one of Nelson Mandela's speeches that saved South Africa from civil war. Unfortunately such defensible P-Rhet is so rare these days that it can produce the gloomy response of a media analyst like Eric Alterman. Reporting former Czech President Havel's speech to a joint session of Congress, in February 1990, he writes:

Havel entered the hall to a thunderous standing ovation. It was quite a moment, and even the tough guys in the press gallery were fighting back tears. This modest, diminutive playwright, fresh from facing down the guns of the Soviet empire and leading his country in a democratic revolution, had been invited to share his wisdom in the hall that sits at the rhetorical center of what was now, undisputedly, the most powerful nation in the history of the world. Never in my adult life had I witnessed so unambiguous a victory for the forces of sweetness and light. . . . He explored many of the great themes of

personal and political responsibility with uncommon wit and origina-
lity. . . . I was being addressed by a political leader who felt no com-
pulsion to speak down to his audience, to insult its intellect with
empty-headed rhetoric and pander to its egocentricity with kitschy
encomiums.

Putting aside Alterman's confession of how depressed he felt when
he started thinking about the rarity of such rhetoric on our scene,
consider Havel's own lamentation about the decline of P-Rhet.
Toward the end of his presidency of the Czech Republic in the fall
of 2002, he discussed (without using rhetorical terms) what he sees as
the decline of the good kinds. Expressing his hope for a return to the
right kind, he "heralds" a hope for "a more humane world, one in
which poets might have as powerful a voice as bankers."[20]

What are the possible cures for our massive practice of and surrendering to political rhetrickery, by both leaders and protesters? While
admitting that nothing will ever fully clean up the mess, I can hope
that more of us will pursue the following two points summarizing
this chapter, this book, and the ideals I wish I myself obeyed more
rigorously:

1   We must train ourselves to judge P-Rhet fairly, by really listening
    to the enemy and imagining ourselves into the enemy's true
    motives. We must judge no piece of P-Rhet according to
    whether the judge and rhetor share the same "side" or whether
    a given audience was won over. Always include the question,
    "Did the rhetor LISTEN to all the audiences crucial to the case?"
    Like a genuinely admirable legal judge, the critic should consider
    the "evidence for *and* against the case," not whether the judg-
    ment will yield personal profit or confirm personal prejudice or
    get a narrow audience to shout "Bravo!"
2   We must train ourselves to practice P-Rhet fairly, rhetoric that
    invites serious LR from our opponents. Instead of threats that

increase their hatred or mistrust, we must learn how to offer evidence that we are sure deserves to be listened to.

Obviously the rhetoric of the political world, more complex than ever before, cannot be fully cleansed, no matter how many of us pursue those two "commandments." Conflicts will never be totally escaped. Even threats of violent alternatives to LR will perhaps never disappear, *Homo sapiens* being what you and I are. For all we know, the horrors of World War III *will* arrive.

What is clear is that our future depends on victories of LR over violence. We are threatened with expanded warfare (probably leading to the catastrophic use of WMD). Now that we live with "media globalization" and "globalization of weaponry" (not to mention current "warfare" about commercial globalization), our very survival, whether as democracies or tyrannies, depends on just how many citizens of the world – leaders or protesters – are trained to be skillful in their listening, and thus more skillful and ethical in their responses.

7

Media Rhetrickery

How is the world ruled and led to war? Diplomats lie to journalists and believe these lies when they see them in print.

Karl Kraus

If you tell a lie often enough, the public will come to believe it.

Paul Josef Goebbels

As the Steady-Camera followed Bush's triumphant walk . . . at the end of his speech, changing angles and aspects, making larger than life the handshakes and smiles and pats on the back, I couldn't help thinking of how much Riefenstahl [who chronicled the rise of the Third Reich] taught us about how powerful a political tool the moving image can be.

Journalist who has asked not to be identified

I'm tempted to begin again with a bit of rhetrickery of my own: "Our totally commercialized media, satanic slaves of commerce, are irredeemably seducing us downward 'even to the edge of doom.'" Doesn't that sound a lot like what we meet every day, especially in television talk shows? "Totally?" "Satanic?" Absurd. "Irredeemably?" Who knows? "Edge of doom?" Where's that? And why engage in literary quoting, when you're talking about politics?

I do fear that the picture is getting worse by the day, but media-rhetoric (here MR) varies so much from country to country and medium to medium and day to day that no full claim about decline could ever be demonstrated.

What cannot be doubted is that we are now flooded daily with news distortions, often just careless but too often deliberate. As I was writing a draft, back in late May 2003, some of the media were finally acknowledging how the American military officers and their media servants had invented a massive hoax about the "rescue" of Pfc. Jessica Lynch, after she was captured in Iraq on March 23. The brouhaha had all been about a bold military rescue from Iraqi abusers of the first female prisoner of war in our history, one who had herself shot back nobly. Only after two months was there open admission that though she was in fact captured and released, she had not been engaged in battle, and the military rescue had not occurred: the doctors had cared for her and turned her over to our team. The fake account had quite probably been designed to increase support for the war – perhaps even to gain media credit with the administration (a feeble echo of the later manipulation of President Bush's visit to the UK and his Thanksgiving turkey trip to Iraq). The admission of the deception has had little publicity, even now that Lynch has denied many "facts" in the reports. A majority of Americans will no doubt go on believing that she was rescued in a military coup, assisted by her own gun firing.

Similarly, it took months for the media to begin admitting how they aided the administration in spinning the justifications for the war. Though by mid-summer even the president was taking some blame for the errors in his State of the Union speech about weapons of mass destruction (WMD), most of the media continued to pretend that it had all been accidental: nobody except political enemies has wanted to blame the top brass.

As Paul Krugman put it, in a *New York Times* column, long before the scandal about Bush's "sixteen words" describing Iraq's purchase of Nigerian uranium:

> One wonders whether most of the public will ever learn that the original case for war has turned out to be false. . . . Each potential find [of possible WMD] gets blaring coverage on TV; how many people catch the later announcement – if it is ever announced – that it was a

false alarm? Each administration charge against Iraq received prominent coverage; the subsequent debunking did not.... In September Mr. Bush cited an International Atomic Energy Agency report that he said showed that Saddam was only months from having nuclear weapons. "I don't know what more evidence we need," he said. In fact, the report said no such thing – and for a few hours the lead story on MSNBC's Web site bore the headline "White House: Bush Misstated Report on Iraq." Then the story vanished – not just from the top of the page, but from the site.... A democracy's decisions, right or wrong, are supposed to take place with the informed consent of its citizens. That didn't happen this time. And we are a democracy – aren't we?

What is most frightening is that Krugman has been subjected to innumerable threats of physical attack, because of his "unpatriotic" columns.

The attempt to address media corruption presents at least three major problems, in addition to the problems met in chapter 6. First, the term "media" is radically ambiguous. For some these days the media are only television. Some would add advertising. For some the term "media" includes all printed journals except serious scholarly writing. But if we think of those who "mediate" between what actually happens and how we learn about it, MR should surely include all who transform reality by reporting and misreporting realities – even teachers in the classroom stimulating discussion of the day's events. Surely MR should include bestselling books that openly engage in reporting public events or attempt "histories" about them? So for us here, the media will include all who mediate – including, I admit, much of my superficial reporting in this book.

A second problem, which I must mainly ignore, is my inescapable ignorance of MR outside my corner of the American scene. I read many indictments of media in other countries, including the claim that *Le Monde* is corrupted by corporate interests.[1] But for all I know the ethical quality of MR has improved 100 percent in countries X and Y while becoming scandalous in the United States. Obviously MR's *technical* quality – mastery in the art of hooking with invented and transformed images and recordings – has improved everywhere, especially in advertising. So although I'm aware of many lamentations about decline in the UK, France, Germany, and the rest of the world, I cannot judge whether the lamenters are justified. The center will have to be what floods my life here in the United States – only a fraction of it coming from Britain (oh, yes: I read *The Economist* sometimes, and – a bit more often – the *TLS*; when I'm in England, I of course read everything). I do have a dim hope that some reader in the UK or Ireland or Zimbabwe might be tempted to have a close look at the MR miseducation committed there, and write a book about it.

The third problem is an amusing paradox exhibited by the flood of MR. Much of my argument about bad MR depends on what I've learned from responsible MR. How can I trustingly quote a journalist's exposé without demonstrating that the media are sometimes OK? (Rhyme intended.) Shouldn't I trust the *Chicago Tribune*, usually "conservative," if it includes a column entitled "The Media Inspire Distrust," with the following opening paragraph?

> A pervasive cynicism seems to be growing about the ability – or even the desire – of major news organizations to provide accurate, object-ive, unbiased reporting on stories that have significant impact on people's lives. I've pondered this trend since the last class of the journalism course that I taught this spring at the University of Illinois at Chicago. "Everything is subjective," one of my students said.... None of the other students in the lively discussion disagreed. Indeed, then and in previous classes the students unfailingly expressed doubt that journalism had much to do with objective truth in any but the most superficial ways.[2]

What's more, can MR be indicted if it includes statements like this one from Jack Fuller, president of the Tribune Publishing Company?

> People are looking for more coherence, not less. They want guidance about the meaning of things.... Part of the challenge of those who pioneer the new medium will be to devise ways in which it can meet

the audience's yearning for a sense of meaning. This will require journalists to embrace and master the lessons of rhetoric, because their task is nothing less than to create a whole new mode of expression and persuasion.[3]

Even the *New York Times*, on which I depend day by day (always of course with absolutely profound, wise, unbiased skepticism), was betrayed recently by the dishonest and undisciplined behavior of two of their reporters. But can a journal that then included serious thoughtful attacks on itself, with strong apologies, be really in bad shape? When we add journals like the *Nation*, the *New Republic*, the *Progressive*, and even *Newsweek* (I resist naming British journals), with their regular exposures of media flaws and political misbehavior, the whole charge seems even weaker.

So I must ask that as you read my blasts on the media here, ask at every moment, "Where did you get your evidence?" And please, whenever you are tempted to offer evidence against any of my claims, ask yourself, "Wasn't the source of *my* evidence also a branch of the 'media'?"

What is beyond doubt is that in the United States, and surely throughout much of the world, we are harmed daily by the floods of careless or even deliberately harmful MR. To repeat my claim in chapters 5 and 6, we are all – not just our children – miseducated daily.

Here is how William Safire, usually a downright defender of the rightwing corporate world, puts his sense of alarm:

You won't [these days] find television magazine programs fearlessly exposing the broadcast lobby's pressure on Congress and the courts to allow station owners to gobble up more stations and cross-own local newspapers, thereby to determine what information residents of a local market receive.

Nor will you find many newspaper chains assigning reporters to reveal the effect of media giantism on local coverage or cover the way publishers induce coverage-hungry politicians to loosen antitrust restraint.

... [As for political selling], the big bucks go into broadcast TV, with its unmatchable cost per thousand viewers.... The leading 20 Internet sites and biggest cable channels are already owned by the expansive likes of G.E.-NBC, Disney, Fox, Gannett, AOL Time Warner, Hearst, Microsoft, Dow Jones, The Washington Post and The New York Times. (Is there anyone I haven't offended?) ... [T]he truth is that media mergers have narrowed the range of information and entertainment available to people of all ideologies.[4]

And here is how Michael Ignatieff summarizes the British media scene:

In place of thought, we have opinion; in place of argument we have [shoddy] journalism, in place of polemic we have personality profiles ... in place of ... public dialogue, we have celebrity chat shows.[5]

Such claims are found "everywhere," again underlining my paradox: MR is awful, yet the media are full of warnings against the awfulness of MR. A recent study (reliable?) has shown that only 36 percent of Americans believe that news organizations get the facts straight – in contrast to 55 percent in 1985.

Here I must concentrate on less questionable claims. Because there is so much untrustworthy MR flooding our world, everyone everywhere now is threatened by two forms of rhetorical miseducation: *unconscious* misleading through sheer carelessness, and *conscious, deliberate* misleading induced by one or another of the four motives (not limited to the media) that we come to below.

Unconscious, Undeliberate Miseducation

Nobody is surprised when sheer careless errors are discovered. The better magazines and newspapers often offer a tiny section of "Corrections" in each issue. Books that are full of misquotations and plagiarisms get exposed by reviewers. As we'll see below, readers on the left publish books exposing shameful carelessness revealed on the right, and vice versa. But meanwhile the misinformation overrides the criticism: millions of citizens – especially, I'm sure, the younger ones – fail to get the message that too much of what the media feed us, even the statistical "proof," is fouled food, some of it poison serving Mammon. A recent article reveals how faking of photo images has increased, and how the fakes are naively accepted by millions as the media tout them. The author speculates that even when the fakery is exposed, most viewers do not find out about it. Examples are offered on both sides of the political debate: viewers took as legitimate the faked portrait of President Bush holding a child's book upside down, as he pretended to be reading it, and viewers took seriously a faked portrait of Senator John Kerry talking with Jane Fonda.[6]

In January 2003, there was an announcement of the annual prize, awarded by the Statistical Assessment Services, for the "2002 Dubious Data Awards" – the "ten most misleading, inaccurate, or downright lazy" bits of news coverage during the year. The errors revealed are shocking, but obviously similar "winners" could be found for every year since MR was invented. (When was that? Was it the day way back when "we" invented language – the first "medium" – and discovered how much fun it is to relate unverified gossip? It was certainly long before printers were invented.)

A strong reinforcement of MR carelessness is the naive, biased carelessness of us receivers. All of us – to repeat – are thirsty for evidence supporting what we already strongly believe, and when it is offered we too often take it straight. Polls in mid-summer 2003 showed that more than half of Americans believed that Osama bin Laden and Saddam Hussein were in close collaboration on the September 11 attack. How many changed their minds when President Bush finally rejected that myth in September 2003? Similarly, many Americans who hate our government, whether on the extreme left or anti-government right, have swallowed the absurd claim that Bush planned the attacks. Apparently this myth is even more widely embraced in Europe and the rest of the world, often with the addition that Jews commanded Bush to engage in the attack.[7]

135

Anti–Semites around the globe are still sucked into the crazy Protocols of Zion myth. Even so–called "objective" academics are caught time after time succumbing to fake "evidence" claiming to support this or that ideologically motivated hypothesis. As I have confessed here before, I myself am guilty of that, often tempted to embrace uncritically any printed or spoken hint of "evidence" that President Bush has lied or fumbled the ball. I try to discipline that bias and ask, "What's the evidence?" – but I often fail. Thus we can hardly blame the media for all of the miseducation. Who can blame them for appealing to those of us who will blindly accept their distortions?

In any case, there is no need here to collect evidence of fake claims of evidence: everybody recognizes them – at least when they are committed by opponents. A statistician friend of mine often laments that the "statistical studies" headlined week by week are mostly unreliable because the researchers have been careless – either deliberately dishonest, sometimes bribed, or badly educated. And an hour later another colleague, attempting to disprove some claim of mine, snarls: "Haven't you seen the report in the *Wall Street Journal* of the study proving statistically that . . . ?!"

Conscious, Deliberate Miseducation

Aside from carelessness and inadequate training, what produces the largest number of errors? Obviously it is deliberate lying, subtle or blatant, or deliberately falsified labeling. How should we react to a world in which a famous radio commentator, Rush Limbaugh, labels as "Communists" all who oppose our preemptive war strike – a world in which some on the left label all supporters of President Bush as "Fascists" and "Hitlerian"? This flood of error in what Dennis Hans and others have called "the disinformation age" is not just ignored in our schools. It is downplayed almost everywhere.

I see mainly four sources of the deliberate distortions, the second and third overlapping with number one, and all of them overlapping with political motives I've already deplored.

(An inherent problem in journalism is too complicated for full treatment here: the contrast between "objective reporting," "editorializing," and "opinion page" commentary. Reporters writing for the "front page" are expected to rise above their biases and report the facts; editorial writers can ignore the facts and express anonymous opinions; op ed page commentators can straddle those two borders, confessing their biases but simultaneously at least pretending to be "objective." All three of these areas are too often corrupted by the four motives we come to now, though the worst harm occurs in the first area, where the claim to objectivity disguises the misleading. The public damage occurs whether the distortions are committed consciously or unconsciously.)

1   Money

"I'm willing to accept bribes for giving rhetorical support to any position, or to be ordered by my bosses to back corporate interests, downplaying news about misbehavior by politicians or executives. By embracing the dictated position, regardless of fact or reason, I can maybe become rich, or at least get a raise."

In *Blinded by the Right: The Conscience of an Ex-Conservative* (2002), David Brock reports scores of occasions when he was seduced or bludgeoned into spreading deliberate lies supporting the "conservative conspiracy" against President Bill Clinton, often being paid hard cash. Rightwing critics have claimed that the book is full of lies (which it may well be – in order to help the book sell). But Brock tries hard to project a new persona, one that resists Mammon's orders, and his evidence of deliberate cheating, often for financial reward, by him and others, is overwhelming.

Mammon's skill in destroying objectivity is especially clear in the case of CNN. When Time Warner bought out Ted Turner in the mid-1990s, CNN began showing signs of paying more attention to its commercial interests. The present competition for ratings between FoxNews and CNN has driven each to "take sides" while radically changing their formats. They now exhibit a much flashier, hipper, more Internet-like style, in order to capture a larger audience. Their objectivity in reporting has certainly declined; the CNN that covered the first Gulf War was radically different from what we have observed since the March 2003 strike on Iraq. And media critics from both the right and left are claiming that the CNN-commercial-sellout is occurring in all the major networks – sometimes in even worse form.

2   Political Support and Personal Safety

"For the sake of safety in my job, or government support for my company, I must not express my honest opinions about this or that political move. Hiding behind the defensible standard of 'objectivity,' practicing 'self-censorship,' I must either portray myself as neutral, reporting both sides fairly, but actually maintaining a biased non-balance, or project an aggressive air of support – regardless of what I believe."

We will never know how many journalists in Nazi Germany detested what Hitler was doing but didn't dare talk about it. We will never know how many journalists who sounded neutral about or even favorable to the Iraq war were in fact opposed to it – though we can hope for some open confessions. Even in countries that profess freedom, journalists obviously suppress or moderate their true views, though they are usually a bit freer to be honest than journalists were under Fascism or Communism. (For more about this see the section on LR-d in chapter 3, p. 48.) In proudly "free" America, journalists in almost every major controversy have confessed – after the event – that they had lied to protect themselves.

The subtle punishments for disagreeing are real. As Todd Gitlin summarizes the widespread silence of journalists, and their bosses, about their opposition to preemptive strike, "It would have had to be put on the agenda by themselves – as something they cared about – which is something they are loathe to do." There has been a flood of reports of journalists being punished for openly protesting the Iraq attack. No doubt some reports have been exaggerated, perhaps even invented. But there is no question that journalists became far more anxious about open declaration of views after the war began than they were before the attack loomed. Only as evidence has mounted that the "war" is continuing, and that its justifications were shaky from the beginning, have more and more journalists risked speaking out. (Most confessions still come in the form: "I really believed in the attack then, and now I see that I was wrong.") And like Krugman, they continue to be physically threatened.

Sometimes the suppression is from the top, as when political powers prevent journalists from obtaining the information they seek – a power abuse that deepens whenever war or threat of war occurs. Recently some reporters have revealed how much suppression of evidence there was in the Gulf War, and research has uncovered how the media suppressed evidence that President Johnson was lying about events in the Vietnam War. Many knew he was lying, but they also knew that to speak out would be dangerous.

Sometimes the fear is only local: my employer may fire me. After escaping from a "business media" job, James Ledbetter describes how his employers required him to conceal the truth, summarizing the situation like this:

> Indeed, too often the news magazines and Websites acted as incurious cheerleaders, championing executive and innovative companies without questioning their books. . . . The mainstream media, too, did its share of hyping the "technology boom," required to conceal the evidence that the bubble was bursting.[8]

The distortions by political extremists are perhaps the worst. Kathleen Hall Jamieson and Paul Waldman report an unquestionable case of media reversal of fact:

> Mr. Gore's statement that he had played an important role in the legislation that brought about the Internet (an ordinary, more or less factual piece of political bragging) was quickly transformed into the absurd claim that he had "invented" the Internet, which was then repeated endlessly by journalists who never bothered to check the original quote.[9]

None of this should be interpreted as confined to blaming the journalists. With the worldwide threats of violent punishment for speaking out, how can any journalist be blamed for being cautious. As *The Times* reported, "The statistics are dreadful: more than 400 writers were murdered between 1999 and 2002. . . . [It is] what the UN Commission on Human Rights calls 'censorship by killing.' Last year alone, 30 journalists were killed and another 1,140 writers were attacked worldwide."[10] Whatever the threats, from death to imprisonment to mere job loss, it is appallingly clear that although fewer journalists are threatened or attacked in "democratic" countries than in autocracies, the fear of punishment threatens honest reporting everywhere.

3   Celebrity

"I want to 'make it,' to get to the top of this so-called profession."

The pursuit of fame overlaps obviously with the first two motives. Fame yields money; serving the political or industrial bosses yields money. And money yields fame.

For those working in most corners of our media the pursuit of personal fame leads to overemphasis on reporting "the famous." Fake or trivial stories about celebrities can make more of a splash than most true stories about important matters. Managers of corporations like Fox, running FoxNews, know that to spend media time on major issues affecting the real welfare of the nation will yield smaller profits than front-paging minor "celebrity" issues: the trial of Princess Diana's butler, accused of stealing her leftover artifacts, or the revelations of one of her lovers; the endless concentration on ex-President Clinton's sex life. And so on. "Let's just drop scientifically demonstrated threats about global warming and other environment disasters, or the brutal facts about worldwide starvation, or the rising inequality of educational opportunity, or the corporate scandals, or the shocking violence in the inner cities, and play up what will attract the most attention. At the same time we must give the impression of dealing

140

with larger issues, especially in our talk shows, where we'll display speakers for the 'other side.' But we'll make sure that as they try to express their opinions, they'll be surrounded by those hired to be on our side, shouting the 'bad guys' down."

The branch of our media most likely to attack these three corrupting influences is fiction. Novelists can still manage to get publishers to accept powerful indictments. (Is that because publishers know that such indictments will sell?) A wonderfully effective satire against media sellout is Ian McEwan's *Amsterdam*. One of the two doomed characters is editor of a newspaper in financial trouble. He learns of some scandalous behavior by a prominent political leader, decides after considerable conflict to feature it on the front page, and suffers disastrous consequences – largely because another medium publicizes the scandal first. Though attacking media corruption is not the center of the book, it does both underline the paradox (we depend on media for attacks on media) and the claim that media success is sought for celebrity.

4 Dogmatic Commitment

"I will passionately, or at least implicitly, defend my one true position; I will honestly, sincerely support my side while ignoring what my opponents say."

This kind of commitment, almost always leading to distortion, is to me by far the closest to being defensible. The dogmatist, practicing win-rhetoric rather than LR, feels full of integrity and can either ignore or openly "refute" the evidence that contradicts the dogma. When it is practiced openly as "advocacy journalism" – that is, when the reporter confesses all basic commitments – such passionate certainty can produce some of our best journalism. The journalists, like Murray Kempton and I. F. Stone in the old days and Jack Newfield and Paul Krugman now, do a kind of research that looks only for support of their cause, report the results carefully and honestly, but never mask the bias. The reader is thus given the required clues for the need to read the claims critically.

141

Blind dogmatism in contrast simply ignores the other side, yet speaks as if totally objective. When in England in April 2003, working on a draft of this chapter, as I suffered the daily floods of cheap MR, right and left, I felt increasingly dismayed by how the actual war was producing a war of words, with neither side acknowledging counter-arguments. In the London *Observer* I read a journalist's justified complaint about a "torrent of hate mail" he had received because he questioned the war; he did not hint that anything he had ever said might be at least questionable. Another journalist, on the right, was reported as "savaging" a "Saddamite buffoon still panting his orgasmic paeans to the impenetrability of Baghdad's defenses." Working in this spirit, you feel that you win not only "out there" but also in your own soul. You are not cheating and you are not to be subjected to critical inquiry. You are serving your God, or at least "the Truth."

To me the most outlandish defense of dogmatic proclaiming comes when immoral argument is defended because the cause is just. Here is how leftish Eric Alterman puts his justified charge against the "Internet gossipmonger Matt Drudge."

> [T]he downside of the punditocracy-gossip merger was the seal of approval it offered to information that was frequently false, malicious, and proffered by sleazeballs. . . . Tim Russert allowed the generally excellent Meet the Press to fall victim to these dangers when he invited . . . Drudge to join an august panel [of pundits]. . . . Drudge . . . defends himself . . . by arguing that he has no professional standards whatever. He proudly admits to publishing the purloined work of other journalists who are still in the process of verifying their stories. Respectfully questioned by Russert, he used his NBC-supplied microphone to berate real reporters for failing to use his own sleazy insinuating tactics.[11]

Unfortunately Alterman reveals here another version of the media paradox; he weakens his attack by revealing his own carelessness in argument, pursuing his own dogmatic commitment. Drudge can answer, "You are just engaging in shoddy slander, with words like

142

'sleazeball' and 'sleaze' and 'insinuating'; your attack contains no solid, documented, carefully structured argument against me. I actually threw your book away after the first few pages, because your evidence mainly consists of epithets." Drudge would be wrong in ignoring the book; *Sound and Fury* is full of genuine evidence of outlandish rightwing bias. But, like most of us, Alterman too often falls into the very fault he is attacking.

Whether or not you agree with me that an increasingly large slice of the media reveals deception, I hope you will agree that we would be better off if more journalists were trained more effectively in, and thus devoted to, thinking about and fighting against these four corruptions.

As many of my quotations here have already shown, it is hard to draw the line between media corruption and the political corruption we saw in chapter 6, since politicians inescapably depend on being able to buy, or at least deceive, the media. And the line drawing is complicated even further by the fact that everyone, including you and me, has to deal with the Machiavellian choices among "goods" and "evils" that I described on p. 120. But everywhere we look we see evidence that the success of corrupt political rhetoric depends on the media, which in turn are corrupted by political bias. As Alterman puts it:

> Our politicians' rhetoric is so riddled with misinformation, mindless cliché, and meaningless spectacle that it has ceased to have any relevance to the problems it alleges to address.... The forms of American political communication – nine-second television sound bites, negative advertisements, and ceaseless fundraising – have buried even the possibility of fruitful debate.... Because American politicians' words are so thoroughly uncoupled from the things about which they speak, the role of setting the parameters of our national debate, of determining what problems require urgent attention and what issues may prove to be important to the national interest, must fall elsewhere. In our case, that means the media.[12]

Alterman's case can be dramatized with two final examples of attempted attacks on bias.

Actually we are flooded with charges of shameful bias, from both the right and left.[13] A bestseller by Bernard Goldberg, *Bias: A CBS Insider Exposes How the Media Distort the News* (2002), is centered on attacking the three major US TV networks. CBS is especially demonized for its "liberal" bias and for its mistreatment of Goldberg as a conservative employee. Goldberg does acknowledge – but only once – that bias is inescapable, found on all sides:

> Does anyone think a "diverse" group of conservative journalists would give us the news straight? I sure as hell don't. They'd be just like the Left. Except, they'd let their conservative biases slip into the news, and they'd swear on a stack of Bibles that they were mainstream...just as liberals do now.
> It's the human condition. (p. 126)

As his own biases "slip into" almost every paragraph, his book – and its wild success among those longing for evidence that journalists are mostly lefties – is one of the most discouraging demonstrations of our plight. He does include some genuinely disturbing examples of how his employers at CBS misbehaved. But as he rightly attacks their mistreatment, he loads the book with evidence that *he* cannot be trusted: he listens to hardly anyone. First of all, he makes no attempt to distinguish among versions of liberalism: everyone who disagrees with any of his views is suspect. Even worse, he offers not a single citation identifying sources for his wild allegations. And he gives only a hint or two of the rightwing bias exhibited outside the three "liberal" networks he targets: *all* the liberal left is equally biased.

Using as his main example CBS's legal objection to his violation of a contract, he ignores the fact that as he writes, scores of radio talk shows are exhibiting rightwing bias much more appalling than any he describes. The book simply pours out slick, unsubstantiated claims that he is above it all and the "liberal" media are down below. That it continues to be a bestseller is to me disturbing evidence for my thesis here.

On the other political side, Eric Alterman also exhibits a great deal of bias in a more recent book, partly devoted to discrediting Goldberg: *What Liberal Media? The Truth About BIAS and the News* (2003). As we have seen, Alterman is openly "left" on most issues. But he is clearly justified in his charge against Goldberg:

> To those who do not already share Goldberg's biases, his many undocumented, exaggerated assertions have the flavor of self-parody rather than reasoned argument. Among these are such statements as: "Everybody to the right of Lenin is a 'right-winger' as far as [liberal] elites are concerned." Opposition to [President Bush's] flat tax, he claims, comes from the same "dark region that produces envy and the seemingly unquenchable liberal need to wage class warfare." (p. 5)

The contrast between Goldberg and Alterman is dramatized perhaps most strongly in the matter of supporting evidence. Goldberg provides no footnotes or index: it is all mere assertion. Alterman provides 646 footnotes – most of them convincing – and a full index. And he invites us to check almost every assertion. That of course does not prove that he is fully objective, but at least it shows that, unlike Goldberg, he expects the kind of reader who will want to do some checking.[14]

By performing or reporting genuine research of the kind Goldberg totally neglects, Alterman catches him again and again engaging in rhetrickery – as Goldberg could only occasionally catch Alterman. But Alterman's critique of Goldberg is no more than a prefatory addition to his book (it was mainly written long before *Bias* appeared). His main point comes closer to mine: to fight off the casual reduction of the world into "right" and "left," "conservative" and "liberal," with neither side listening. He discerns bias afflicting the media everywhere:

> Any number of biases – liberal, conservative, religious, ethnocentric, humanist, heterosexist, age-ist, class-ist, racist, able-ist, weight-ist . . . can creep into a story despite the best efforts . . . to keep them at bay. The key question to ask is not whether examples of bias can be found,

but exactly where is bias pervasive and what is its effect on the news and American public life?

[O]n most social issues, conservatives have a case. Elite media journalists, like most people in their education brackets, . . . rarely come into contact with religious fundamentalists. . . . If religion were the only measure of bias then conservatives would have a strong case. (p. 104)

Even worse than the worst of such printed attacks from left and right are the television talk shows that I call Crossfirism. It is impossible to quote from much of those shows, because both sides are mostly shouting unintelligible charges. But I can offer the results of my own rigorous scientific study. In the past month I have spent eight and a half painfully wasted hours watching some of these shows, and I can honestly, scrupulously, objectively report that not once has *any* participant said anything like, "Oh, I see now that you're right; I've been wrong. I hadn't known about . . . or thought about . . . or seen X, Y, or Z. Listening to you has changed my mind." And every program has ended with their shouting at each other all at once, with no viewer able to make out more than an angry word or two. My detestation is of course increased by my biased objection to the fact that the losers in the shouting are usually critics of the rightwing; but that confession does not weaken the charge that the programs are miseducating all of us, in every moment of viewing.

Bias aside, I hope that my main point is clear: everyone on all "sides" who thinks about the media for more than five minutes, as insider or outsider, emerges with a sad warning: "I must be more careful! I must think harder about what I read and see. Most who pretend to address me have their attention mainly not on my welfare but on how to capture me, regardless of the truth or importance of their claims. Even when I feel that I have been responsibly informed, I often have not been, and my thinking has been corrupted."

The case can perhaps be qualified slightly by the fact that more of us these days are in one sense "aware of current events" than ever before. Because we all watch at least a bit of TV and glance at the headlines and photos on the front page, we all "know" about what is prominent in "everybody's" mind at this very minute. Our great great grandparents mostly knew nothing about non-local news until it was too late to do anything about it. In contrast, we are "informed" quickly, sometimes instantaneously. Does that fact suggest that we suffer less miseducation than did our forebears? Whatever the answer, we are – to repeat one last time – really misinformed, and MR, even in the form of thoughtful books, too seldom gives us real help in thinking clearly about the various events. Everyone on all sides of almost every controversy simply blasts out conclusions, with no attention to the steps that support those conclusions.

The cure? It will hardly surprise you to hear me echo chapter 5: flood our schools, from grade one onward, with Rhet-Ed that stresses LR: training in how to deal critically with MR! If that could happen, everyone would grow up somewhat more skillful in protecting against deception. And our informants, whether ranking as pundits or not, would be less inclined to deceive.

Postscript

The media revolution I have stressed here is dramatically underlined by the transmission in May 2004 of politically crucial "international" broadcasts: first of the many images portraying, to a universal audience, American troops torturing Iraqis; then of an Iraqi beheading an American. President Bush and Secretary of Defense Rumsfeld have found themselves addressing *international* audiences, in an effort to diminish hatred of Americans, while many Americans have found, in the image of the beheading, further justification for our presence in Iraq. The revolution I described is even more dramatic than I realized.

Part III
Reducing Rhetorical Warfare

Rhetoric is not just what Richards calls "the art of removing misunderstanding"; it is the communal art of pursuing new truth.

Anon

Recipes for curing rhetorical ills have been offered ever since *Homo sapiens* suffered the first failure to communicate. All of the great rhetoricians worked to provide cures. Too often, however, their emphasis was on win-rhetoric rather than on listening-rhetoric: how to *persuade better* rather than how to *join and thus progress together.* They were right in insisting that we all need to learn how to persuade more effectively, but what the world needs even more are ways of probing beneath pointless disputes: methods of discovering shared ground beneath surface warfare.

To illustrate how listening-rhetoric can diminish harmful controversy, especially in its deepest form, rhetorology, we could explore any current ideological battle: between Christians and Muslims; Catholics and Protestants; Mormons and Baptists; supply-side and demand-side economists; postmodern Marxists and rival socialisms; Democrats and Republicans; "hawks" and "doves"; Darwinists and creationists; postmodernist academics and traditionalists. A close look at any of these oppositions would illustrate how rarely partisans listen to the case for the other side. And a detailed probing of any one of them could illustrate my claim that rhetorology can yield more than a mere truce: not just a bargain, but genuine joint inquiry, based on mutual trust and a sense of – or at least hope for – actual progress.

Everyone who attempts LR soon learns how tough an assignment it can be. One of my more revealing failures occurred when I was arguing with six colleagues back in March 2003. My claim was that President Bush should not attack Iraq without full UN support. Four of the six were against me. Attempting a bit of rhetorology, I stopped preaching my case and instead took this move: "Hey, wait a minute. Let's see if we can't find something on which we all agree. Wouldn't we all agree that it's always better to reduce the number of one's enemies rather than increase them?" After a moment or two discussing what the word "enemy" means, they all agreed. Then I said, "Then why can't we agree that as the number of those who hate us, worldwide, is increased by our policies, we are making a mistake?" At which point the most ardent of the Bush defenders almost shouted at me: "Don't you see that the best way to reduce the number of enemies is to kill them?"[1]

My failure at that table illustrates the absolute limits of the rhetorical strategies I am defending. For a brief moment I thought we had found "common ground," but it turned out not to *be* common ground. My phrase "reducing the number of enemies" had carried two radically different meanings. The case illustrates the fact that the effort at genuine, deep listening has fewest successes when violence and war are at stake.

No one can ever offer a full cure for our pointless controversies, let alone violent threats. All we can hope for is that more of us more often will pursue ways of listening. Even if we cannot quite achieve the biblical exhortation to love our neighbors as ourselves, we can sometimes discover that they deserve as much attention as we do.

From the stack of tempting examples, I now choose the warfare between science and religion. Theologians have always pursued beliefs that they were sure *ought* to be shared by all; scientists have always believed that they stand on at least some common ground that *ought* to be shared by all. (Many scientists don't talk about that point; they just assume it; many others are aware of just how shaky some of their "unquestioned" assumptions can be.) Often through history the conflict of assumptions has led to open war, with disciples of God issuing death penalties on scientists and scientific cults, like the Illuminati, actually assassinating priests and infidels. The conflict is usually far less violent these days than in the time of Galileo, but it is still a major threat to any hope we have of moving together into mutual understanding.

8

Can Rhetorology Yield More Than a Mere Truce, in Any of Our "Wars"?[1]

The main reason religion needs to be privatized is that, in political discussion with those outside the relevant religious community, it is a conversation-stopper.
Richard Rorty, "Religion as Conversation-Stopper"

Although scientists may officially eschew metaphysics, they love it dearly and practice it in popularized books whenever they get the chance.
Jeffery Wicken

Science without religion is lame, religion without science is blind.
Albert Einstein

Science is constituted through interactions that are essentially rhetorical.
Alan G. Gross, *The Rhetoric of Science*

As in most controversies, those who attack either religion or science usually make their case without showing any serious evidence that they have listened to their opponents: religion is superstition, utterly fake; science is the cruel enemy of human values. Fanatical non-listeners thus waste book after book, article after article, attacking selected extremes, while dogmatically preaching some version of their own side.

Even those who argue for some degree of genuine overlapping are often carelessly biased. One example is a recent article that

153

attempts to show not only that the overconfidence of some scientists resembles religious dogmatism, but that *all* scientists are "gnostics" in the sense that they are certain that they are the only ones who have the truth, or at least the right road to truth.[2] For this author the only common ground shared by scientists and religionists is dogmatic excess!

Before attempting to exhibit science and religion as half-siblings, we must first look at how each of them has related to, or quarreled with, rhetoric. The relations have been quite different. That rhetoric and religion are inescapably akin has been obvious to everyone who has thought about it; even theologians who separate rhetoric from truth would concede that religions depend for survival on *preaching*, on being *evangelical*. No pastor can do well without a mastery of religious rhetoric. In contrast, rhetoric and science are most often seen as in no way related; they are as strongly divorced as are science and religion. As I said in chapter 2, it wasn't until the late twentieth century that scholarly works began appearing about the rhetoric of science, and I have found that none of them strive, as I do here, to relate the *rhetorics* of science and religion.

Religion and Rhetoric

Some classicists saw rhetorical probing as the proper route to the right kinds of religious thought. Others, like St. Augustine, felt deep conflict between their training in rhetoric and their religious certainties, while still acknowledging their inescapable reliance on rhetoric. In modern times most religionists have seen rhetoric as at best the mere altar boy to the priest.[3] While serious religious method, whether theology or prayer, can yield truths, rhetoric is what you use to spread them to the world.

This ambiguous relation between religion and rhetoric is curious, especially when viewed in the light of how opponents of religion have tended to regard the two as almost identical. For many, since religion is mere irrational faith, its language can be nothing *but* rhetoric, often mere rhetrickery. Aggressive prophets of a positivistic worldview have used the same tactics against both rhetoric and religion. Religion and rhetoric, those twin dark burdens of ignorance inherited from the prescientific past, can both be simply dismissed. Neither of the two ways of tying rhetoric to religion – as dutiful altar boy or as forlorn doomed twin – can tempt anyone to inquire seriously into their deeper relations. But when rhetorical studies are seen as an indispensable and universal path to escape misunderstanding, and when religions are seen not as benighted, superstitious inheritances from the dark ages but expressions of a universal human need for explaining the world and escaping its horrors – the pursuit of deeper understanding of what is to be worshipped, and how – we already see a new reason for claiming their inseparability. This may explain why one finds these days so many discussions of "rhetoric and religion" or "the rhetoric of religions."

Especially since Kenneth Burke's *Rhetoric of Religion*, such studies have flooded the academic world. Anyone who pursues our topic behind the contrasting and often deceptive labels, playing with synonyms, probing the theological and scientific "rhetoricians" who avoid the language, will find thousands of discussions of how rhetoric, under somebody's definition, either serves, or leads to, somebody's definition of religion.

Science and Rhetoric

When we turn to science, we find a much more rigorous divorce from rhetoric. Most scientists still think of it as having nothing to do with their serious inquiry; again it is often nothing but rhetrickery. The recent appearance of many books and articles on "the rhetoric of science"[4] has produced many angry responses from those who fear that the very phrase undermines the claims of science. Even scientists who feel some attachment to religion think of rhetoric as somehow irrelevant.

Do the Diverse Rhetorics Overlap?

Because of these contrasting relations with rhetoric, many on both sides will consider the following two claims a bit peculiar, if not plain silly:

- Science (or pure reason, rationality, hard thought) is not really more completely divorced from rhetoric than is religion.
- The warfare between science and religion, between reason and faith, between rationalists and religionists, has been seriously reinforced by the neglect of genuine rhetorical inquiry.

My hope is to move at least some ardent defenders of religious commitment, and some scientists who think they'll soon have the ultimate "Theory of Everything,"[5] to acknowledge that they have been mistaken in dismissing their opponent. It's not that they are wrong to defend religion or to pursue scientific thinking to the hilt but that they were wrong to see such thinking as the only legitimate kind. To put the thesis of this chapter in the most forceful rhetorical terms, then, I'll just ask all you readers who think of yourselves as scientfically minded: "Are you sure that your arguments and convictions are in opposition to religion?" Then, to all of you who think of yourselves as deeply religious, I ask: "Are you sure that your deepest beliefs contrast sharply with those held by scientists?"[6]

I will not be making the extreme assertion that rhetorology can totally unite any one particular religious denomination with the full scientific endeavor. While I admire Cardinal Newman's *Grammar of Assent* (1870) for its probing of rhetorical matters, I don't follow him in the claim that honest rhetorical thought will actually lead to one triumphant denomination – his brand of Catholicism. Instead, I claim only that a full rhetorology can lead us to recognize at least seven fundamental similarities between the rhetorics of science and religion. If half-siblings seems too strong, at least they belong to the same clan.

On both sides many will think such a quest absurd. Some who are passionately religious might say:

> Your quest really is silly. It's all right, of course, for you to have your fun pursuing your coinage, rhetorology. It's a good thing to have serious study of inescapable conflict among fallen creatures as they pursue, ever since Babel, their always multiple, limited, and conflicting ends in history. But we have religion and theology, providing the right kind of worship and valid study of a perfect Being who is beyond conflict, the Author of our being who is not dependent on our contingencies and not – except in rather peculiar ways – dependent on history. That God has indeed taught us certain rhetorical forms – the rhetoric of prayer, for example, or of the homily – and He may teach us how not to talk ("Thou shalt not bear false witness"). But is it not absurd to hope that the study of how we do talk will lead us to a Divinity who will not just forgive but embrace atheistic scientific inquiry?

Meanwhile the passionately scientific critic will be making almost the same points in different language:

> Your quest here is not just silly, it's dangerous. We've always believed that shoddy rhetoric and naive religious belief are tied together. What's new about that? You're just working in a closed circle of self-validating nonsense. And in so doing you undercut drastically the unique value of genuine scientific inquiry: the only human endeavor that escapes the corruptions of human bias.

Every effort to relate science and religion, whether rhetorically or metaphysically, can be accused of being overly ambitious. There has been an astonishing flood of books and articles in recent decades attempting to find some meeting ground. I have a shelf more than eight feet long containing books and articles on the subject, most of them published since Fritjof Capra's *The Tao of Physics*, in 1975.[7] The Temple Foundation is now giving huge cash awards for the best books relating science and religion, and I am told that the Foundation is flooded with applicants and recommendations.

No matter how we label the oppositions – reason vs. superstition, dogmatic rationalism vs. genuine human values, secular humanism vs. religious fundamentalism, atheism vs. theism – the conflict between hard thought about natural laws and hard thought about the source and grounds of nature and value will almost certainly outlive you and me and our grandchildren. Even those analysts who attempt to produce at least an armistice cannot promise that the threat of further warfare will ever disappear. And we may even see further examples of open violence, as when a pious believer concludes that it's a holy act to murder a doctor who is committing evil abortions.

Rival Approaches

Battles among various versions of science and religion are overwhelmingly diverse. Some books still echo earlier portrayals of a flat-out war, with science the proud victor over religion; the superstitious enemy of truth just dies. Michio Kaku's *Visions: How Science Will Revolutionize the Twenty-First Century* (1997) predicts science's solution to every "why" question and every religious need; Kaku even includes the zany idea that science will develop genuine immortality, by downloading your brain and reinstalling it in some other body later. But many authors recently have sought some truce or accommodation or even full conciliation. Not long before he died, Stephen Jay Gould, perhaps the most popular of all biological rhetoricians, published a book, *Rocks of Ages: Science and Religion in the Fullness of Life* (1999). Gould claims total validity for both religion and science, but his major claim is that there is absolutely no overlap, because their rhetorics – a term he doesn't use – are totally distinct. He even invents the acronym NOMA, for Non-Overlapping MAgisteria. The reason there is no overlap is that rational inquiry is for him on the science side; rhetoric is on the religion side, *unprovable* faith.

158

A surprising number of the new books, in contrast to those extremes, echo Cardinal Newman by reconciling science with one particular religion. John Polkinghorne, a brilliant particle physicist and priest, claims no conflict whatever between his version of hard science and his version of Christianity.[8] Some, like Ian Barbour, avoid such difficulties by digging more deeply into scientific method and theological arguments, claiming to find, in the tradition of Whitehead and Hartshorne, a meeting ground (process theology, leading to "panentheism").[9] And of course many studies are more superficial than Barbour's, pursuing one or the other of the three most tempting approaches: diplomacy, tolerance, or utter relativism: there's no such thing as truth, so why bother?[10]

For some sociologists the differences, not just between science and all religion but among diverse religions, are finally irreconcilable. In "Is There a Place for 'Scientific' Studies in Religion?" Robert Wuthnow argues that

> the role of scientific studies should not be ... to discover what is common among the various religious traditions, but to understand what is different and to gauge reactions to those differences. ... To their credit, social scientists who study religion today are much more likely to insist on in-depth analysis of specific traditions than to settle for superficial generalizations.

He claims to be probing "in depth" – but his quest is only for the differences.[11]

Putting aside the obvious differences, what are the shared unquestionable convictions of the combatants: the assumptions, commonplaces, *topoi*, firm platforms or "places" on which they stand? (For simplicity, I'll follow Stephen Toulmin and call them the "warrants" taken for granted on all sides.) If disputants really probed for shared warrants – if they really listened – would they find far fewer real differences? Will they find what John Dewey pursued in his book – *A Common Faith* (1934)?

As is obvious by now, any such quest is based on a prejudice: the assumption that, after all, there *must be some warrants that are shared.* I have been a passionate lifetime believer in science − of different kinds at different stages of my life. I have been also a lifetime pursuer of religious truth − again of radically different versions: from beginning as a devout orthodox Mormon, through increasing doubt to professed atheism, to a recovery of religious belief that some might call mere pantheism, or perhaps Deism. I still call myself genuinely religious, though I have often had to use metaphorical, symbolic, or mythological dodges when arguing with a fundamentalist Christian about whether the earth was created in six days, or whether Jesus was really dead for three days and then resurrected, violating everything we think we know about biology.

Can I really call myself fully religious, while being fully committed to whatever natural truth is thoroughly demonstrated? The answer depends a lot on definitions of terms.

Why Mere Verbal Definitions Give Little Help

It is hard to think of any terms more slippery, more polymorphous, even perverse, than "religion," "religious," and "religiously," let alone "spiritual" or "devout" or "belief." (As chapter 1 revealed, "rhetoric" is a good rival; even "science" has no single definition.) For some, religious terms refer simply to passionate commitment, to anything: "I watch *60 Minutes* religiously." For others religion is synonymous with what their enemies call *super*stition: belief in a superpower who can be appealed to for rescue from the human mess.

William James struggled with this diversity when preparing his Gifford Lectures on *The Varieties of Religious Experience* (1902 − and many later editions). At times he almost gave up on the project, but he finally settled on a psychological definition: religion is "the feelings, acts, and experiences of individual men [and women] in their solitude, so far as they apprehend themselves to stand in relation to whatever they may consider the divine."

Abandoning all such attempts at full verbal summary, I move here beyond "feelings and experiences in solitude" to a list of seven *shared* warrants – the stable platforms that most who call themselves religious and most scientists consciously or unconsciously stand on as they present arguments.

That the search for shared warrants is not easy is dramatized by the experience of my friend, divinity professor David Tracy. As a Catholic theologian, he met annually for several years with leaders of other "great religions" who were hoping to find common ground. Returning each time from the discussion with Buddhists, Muslims, Jews, Catholics, and Hindus, Tracy would seem a bit discouraged: "We found little or nothing we could all agree on this year." But one year not long ago he came back looking positively optimistic. When I asked what they had *all* agreed on, he said, as I remember it, "We all agreed that something is radically wrong with creation."[12] Would they have needed even longer to come to agreement if scientists had been there? Well, if I'm right in what follows, they might have come to an agreement even sooner.

Warrant One: The world as we experience it is somehow flawed.

Something is wrong, deficient, broken, inadequate, lacking. Something is rotten not only in the state of Denmark, but everywhere. As the popular bumper sticker puts it, "Shit Happens." This or that corner of the world is falling apart as I write this sentence. Millions are suffering intolerably.

In one form or another everybody in the world believes in, and actually relies on, this warrant. We ignore it mainly in our moments of ecstatic happiness, when everything *feels* wonderful. But a moment or day or week later, we quickly fall back into acknowledging what David Tracy's group conceded: *something* is wrong, or something *went* wrong, with creation. For the purest of scientists[13] what is *explicitly* wrong is our ignorance of a truth we should be seeking. But even they live, day by day, in a world that exhibits multiple flaws, such as the failure of Congress to grant the money needed to finish

161

this or that billion-dollar project, or the misbehavior of a lab assistant, or the cheating of a colleague. And more and more scientists these days face the threat that there is possibly an inescapable conflict in the whole of things: for example, the contrast between what gravity theory tells us and what quantum physics reveals. But even if that scientific "flaw" is finally removed, there will still be, for everyone, a range of flaws in the world as now experienced.

Implicit in the notion of wrongness is an inescapable value judgment: to judge anything as "wrong" one has to embrace some notion of something righter, which leads us (following Kenneth Burke's accounts of perfectionism) to . . .

Warrant Two: The flaws are seen in the light of the Unflawed, some truth, some notion of justice, or "goodness," or of some possible purging of ugliness or ignorance; standards of judgment of the brokenness exist somewhere.

Though some scientists may already be bridling here, wouldn't most embrace this warrant? They have standards of scientific truth and personal integrity in the pursuit of knowledge which will repair our ignorance. As many of them have fulminated against various post-modernist questionings of "truth," they are implicitly confessing that they embrace this warrant. As they attack scientists who cheat, they express the faith that scientific cheating is genuinely, universally, morally wrong – a faith that they could never demonstrate with hard research. Their standard of honest research was not just invented by them; it is in a sense "eternal," awaiting human discovery. Which leads us to . . .

Warrant Three: There is some supreme order or cosmos or reality, something about the whole of things that provides the standards according to which I make the judgments of Warrants One and Two.

Almost all who call themselves religious, and most scientists, even the most ardent atheists, believe in Warrant Three: there *is* a cosmos, often thought of in terms that resemble astonishingly what many theologians have called Supreme Being. Scores of books have reported the quest for a *final theory* that will explain *everything*. Why? Because "everything" is really *there*, waiting to be explained – and it is also *here*, supporting our pursuit of it. As Matthew Arnold's definition puts it, religion is belief in some power "greater than ourselves, making for righteousness."[14] His word "righteous," connoting something like dogmatic or arrogant, will put some people off these days. But what Arnold meant was "something righter than wrongness," and every scientist has to believe in that; otherwise the quest for truth is pointless. There is a larger "truth" awaiting discovery, a Totality of Truths that includes and judges the particular truths found in this or that research project.

These three warrants, intertwined, are nicely revealed by the David Tracy anecdote: something *is* radically deficient in the world as we see it – because we all agree that "things could and should be better." His report of the discovery was not just that "Something is wrong with the world I live in," or "There's a lot of stuff around me that I personally disapprove of or grieve over." Everybody believes that: something could and should be better about my world – even if it is only that "I ought to have more drugs available" or "I don't have enough corpses yet buried in my cellar" or "Why can't I get every day the feelings I get in that new entertainment church on Sunday morning?" That is why M. Scott Peck made the mistake of taking my case too far. In his bestselling book *The Road Less Traveled* (1978), he argued that *everybody* in the world is religious, whether they know it or not. To me he corrupts the notion of religion by reducing it to the one warrant: passionate caring about *something*. (For a small minority of those who think of themselves as religious, ecstasy is the only warrant; for some ecstasy-pursuers religion is all just personal feeling. I'm tempted to call such people "me-ligionists" – what Jacques Derrida called "irresponsible orgiasts.") But Peck was right about the universality: even in moments when we are feeling total bliss about this or that reward of life, if someone interrupts and asks, "Is *everything* fine in the world?" we have to confess that millions are

163

starving, hundreds of innocents are at this moment being killed, somewhere, hundreds will die today in a car crash or plane crash or suicide bombing or a new war. Even the most blissful me-ligionists may concede, when questioned, that something is after all wrong: too many in the world don't accept their celebration of this or that liberating feeling.

Thus almost all of us on all sides embrace the relation of the first warrant to the second and third. Warrant One implies a value judgment: "Something went wrong with creation," or "Something *ought* to have been righter," or at least, "I can see what would have been better." It's not just, "I don't like some things about it," but rather, "Some things are wrong when judged by what would be right, by what a full rightness would demand, by what the whole of creation as I see it – my cosmos, my God, my view of nature – implies as the way things should be but are not."

In the language of Christianity and Judaism this point is put as "the Fall," a temporal decline from what had been perfection. Some religions, even some branches of Christianity, deny that: "It" has been flawed eternally. But the three warrants do not need to be taken temporally. As Kenneth Burke makes clear in *The Rhetoric of Religion*, stories about temporal rising and falling can always be translated into non-temporal, vertical ladders: *temporally*, we were up there, fell down, and now we're down here trying to climb back up; *non-temporally*, we've always been a long way down the ladder, trying to climb up a bit with no hope of ever fully comprehending what is "at the top."

Thus lamentation about the universality of brokenness moves toward religion (and the implicit religion of scientists) only when it is linked with the second and third warrants – only when the lamenter realizes not just that shit happens but that shit's happening, and its definition in relation to what is not awful but good is somehow built into the very structure of things: some cosmos, a Something without which there would be Nothing. Disaster has always happened, from the beginning (or, as Bible literalists claim, *almost* from the beginning), but there was/is a place from which the fall can be judged as a fall. It is defined by an elusive notion of its opposite, an order or cosmos which in some sense judges the happening as faulty and imposes "oughts" upon us. "Your laboratory research was tragically flawed; you *ought* to have known better." "Your colleague has violated scientific standards, and you *ought* to have warned her about it, or reported her lying to the authorities."

Warrant Four, emerging from the first three: All who are genuinely religious (not just complaining) will somehow see themselves as in some inescapable sense a part of the brokenness.

It's not just other people – those terrorists out there, say – who are out of joint. *I* am. I'm not as good or kind or effective or smart or learned or organized or courteous or alert or wise as I ought to be. Even the best of us, even the strongest, the purest, the humblest, are inherently lacking, deficient, in need of further repair, or as religionists put it, we are sinful or guilty. I am an inseparable part of a cosmos that includes this flawed fraction of itself, me, thus including in that fraction a sense of regret about my flaws.

In all honest scientists, this warrant is revealed as lamentation about personal ignorance: what I don't know and *ought* to know![15] And my guess is that many exhibit it as they curse themselves daily for their scientific deficiencies and failures.

Warrant Five, following inescapably from the first four: The cosmos I believe in, the cosmos I may or may not feel gratitude toward for its gift of my very existence, the cosmos that is in its manifestations in my world in some degree broken – my cosmos calls upon me to do something about the brokenness.

I must do what I can in the repair job, working to heal both my own deficiencies and to aid my fellow creatures in healing theirs. For many scientists, this can mean no more than, "I have a duty to work at removing my own ignorance." But more often even for "atheistic" scientists it becomes a moral command to remove *the world's* ignorance. For some official religions, as in versions of Judaism and in the version of Mormonism still naggingly active in my soul, it produces floods of daily self-reproach: that which I have done I should not have done, and that which I have not done I should have done. In many denominations it produces missionary work; for many scientists it produces a lifetime vocation to teaching: the widespread ignorance of scientific truth is as appalling as "sin" is to devout religionists.

A major example of earlier scientific "fixing" was the alchemist's efforts to repair, with their science (or artistry), a universe not created by a perfect or imperfect God but by a perfect or imperfect Demiurgos. Modern scientific "cures" range from environmentalists' projects to some hopes for genetic engineering: obviously our bodies ain't what they ought to be, and maybe we can remove the flaws.

Beneath all the varieties of cure, we see this one indisputable meaning of life: a purpose that transcends – and influences – our particular feelings of the moment. Has anyone here ever met a genuine scientist who does not share this sense of a passionate purpose for improvement – of *something*?[16]

Warrant Six, an inevitable moral corollary of the other five: Whenever my notion of what my cosmos requires of me conflicts with my immediate wishes or impulses, I ought to surrender to that higher value.

Rather than pursuing what is easiest or most pleasant or most reassuring to my present sensations or wishes, I obey or pursue *It*. Our impulses, our immediate wishes, *ought* to be overridden whenever they conflict with responsibility to cosmic commandments. We have obligations not just to others but to the Other. Religious talk dwells on this, while for scientists it is usually only implicit. But next time you meet a scientist who is furious about a colleague who has cheated, ask him or her why cheating is *really* wrong. If I am a genuine scientist, and I am tempted to make a reputation or fortune by falsifying my results, I have an absolute command, not just from my conscience but from my cosmos, to combat that temptation. If

I feel that my culture is condoning such selling out, I must combat that cultural drive. (That more and more researchers are becoming "sinful," according to this standard, by selling out to pharmacy companies, is relevant here but not crucial.)

None of us escapes the conflicts among three cosmic demands: "Pursue Truth!" "Pursue Goodness – the welfare of others." "Pursue Beauty." Many physicists engaged in the Manhattan Project (by no means all) have reported that their work on the bomb almost tore them apart, not just because of the conflict between the "command" to pursue scientific truth and the fear of human disaster, but because of the conflict between two versions of "goodness": ending the war vs. refusing to kill hundreds of thousands of innocents. Nobody escapes the "choose the lesser evil" problem discussed above (p. 120), but "choose the better Good" is even tougher. Nobody escapes the hard fact that something larger than our personal comfort or preference issues "commandments."

Warrant Seven, a warrant that everyone, not only William James, would make essential to all religions: The psychological or emotional feelings connected with all of this.

All genuine religions either openly or subtly offer spiritual "highs," moments of deep spiritual feeling – not just the excitement provided by some me-ligions but the deeper bliss that results from contact with the ultimate: the cosmos, the whole of things, God, Being, Nature, the source of all of our "commandments." I could fill the rest of this chapter with quotations from scientists about how thrilled they are when they make full contact with what they consider reality or scientific truth or the challenge of the ultimate mysteries of beauty: both words, "mystery" and "beauty," fill Steven Weinberg's book, *Dreams of a Final Theory* (1992). Scientists feel in such moments that they have joined a "power bigger than themselves that makes for rightness – truth." (I have to admit that many scientists I've chatted with about this feeling admit that they share it, but flatly deny that it has anything to do with religion.)

Most religions offer in their myths explicit acknowledgment of finally irresolvable mystery: what some medieval theologians called Incomprehensibility. The Wholeness of the invisible cosmos is beyond rational demonstration. The Order is always some kind of numinous *mysterium tremendum*.[17] Many scientists get off the boat here: we'll finally master it all. But others have captured something of this mystifying wonder, admitting that no human being will ever grasp the "incomprehensible" whole. But even those who aggressively claim that "in principle" science is the only faith that can capture it all usually reveal a spiritual sense of awe or glory or gratitude for that "all."

The Neglected Blessings

Many religionists will feel impatient because these seven warrants leave out so many rewards that feel important to them: this or that blessing that "my religion considers essential and that scientists question." And many scientists may cringe at my attributing the warrants to them. On other occasions I have discussed those diverse blessings, the diverse psychological or emotional rewards in addition to the spiritual highs of Warrant Seven: the bliss of joining a community, of consuming the blood and flesh of Christ, of proudly obeying commandments about how to dress, of dutifully reading scriptures, of finding reinforcement for courage or humility or other virtues, of the escape from despair about the disaster-laden world through hope for eternal life.

The so far unmentioned blessing that for many religionists would be at the top, perhaps most challenging to my rhetorological project, is reliance on intervention by a providential God: the hope, comfort, and sense of loving protection provided by a God willing and able, with miracle, to violate the natural laws "worshipped" by scientists. For many on both sides this is not only one of the warrants of religion but absolutely the number one definition of religious belief: if you believe in a Great Meddler, you are religious; if you do not, you're an

168

atheist. And for many scientists even a hint of such providential intervention violates the very notion of genuine science.

Fortunately, this belief is not essential to many of the most serious theologians even within the Christian–Judaic tradition. They have condemned praying for providential, meddling gifts as a reduction to a kind of cheap bargaining or bribery: our reason for obedience to our God becomes, many have lamented, merely an attempt to get paid back at the end.[18] Which leads me to . . .

But SPACE again suddenly shouts at me: "You're about to make this chapter so long that you'll have to cancel other chapters!" So I must end with three rough questions:

- Are not even atheistic scientists "religious" as they exhibit, explicitly or implicitly, the seven warrants? As they passionately pursue Truth, driven by a conviction about or faith in a cosmos that includes truth and the moral command to pursue it, do they not join "believers" who believe without "scientific" proof? Can any committed scientist give up the notion that "some power, greater than ourselves," some Cosmos, Being Itself, *provided* the conditions of his or her research, and still provides, daily, the whole range of possibilities that life itself yields? Of course that Supreme Being also provided the conditions that led to all of our disasters – which lands us in the messy waters of theodicy – how to pardon Supreme Being for creating the conditions that led my test-tube to break just when its contents were most needed. Perhaps agreement that this is a deep problem in all religious belief provides another *warrant* on which we all join. But it's not a proper subject for this book.
- Should not even the most devout religionist concede that whatever truth science fully demonstrates is a part of what their God grants us?
- Finally – and most importantly – a version of the question underlying this whole book: Can we hope that by practicing rhetorology of some kind – LR in its most committed form – we might diminish some of the pointless demonizing that diverse

169

quarrelers commit? Can we not diminish the widespread effort to destroy enemies that don't even exist? Cannot serious rhetorical study, even if you reject my coinage for it, diminish the damage that too many of us inflict on too many victims too much of the time? As rival rhetorics create and defend rival "realities," cannot they concede that some rivals may be revealed as superior, if really listened to?

In short, even if you reject my "joining" of science and religion, I hope that you will at least be tempted to experiment with rhetorology on some other conflict that plagues your life.

Conclusion

Still we are in the dark about rhetoric.
Socrates in Phaedrus, defending "dialectic"

Wherever there is persuasion, there is rhetoric. . . . And wherever there is "meaning," there is "persuasion."
Kenneth Burke

Can anyone really question my repeated claim that the quality of our lives, moment by moment, depends on the quality of our rhetoric? Even our survival, now that mass destruction threatens, depends on the rhetoric of our leaders and our responses to them. Thus our children's future depends on how they are taught rhetoric.

If you prefer other terms for it, I will try hard to listen to you: effective communication, practical reasoning, responsible argument, serious discourse, attentive symbolic exchange, productive dispute. But whatever the terms, the fact remains that in every domain of life, the tradition of rhetorical studies offers assistance in improving our rhetoric: in removing misunderstanding, rejecting violence, discovering common ground underlying our conflicts, and finding methods for pursuing those goals effectively. Especially important for that project is the effort here to invite all students of "effective communication," regardless of their preferred terminology, to discover how much they might gain by emerging from their narrow corners and learning from other inquirers. In the academy, genuine "interdisciplinarity" can be achieved only by genuine listeners.

Unfortunately, as this book painfully reveals, none of this hope can be reduced to simple rules; there is no one road map leading us out of the deserts and swamps and massacres that rhetrickery lands us in. Even if every one of us promised to practice LR, or even rhetorology, in all disputes, human conflict would remain with us, sometimes in violent form. Yet the history of rhetoric teaches that learning to listen, and encouraging our opponents to listen, can *sometimes* yield moments of sheer illumination: a trustful pursuit of truth replacing what had appeared to be a hopeless battle.

Thus this manifesto, as you have seen throughout, exhibits a kind of aggressive universality. Just as philosophers have always thought that more widespread philosophical study might save humankind, and theologians have been certain that embracing the right belief would do it, I am certain that more attention to rhetoric, including philosophical rhetoric, might save – well, certainly not *all* of us, but many of us in many corners of the world. Whether you are inside the academy or outside, doing politics or business, practicing philanthropy or chicanery, now is the time to start studying critically the floods of good rhetoric and rhetrickery that sweep over you daily. Your fate, like mine, depends at least partly on the quality of your listening to the rhetoric that hits you, and the quality of your responses.[1]

Notes

Preface

1 Thomas O. Sloane, "The Mystery of Rhetoric Unveiled: A Memoir," in *Rhetorica Movet: Studies in Historical and Modern Rhetoric in Honour of Heinrich F. Plett*, ed. Peter L. Oesterreich and Thomas O. Sloane, 1999, p. 523.
2 Term borrowed from Jon Leon Torn, "The Crippled Servant: Rhetoric as an Essential Problem of Modernity" (speech at Pennsylvania State Conference, "Rhetoric's Road Trips: Histories and Horizons," July, 2003).
3 *The Philosophy of Rhetoric*, 1936; 2nd ed., 2001.

Acknowledgments

1 "Patient Compliance, The Rhetoric of Rhetoric, and the Rhetoric of Persuasion," *Rhetoric Society Quarterly* 23, 3–4 (Summer/Fall 1993), p. 90.

1 How Many "Rhetorics"?

1 For a first-class, brief distinction between good and bad rhetoric, see Umberto Eco's "Political Language: The Use and Abuse of Rhetoric," in his *Apocalypse Postponed*, ed. Robert Lumley, 1994.
2 For an interesting probe into how hand gestures work rhetorically, see Susan Goldin-Meadow, *Hearing Gestures: How Our Hands Help Us Think*, 2003.
3 For an up-to-date reinforcement of decades of attacks on the fact–value distinction, see Hilary Putnam's *The Collapse of the Fact/Value Dichotomy, and Other Essays*, 2002. For an outdated list of such philosophical attacks, see the appendix

to my *Modern Dogma and the Rhetoric of Assent*, 1974, listing scores of careful revivals of genuine reasoning about values.

4   George Campbell, *The Philosophy of Rhetoric*, 1776; modern edition ed. Lloyd F. Bitzer, 1963, p. 1.

5   See Jane Sutton and Mari Lee Mifsud, "From Antistrophe to Apostrophe through Catastrophe," *Rhetoric Society Quarterly* 32, 4 (Fall 2002), pp. 29–50.

6   Eco, "Political Language," pp. 75–86.

7   Many rhetoricians have sought some term for genuine listening. Some have pursued it in the domain of "aesthetics," where poetry or music depend on vital listening. Judith Halden-Sullivan calls listening the "practice of nearness." Gerald Graff, in *Clueless in Academe*, 2003, invents the term "Arguespeak," which out of context sounds more contentious, less devoted to listening, than Graff intends.

8   Others have suggested other terms for this or that territory that tends to feel excluded by the term "rhetoric": Jay Kastely's "rhetoricality," for example, "a generalized rhetoric that penetrates to the deepest levels of human experience" (John Bender and David E. Wellbery, *The Ends of Rhetoric: History, Theory, Practice*, 1990, p. 25).

9   For a challenging study of what genuine listening – probing the soul of a fellow rhetor – can mean, see Plato's *Phaedrus*, especially toward the final third (*The Dialogues of Plato*, trans. B. Jowett, 1937 [9th printing]), pp. 272–7.

10   *Changing English: Essays for Harold Rosen*, ed. Margaret Meek and Jane Miller, 1984.

11   In recent decades studies in many branches of the social sciences have stressed, usually with "constructionist" rather than "rhetorical" terms, how reality gets made by what we say. For one thoughtful probing of the realities made by, *constructed* by, rhetoric, see Jonathan Potter's *Representing Reality: Discourse, Rhetoric, and Social Construction*, 1996.

12   One friend has already attacked this view as naively absolutist: "Don't you see that many past cultures would have collapsed if they hadn't had slavery?" So if you don't like my examples of permanent values, please probe your own list. You think that to call faking scholarly evidence morally wrong is merely a human invention, not real? The claim that nuclear war is bad is not truth but mere assertion? Of course the *judgments* vary from culture to culture, but that does not change the realities.

13   Aristotle's key term for how rhetoric discovers truth was *inventio*, often mistranslated as implying invention in the sense of making stuff up. *Inventio* received its most influential development in Cicero's *De Inventione*. Only occasionally does Cicero acknowledge that *inventio* must be translated with two different concepts: not just making up new truths but *discovery* of truths

already "there," awaiting our discovery. See Walter Watson's entry on "invention" in *The Encyclopedia of Rhetoric*, ed. Thomas O. Sloane, 2001, pp. 389–404.

14 For a serious probing of "discourse communities," concentrating on how to build the proper *academic* discourse community, see Patricia Bizzell, *Academic Discourse and Critical Consciousness*, 1992, esp. chapters "What is a Discourse Community?" and "Beyond Anti-Foundationalism to Rhetorical Authority: Problems Defining 'Cultural Literacy.'" See also *ALT DIS: Alternative Discourses and the Academy*, ed. Christopher Schroeder, Helen Fox, and Patricia Bizzell, 2002. For a short account of the popular phrase "rhetorical situation," see Mary Garret and Xiaosui Xiao, "The Rhetorical Situation Revisited," *Rhetoric Society Quarterly* 23, 2 (Spring 1993), esp. pp. 30–2. Perhaps the most important (and most neglected) exploration of rhetorical domains was by Giambattista Vico, pursuing *sensus communis*, the common grounds a given community shares, as the solution to wild controversy (vol. 3 of his *Scienza Nuova*, 1725).

15 For a brief summary of how social scientists have quarreled over the necessity of hard, empirical data, see Jennifer Hochschild, "On the Social Science Wars," *Daedalus* (Winter 2004), pp. 91–4.

16 *Social Text* 46/47, Spring–Summer, 1996.

17 Alan D. Sokal, "A Physicist Experiments with Cultural Studies," *Lingua Franca*, May–June, 1996.

2   A Condensed History of Rhetorical Studies

1 Journals with "rhetoric" in the title include *Rhetorica*, *R&PA* (*Rhetoric and Public Affairs*), *RSQ* (*Rhetoric Society Quarterly*), *Rhetorica* (*International Society for History of Rhetoric*), *Philosophy and Rhetoric*, *Kairos: A Journal of Rhetoric, Technology, and Pedagogy*, *Advances in the History of Rhetoric*, and *Rhetoric Review*. Journals without "rhetoric" in the title but with frequent essays explicitly about rhetoric include *Quarterly Journal of Speech*, *CCC* (*College Composition and Communication*), *JAC* (*Journal of Advanced Composition*), *Western Journal of Communication*, *Central States Speech Journal*, *Narrative*, *Pedagogy: Critical Approaches to Teaching Literature, Language, Composition, and Culture*, and several others. Others that I wish would more explicitly acknowledge their kinship are *Informal Logic*, *Argumentation*, *Journal of Symbolic Logic*, and *Philosophy and Literature*. There are a few Network sites, such as *H-Rhetor* and *Rhet-Net*. A major "journal," unprinted but with all essays critically monitored, is *POROI* (*Project on Rhetoric of Inquiry*), an "Interdisciplinary Journal of Rhetorical Analysis and Invention," available at http://inpress.lib.uiowa.edu/poroi.poroi/index&so In England

I find no journals explicitly about rhetoric, though I'm sure there are scores of articles every year about rhetoric, appearing in journals with non-rhetorical titles. On the continent, I find *Rhetorik* (once a year?), in Tübingen, and *Logo: Revista de Retorica y Teoria de la Communicacion*, in Salamanca. The vast majority of rhetoric articles by Europeans appear in *Rhetorica* (the ISHR journal): over 300 articles in four languages over twenty years. I am indebted to Fred Antczak and Tom Conley for some of this information, plus some further signs of rhetoric's revival on the continent. Here is Conley: "There are dozens of rhetoric articles that have appeared in *Vetus* and *Novum Testamentum*. There is a 'Center for Rhetoric Studies' in Sofia, and three years ago, Jakub Lichanski published his *Retoryka od renesansu do wsypolczesnosci – Tradycja i Innowacja (Rhetoric from the Renaissance to Modern Times: Tradition and Innovation).*"

2   I'm hoping that the major universities may soon imitate the full program at the University of Copenhagen, one that concentrates on rhetoric from college entrance to the doctorate.

3   George A. Kennedy, *Classical Rhetoric and Its Christian and Secular Tradition from Ancient to Modern Times*, 2nd ed., 1999; Marc Fumaroli, *Histoire de la rhétorique dans l'Europe moderne, 1450–1950*, 1999; Terry Eagleton, "A Small History of Rhetoric," in *Walter Benjamin: Or Towards a Revolutionary Criticism*, 1981. The French scholar Antoine Compagnon, concentrating on France and America, limited his splendid history to the decline (*Éclipse*) toward the end of the nineteenth century, and the revival (*réhabilitation* and *renouveau*) in America in the twentieth century. James A. Herrick's *The History and Theory of Rhetoric*, 2001, is "only" 300 pages.

4   *De Doctrina Christiana*, Book iv.

5   Descartes's relation to rhetorical studies was complex and is still debatable. See Stephen Gaukroger, *Descartes: An Intellectual Biography*, 1995, especially pp. 120–4.

6   *An Inquiry into the Nature and Causes of the Wealth of Nations*, 1776; 2nd ed., somewhat revised, 1778. The edition I now rely on is edited by Edwin Cannan, 1976.

7   First published as *Lectures on Rhetoric and Belles Lettres Delivered in the University of Glasgow by Adam Smith. Reported by a Student in 1762–63*, ed. John M. Lothian, 1963; 2nd ed., 1983.

8   One draft had the title *New Science Concerning the Principles of Humanity*; the third edition had the title *Principles of New Science . . . Concerning the Common Nature of the Nations*, 1744.

9   It's hardly surprising that Whately's *Elements of Rhetoric* (original 1828) is now published only in America, ed. D. Ehninger, 1963. For an account of Jebb's work on rhetoric, see Carol Poster's review of *Collected Works of Richard Jebb*, ed. Robert B. Todd, *Rhetoric Society Quarterly* 33, 4 (Fall 2003), pp. 97–110.

10 For a full account of the astonishing rise and fall of rhetoric in musical studies, especially in Germany, see Patrick McCreless, "Music and Rhetoric," in *The Cambridge History of Western Music Theory*, ed. Thomas Christensen, 2002, pp. 847–78.

11 For a good brief tracing of the decline, see Gérard Genette's "Rhetoric Restrained": "La Rhétorique restreinte," in *Figures III*, 1972. For a fine brief account of the decades just preceding the "flowering," and afterward, see James L. Kinneavy, "Contemporary Rhetoric," in *The Present State of Scholarship in Historical and Contemporary Rhetoric*, ed. Winifred Bryan Horner, 1983.

12 Speculation about the causes of rhetoric's rise and fall and rise again are endless. One challenging explanation of the "Modernist Return of Rhetoric," by John Bender and David E. Wellbery, sees it as resulting from the decline of five causes of the fall: "objectivism, subjectivism, liberalism, literacy, and nationalism" (*The Ends of Rhetoric: History, Theory, Practice*, 1990, p. 23). These five mostly overlap my list that follows.

13 There are literally thousands of published discussions of how science triumphed – most of them describing the war not as science vs. rhetoric but science vs. religion, with science usually winning. See chapter 8.

14 Georg Lukács calls excessive individualism "subjective idealism." For a first-class probing of the rise of individualism, see Karl Weintraub, *The Value of the Individual: Self and Circumstance in Autobiography*, 1978. For a brief claim that we are not in-dividuals but depend on *living together* – con-vivially – see Polanyi in chapter 4, especially pp. 63–4.

3 Judging Rhetoric

1 For a powerful probing of how Aristotle's *Rhetoric* teaches the inescapable power of *ethos*, and the resulting trust or mistrust, see Eugene Garver, *Aristotle's Rhetoric: An Art of Character*, 1994, especially chapter 6, "Why Rhetoric Needs Ethos."

2 Adam Smith's *The Wealth of Nations* is perhaps the most influential of all books about "bargain-rhetoric," usually of the simple seller/buyer kind. Human beings, he says, have an innate "propensity to truck [*sic*], barter, and exchange one thing for another. . . . [This is] the necessary consequence of the faculties of reason and speech" (opening of chapter 2, vol. 1). As a lifetime professor of rhetoric, he is astonishingly helpful in his analyses of how much our lives depend, in our bargaining-rhetoric, on trust.

3 For a stirring account of "holy" Mormon violence, including records of rhetorical attempts to avert it, see Jon Krakauer's *Under the Banner of Heaven: A Story of Violent Faith*, 2003.

4 See Emiko Ohnuki-Tierney, *Kamikaze, Cherry Blossoms, and Nationalisms: The Militarization of Aesthetics in Japanese History*, 2002.
5 Vico and Gracian citations are from Chaim Perelman, *The New Rhetoric*, 1969 translation, pp. 23–4. See chapter 4.
6 For a clever account of how Churchill conveyed to the British War Cabinet and to the French a "false optimism" about America's entry in the war, accommodating to audiences all the way, see Roy Jenkins, *Churchill*, 2001, pp. 613–15.
7 Summarizing a claim by Chauncey A. Goodrich of Yale College.
8 In my graduate work in "English," I was required to study carefully the speech on Conciliation. These days, though Burke's achievements are still celebrated widely among historians, I find only two references to that speech, among more than 150,000 references to his other work. (And there I go again, relying on totally unreliable "research.")
9 J. M. Coetzee, *Giving Offense: Essays on Censorship*, 1996, p. 39.

4 Some Major Rescuers

1 Nicola Abbagnano, article in *Encyclopedia of Philosophy*, ed. Paul Edwards, 1967 (vol. 6, p. 414). If you are at all confused about what positivism, empiricism, and logical positivism were and who were their founders, just consult this or any other Encyclopedia of Philosophy.
2 For a strong scientific argument of how all reasoning depends on the brain's rhetorical resources – especially our emotions – see Antonio R. Damasio's *Descartes' Error: Emotion, Reason, and the Human Brain*, 1994. His later works make his case even more strongly.
3 Long after drafting my account of Watson and Crick's rhetoric, I discovered that Alan Gross had done a much fuller job on the subject, in *The Rhetoric of Science* (1990). His account is sympathetically reported, though highly questioned, in Susan Haack's *Defending Science – Within Reason: Between Scientism and Cynicism* (2003).
4 There are still a "Michael Polanyi Center" and a "Michael Polanyi Society."
5 See for examples Russell Hardin's two books, *Trust and Trustworthiness*, 2002, and *One for All: The Logic of Group Conflict*, 1995; and legal scholar Cass Sunstein's *Risk and Reason: Safety, Law, and the Environment*, 2002. And on we could go, through the problems anthropologists face in the quest for trust between researchers and alien cultures. When they try to project their mind into others, they are obviously working on the rhetorical problems of audience and ethos and LR. (Clifford Geertz's *Available Light: Anthropological Reflections on Philosophical Topics*, 2000, would provide a key example.) And if we turned to

psychology, we would find an equally threatening morass of tempting examples. Even psychologists who think of themselves as concentrating on emotion, not character, inevitably land in questions of ethos. For a really superficial – but famous – account of how rhetoric depends on psychological matters, see the works of David J. Lieberman, especially *Get Anyone to Do Anything and Never Feel Powerless Again*, 2000. Of course Lieberman never refers explicitly to rhetoric: it's all power – using your power to win, and even to do good in the world.

6   See especially MacIntyre's *After Virtue*, 1981, Williams's *Morality: An Introduction to Ethics*, 1993, and Murdoch's *The Sovereignty of Good*, 1970, and *Metaphysics as a Guide to Morals*, 1992.

7   We could also dwell on many of Weber's other works: for example, his many essays on the role of charisma in all human affairs (*On Charisma and Institution Building*, ed. S. N. Eisenstadt, 1968), or his *The Protestant Ethic and the Spirit of Capitalism*, 1930.

8   Charles Sanders Peirce, *Reasoning and the Logic of Things: The Cambridge Conferences Lectures of 1898*, ed. Kenneth Laine Ketner, 1992.

9   "Faith and the Right to Believe," in *The Writings of William James*, ed. John J. McDermott, 1967, p. 735.

10   Another pursuer of the truth of consequences, Richard Weaver, was much more openly indebted to the rhetorical tradition; indeed, he can be credited with considerable influence in the flowering of the terms we traced in chapter 2. His works, especially *Ideas Have Consequences* (1948) and *The Ethics of Rhetoric* (1953), awoke thousands of readers, especially among political conservatives and defenders of moral reasoning, to the view that rhetorical studies deserve revival because rhetoric *makes* realities, including ethical realities, both defensible and indefensible.

11   A chorus clamors for inclusion: Eric Auerbach's *Mimesis: The Representation of Reality in Western Literature* (1946), which was deeply influential on my own graduate studies back in the late 1940s. As a trained "philologist" Auerbach naturally concentrated mainly on what he considered "style," but he was "resurrecting" the full range of "beauty" at every moment. Northrop Frye's *Anatomy of Criticism* (1957, 2000) deserves a full chapter. Another neglected candidate: Barbara Herrnstein Smith's really splendid probing of poetry's powers, in *Poetic Closure: A Study of How Poems End* (1968). See also Carl Dennis, *Poetry as Persuasion*, 2001.

12   Ann E. Berthoff, ed., *Richards on Rhetoric*, 1991, p. ix.

13   See especially Smith's earlier book, *The Theory of Moral Sentiments* (1759), in which consideration of others – sympathy, trust – strongly rejects total reduction of motives to "the pursuit of one's own interests."

179

14 Perelman also published what might be called another manifesto celebrating rhetoric: *The Realm of Rhetoric*, trans. William Kluback, 1982.

15 "Communication and the Human Tradition," *Communication* (1974), pp. 135–52.

16 In another context I would pursue a suggestion that Burke's remarkable study of religious rhetoric should have led him one step further, to a recognition that his logology (almost a synonym for what I'm calling "rhetorology") finally requires a version of *theology* for its validation. The study of rhetoric does not lead only to a study of God-talk; it leads to a serious embrace of some conception, however loose-jointed or "pluralized," of the Divine. And that notion need not conflict with what scientists pursue. See chapter 8.

17 You will not be surprised to learn that in current references on the Internet, Derrida has five times as many as Burke, who has ten times as many as any of the others I've described. But I can predict, without research, that only a tiny fraction of the 58,000 references to Derrida relate his work to rhetorical studies.

18 See "Jacques Derrida on Rhetoric and Composition: A Conversation," ed. Gary A. Olson, *Journal of Advanced Composition* 10, 1 (1990). Other prominent postmodernists and deconstructionists were also deeply trained in rhetoric, especially Paul de Man and Roland Barthes. See especially Barthes's forgotten essay, "The Old Rhetoric: An Aide-Mémoire," in *The Semiotic Challenge*, trans. Richard Howard, 1988, originally published as *L'Aventure sémiologique*, 1985.

19 Because of the intense, often terrifying, style of his teaching, Mckeon became for some a kind of villain. Robert M. Pirsig, in his fine novel *Zen and the Art of Motorcycle Maintenance* (really all about rhetoric), uses McKeon, only lightly disguised, as the cruel professor whose methods drive the hero into a mental institution.

Part II   The Need for Rhetorical Studies Today

1 Some recent research has claimed that two other primates, chimpanzees and orangutans, predated us in this discovery of the "self" and "others."

2 Dan Siegel, "An Interpersonal Neurobiology of Psychotherapy: The Developing Mind and the Resolution of Trauma," in *Healing Trauma: Attachment, Mind, Body, Brain*, 2003, pp. 38–40.

3 For a valuable summary of how current scientists are pursuing that "moment" when rhetoric in linguistic form emerged, see "Early Voices: The Leap to Language," *New York Times* (Science Times), July 15, 2003, p. D1. Of course

they say nothing about how non-linguistic rhetoric long predated language − or the Tower of Babel.

5   The Fate of Rhetoric in Education

1   *New York Times*, November 12, 2003, p. A23.
2   For a wonderful account, including careful scientific research, of how schools can kill love of learning, see Mihaly Csikszentmihalyi, *Flow: Studies of Enjoyment*, 1974. In an appalling number of cases in his studies, students concluded that their hours in class were the worst of the day.
3   Study by Neeta Fogg, Professor of Economics, Northwestern University. A recent study found that about one in five African-American high school students drops out. Can any reform of education reverse that?
4   According to the *New York Times*, New York City's proclaimed dropout rate "hovers around 20 percent. But critics say that if the students who are pushed out were included, that number could be 25 to 30 percent" (July 31, 2003, front page).
5   Such data are always chancy, and will obviously be changed by the time this book is published.
6   For a careful historical tracing of higher education in England after 1944, see Robert Stevens, *University to UNI: The Politics of Higher Education in England Since 1944*, 2004.
7   Far too many beginning teachers receive bad rhetorical education, and thus drive students away. In many universities, the teachers of the required first-year course in Composition, Writing, or (sometimes) Composition and Rhetoric, are "teaching assistants" fresh out of college, provided with little or no teacher-training or mentoring about how to do the job. My most fortunate experience as a beginning teacher was the University of Chicago's requirement (now on the wane) that everyone teaching any required college "CORE" course meet with the whole staff, once a week, to share methods and problems about the teaching. This weekly close encounter with fifteen or twenty colleagues − all of them facing similar pedagogical problems − taught me more about Rhet-Ed than I could have learned in any other way.
8   Letter to the *New York Times*, December 6, 2003, p. A30.
9   Should I assume that everyone these days remembers Churchill's response when an editor objected to his ending a sentence with "up with"? Memory says it was "That is something up with which I will not put."
10   Cited in Ravitch, *Language Police*, p. 72.

11 Gerald Graff, *Clueless in Academe: How Schooling Obscures the Life of the Mind*, 2003.

12 Public miseducation can of course be found in all countries, whether democratic or totalitarian. An amazing example is the bestsellerdom in France of a book "proving" that the September 11 terrorist attacks were engineered by the US administration. See "French Follies: A 9/11 Conspiracy Theory Turns Out to Be an *Appalling Deception*," a review of Thierry Meyssan's *L'Effroyable Imposture*, by Kirk Hagen, *Skeptic* 9, 4 (2000), pp. 8–13.

13 In a recent talk about his reform plans, Vallas did honorably face the issue of poverty directly: "The insides of public schools are filthy and the outsides look like trash bins," he complained to unionized custodians and maintenance engineers. "Some buildings are sweatboxes. Others are enough to 'scare the living daylights' out of teachers."

14 Dale L. Sullivan, "A Closer Look at Education as Epideictic Rhetoric," *Rhetoric Society Quarterly* 23, 3–4 (Summer/Fall 1993), pp. 71–89.

15 For more hints about teaching methods, see Graff, *Clueless in Academe*, esp. pp. 209–75, and Peter Elbow's exchange with me, forthcoming in *College English*.

16 There are by now scores of books and articles reporting on commercial inroads on "pure" research – especially in medical matters. Drug companies "hire" researchers, in more or less subtle ways, with the result that research for shared knowledge that is important *as* knowledge gets lost. See, for example, *The Big Fix: How the Pharmaceutical Industry Rips Off American Customers*, by Katherine Greider, 2003.

6   The Threats of Political Rhetrickery

1   It's not surprising that from earliest times arguments about political choice have outweighed all other discussions of rhetoric. For a first-class treatment of political rhetoric, see Umberto Eco's "Political Language: The Use and Abuse of Rhetoric," in his *Apocalypse Postponed*, ed. Robert Lumley, 1994. For the best journal specializing in political rhetoric, see *Rhetoric and Public Affairs*. Every journal dealing with rhetorical matters is almost dominated by political concerns.

2   For a useful anthology of diverse probings of public rhetoric, especially from politicians, see *Public Discourse in America: Conversation and Community in the Twenty-First Century*, ed. Judith Rodin and Stephen P. Steinberg, 2003.

3   The chief rival would be conflicts among religions – which too often lead to literal warfare. Our current international mess is at least partly inspired by the

conflict in millions of minds between Christianity and Islam, with the long history of military conflict in the memories of many. And now that the US occupation in Iraq is prolonged, open violence, and perhaps open warfare, between Shiites and Sunnis seems more and more likely. For evidence of how frighteningly close we are moving to religious rather than merely political warfare, see the media coverage of US Lt. Gen. William G. Boykin's speeches claiming that Muslims hate Americans because "we're a Christian nation," that they worship an "idol," and that our "enemy is a guy named Satan." For a penetrating effort to *listen* to the realities of Christianity and Islam, seeking the common ground they share, see Bruce Lincoln, *Holy Terrors: Thinking about Religion after September 11*, 2003.

4   For a clever, brief analysis of presidential rhetoric, especially when it makes use of religious traditions and rituals, see linguist Michael Silverstein's *Talking Politics: The Substance of Style from Abe [Lincoln] to "W" [Bush]*, 2003.

5   See *New York Times*, March 6, 2004, pp. 1ff.

6   Each of the "revolutions" might be said to have begun long ago: with the invention of printing, followed by radio, and then TV; and with the invention of the first explosives capable of killing off those not engaged in hand-to-hand combat. Most sensitive leaders have been aware of the revolutions, inventing terms like President Eisenhower's "military-industrial complex."

7   *Chicago Tribune*, January 19, 2003, Section 2, p. 1.

8   For a close analysis of Blair's rhetorical skills, before the Iraq disasters, see Peter Bull's "New Labour, New Rhetoric? An Analysis of the Rhetoric of Tony Blair," in *Beyond Public Speech and Symbols: Explorations in the Rhetoric of Politicians and the Media*, ed. Christ'l De Landtsheer and Ofer Feldman, 2000. The essay hails Blair as a master of what some call "equivocation," others "the rhetoric of modernization": "the intentional use of imprecise language" in order to "avoid conflicts." The book is an excellent anthology of essays appraising political rhetoric throughout the world, including Japan, the Near East, and the United States.

9   Nobody escapes this problem. When I recently read a charge that all critics of President Bush's war push are "naive idealists," my immediate response was something like, "Now we have further evidence for my anti-war case: Yep, all the supporters are extremists." Only a bit later did I rebuke myself for biased overreaction.

10   *Chicago Tribune*, April 22, 2003, Tempo section, p. 1.

11   *International Herald Tribune*, April 10, 2003.

12   On how wars lead everyone to engage in the "rhetoric of fear," see Rampton and Stauber, "The Uses of Fear," in *Weapons of Mass Deception*, 2003.

13   For fine discussions of political casuistry see Eugene Garver's *Machiavelli and the History of Prudence*, 1987, and *Aristotle's Rhetoric: An Art of Character*, 1994. For a

broader probing of casuistry, see Albert Jonsen and Stephen Toulmin, *The Abuse of Casuistry: A History of Moral Reasoning*, 1988.

14 Isaiah Berlin, "The Pursuit of the Ideal," in *The Crooked Timber of Humanity*, 1990, p. 17.
15 Kerry Patterson et al., *Crucial Conversations: Tools for Talking When Stakes Are High*, 2003.
16 Eco, "Political Language," p. 85.
17 See Jonathan Schell, *The Unconquerable World: Power, Nonviolence, and the Will of the People*, 2003.
18 *Progressive*, November 2003, p. 46.
19 In a longer draft, I dwelt on his mistake in beginning with what sounds like a defense of Timothy McVeigh, the Oklahoma bomber, and his frequent self-centered complaints about journals turning down his articles.
20 "A Farewell to Politics," *New York Review of Books*, October 24, 2002, p. 4.

7 Media Rhetrickery

1 For a careful survey of media-rhetoric in Europe, see Deirdre Kevin's *Europe in the Media: A Comparison of Reporting, Representation, and RHETORIC in National Media Systems in Europe*, 2002. (As I don't have to tell you, the caps on RHETORIC are mine, not hers.)
2 J. Linn Allen, "The Media Inspire Distrust," *Chicago Tribune*, May 25, 2003, Section 2, p. 4.
3 Jack Fuller, *News Values: Ideas for an Information Age*, 1996, p. 221.
4 *New York Times*, January 20, 2003, p. A23.
5 Ignatieff quoted in Jeremy Jennings, "Deaths of the Intellectual: A Comparative Autopsy," in *The Public Intellectual*, ed. Helen Small, 2002, p. 111.
6 *New York Times*, March 11, 2004, pp. E1, 7.
7 See Andrew Gimson, cover story of the *Spectator*, September 13, 2003.
8 James Ledbetter, "The Boys in the Bubble," *New York Times*, January 2, 2003, p. A29.
9 Quoted from a review by Alexander Still of *The Press Effect: Politicians, Journalists and the Stories that Shape the Political World*, 2003, in the *New York Times*, January 8, 2003, p. B11.
10 *The Times*, November 27, 2003, T2, p. 3.
11 Eric Alterman, *Sound and Fury: The Making of the Punditocracy*, 1992; paperback 1999, pp. 274–5.
12 Ibid., p. 2.

13 For example, *Big Lies: The RightWing Propaganda Machine and How it Distorts the Truth*, by Joe Conason, 2003. One major problem with such attacks is that they tend to reduce all distortions to "lying," thus ignoring the fact that the "liars" are often, like President Bush much of the time, absolutely convinced that their erroneous claims are true (or so I speculate). Dogmatists tend to believe the "lies" they tell. The only recent publication I could find in the UK is *Tell Me Lies: Propaganda and Media Distortion in the Attack on Iraq*, ed. David Miller, 2003.

14 Since my writing of the above, Goldberg has published another book, containing a grossly biased attack on Alterman: *Arrogance: Rescuing America from the Media Elite*, 2003. If one adopts my broadened definition of "media," including books about the media, Goldberg's works point up our need for rescuers.

Part III   Reducing Rhetorical Warfare

1 Eight months later, in another argument about why the attacks against our troops are increasing, he flatly denied ever having said what I have reported. But I have a record of it in my journal.

8   Can Rhetorology Yield More Than a Mere Truce, in Any of Our "Wars"?

1 This chapter borrows some from my essay in a volume honoring David Tracy: *Radical Pluralism and Truth*, ed. Werner G. Jeanrond and Jennifer L. Rike, 1991, pp. 62–80. I also quote from various published versions of an essay on the rhetorics of science and religion.

2 Thomas M. Lessl, "Gnostic Scientism and the Prohibition of Questions," *Rhetoric and Public Affairs* 5, 1 (Spring 2002), pp. 133–58. See critical response: "Lessl on Gnostic Scientism: Four Responses," *Rhetoric and Public Affairs* 5, 4 (Winter 2002), pp. 709–40.

3 I don't like that word religionist, but it's hard to find a better one. Call them the believers? Well, scientists are believers too. The faithful? Well, scientists are pursuing their faith. The devout? Sounds pejorative. The theologians? Sounds too exclusive. So it will have to be religionists – even though one of my dictionaries says that that word sometimes means simply "bigots."

4 One of the best treatments of rhetoric in scientific study is Alan G. Gross's *The Rhetoric of Science*, 1990; 2nd ed., 1996. By "going a bit too far" in intruding

rhetoric onto every scientific moment, he has offended many, but he ought to be read by everyone. My bibliography of books and articles on the subject has about 250 titles.

5 For a good (though no doubt by now somewhat outdated) summary of "theories of everything," speculations about how this or that scientific pursuit will explain it all, see Timothy Ferris, *The Whole Shebang: A State-of-the-Universe(s) Report*, 1997.

6 For an amazingly revealing exploration of dogmatic, violent excesses on both sides, I can't resist recommending Dan Brown's *Angels and Demons* (2000) – set mainly in the Vatican and much more than a mere "murder mystery." It implicitly "argues" for a genuine union between science and religion. The heroine, a particle physicist, says: "Faith is universal. Our specific methods for understanding it are arbitrary. Some of us pray to Jesus, some of us go to Mecca, some of us study subatomic particles. In the end we are all just searching for truth, that which is greater than ourselves," and "we are grateful for the power that created us" (p. 110).

7 Fritjof Capra, *The Tao of Physics: An Exploration of the Parallels Between Modern Physics and Eastern Mysticism*, 1975. Here is a painfully reduced list of other key works in the controversy: Peter J. Bowler, *Reconciling Science and Religion: The Debate in Early Twentieth-Century Britain*, 2001; Jacob Bronowski, *Science and Human Values*, rev. ed., 1965; Paul Davies, *God and the New Physics*, 1983; John William Draper, *History of the Conflict Between Religion and Science*, 1874; Amos Funkenstein, *Theology and the Scientific Imagination: From the Middle Ages to the Seventeenth Century*, 1986; Langdon Gilkey, *Naming the Whirlwind: The Renewal of God-Language*, 1969; Stanley L. Jaki, *Science and Creation: From Eternal Cycles to an Oscillating Universe*, rev. ed., 1986; *Religion and Science: History, Method, Dialogue*, ed. W. Warrant Richardson and Wesley J. Wildman, foreword by Ian G. Barbour, 1996. Finally, though Iris Murdoch rejects the term God and most religious terms from her inquiry, I see her *Metaphysics as a Guide to Morals*, 1992; Penguin ed., 1993, as a marvelous candidate for this list; I wish every scientist would read it, following its echoing of Anselm's ontological proof.

8 John Polkinghorne, *The Faith of a Physicist: Reflections of a Bottom-up Thinker*, Gifford Lectures, 1993–4, 1994. See also his *Belief in God in an Age of Science*, 1998.

9 Ian Barbour, *Religion and Science: Historical and Contemporary Issues*, rev. and expanded edition of Gifford Lectures, 1997. Also *Religion in an Age of Science*, Gifford Lectures, 1990.

10 The word "relativism" is almost as ambiguous as "religion." What I have here called "utter" relativism is a synonym for complete skepticism. But for some the term comes closer to the "pluralism" that I've been defending for decades: not "there is no truth" but "there are many genuine truths, truths that only seem to

refute each other." For a splendid questioning of utter cultural relativism, probing the religious issues it raises, see Richard Shweder's "Post-Nietzschean Anthropology: The Idea of Multiple Objective Worlds," in *Relativism: Interpretation and Confrontation*, ed. Michael Krausz, 1989, pp. 99–139.

11 *Chronicle of Higher Education*, January 24, 2003.

12 I wonder how Leibniz would respond to that, as he worked out his theory of "the best of all possible worlds." But of course his whole project was based on the acknowledgment that when judged from the human perspective, a very great deal "went wrong" in creation.

13 By "purest" I mean those who are not in it for money or fame. For too many it boils down to "not enough people are accepting, or paying enough, for my research." "I didn't get my proper share of scholarly citations this year." Even their egotistical worries confirm the claim that "something is wrong with the world."

14 Matthew Arnold, *Literature and Dogma: An Essay Towards a Better Apprehension of the Bible*, 1883, ch. 1. Compare with note 7 above.

15 Thomas Merton saw as the turning point in his life the moment when he realized he had been ignoring Warrant Four: his "religion" before that had never acknowledged his own need for repair. See Robert Inchausti, *Thomas Merton's American Prophecy*, 1998, ch. 2.

16 See Alan Lightman and Roberta Brawer, *Origins: The Lives and Worlds of Modern Cosmologists*, 1990.

17 Rudolf Otto, *The Idea of the Holy: An Inquiry into the Non-Rational Factor in the Idea of the Divine and its Relation to the Rational*, trans. John W. Harvey, 1923, pp. 1–30. See also Jacques Derrida, *The Gift of Death*, 1995, pp. 25–34.

18 See the deeply informative book *Bribes: The Intellectual History of a Moral Idea* by John T. Noonan, Jr., 1984. I can't resist tucking in a true anecdote about providence: a religious friend is really troubled by the question of how his God would allow the sandstorm that occurred in Iraq on March 25, 2003, slowing down the US troops, strike on Iraq. All scientists and most religionists I know would scoff at that notion.

Conclusion

1 You might want to apply my exhortation to the 50,000 rhetorical word choices I've made here – of course not just word choices but choices from among the resources of logos, of pathos, and of ethos. Do many of them strike you as sloppy, or mere rhetrickery? If so, please write to complain, while inviting me to analyze *your* rhetoric.

Index of Names and Titles

To save space I have had to cut many names important to this project. If you are shocked at being omitted, check my Acknowledgments (p. xvi), and the appendices to chapters 2 (pp. 35–8) and 4 (pp. 82–3). If you find yourself still missing, I can only claim that your very existence dramatizes the "flowering" of rhetorical studies reported in chapter 2: in contrast to fifty years ago, by now the "world" of rhetorical studies is much too broad for coverage in any short book.

Abbagnano, Nicola, 178n1
Abuse of Casuistry: A History of Moral Reasoning, The (Jonsen and Toulmin), 183–4n13
Academic Discourse and Critical Consciousness (Bizzell), 175n14
Advances in the History of Rhetoric (journal), 175n1
After Virtue (MacIntyre), 179n6
Ahmed, Mohammed Diab, 118
Allen, Danielle, xvi
ALT DIS: Alternative Discourses and the Academy (Schroeder, Fox, and Bizzell), 175n14
Alterman, Eric, 126–7, 142–3, 145, 184n11, 185n14
Althusser, Louis, 16
Amsterdam (McEwan), 141

Anatomy of Criticism (Frye), 179n11
Angels and Demons (Brown), 186n6
Anselm, 186n7
Antczak, Frederick, xvi, 35, 82, 176n1
Apocalypse Postponed (Eco), 173n1, 182n1
Aquinas, Thomas, 26
Arendt, Hannah, 82
Aristotle, 3, 4, 7, 17, 28, 51, 70, 73, 79, 81, 107, 120, 174n13, 177n1
Aristotle's Rhetoric: An Art of Character (Garver), 177n1, 183n13
Arnold, Matthew, 163, 187n14
Arrogance: Rescuing America from the Media Elite (Goldberg), 185n14
Atwell, Janet, 82
Auden, W. H., 34
Auerbach, Eric, 179n11

Austin, J. L., 67
*Available Light: Anthropological Reflections
   on Philosophical Topics* (Geertz),
   178n5
Axer, Jerzy, 82

Bacon, Francis, 6
Bakhtin, Michael, 82
Barbour, Ian G., 159, 186n9
Barthes, Roland, 180n18
Bartsch, Shadi, xvi
"Battle Hymn of the Republic," 124
Bauder, David, 117
Bayle, Pierre, 80, 81
Bazerman, Charles, 82
Beardsley, Monroe, 70
Beers, Charlotte, 113
Belief in God in an Age of Science
   (Polkinghorne), 186n8
Bender, John, 174n8, 177n12
Berlin, Isaiah, 120, 121, 184n14
Berlin, James, 82
Berthoff, Ann E., 70, 179n12
Bevington, David, 27
*Beyond Public Speech and Symbols:
   Explorations in the Rhetoric of
   Politicians and the Media* (De
   Landtsheer and Feldman), 183n8
Bialostosky, Don, 82
*Bias: A CBS Insider Exposes How the
   Media Distort the News* (Goldberg),
   144
*Big Lies: The RightWing Propaganda
   Machine and How it Distorts the
   Truth* (Conason), 185n13
Bitzer, Lloyd F., 8, 82
Bizzell, Patricia, 82, 175n14
Blair, Prime Minister Tony, 14–15, 111,
   112, 114–15, 183n8
*Blinded by the Right: The Conscience of an
   Ex-Conservative* (Brock), 137

Boston Review, 109
Bowler, Peter J., 186n7
Boykin, Lt. Gen. William G., 182–3–3
Bradford, Vivian, 82
Bradley, F. H., 67
*Bribes: The Intellectual History of a Moral
   Idea* (Noonan), 187n18
Britton, James, 82
Brock, David, 137
Bronowski, Jacob, 186n7
Brontë, Charlotte, 89
Brooks, Cleanth, 70
Brown, Dan, 186n6
Brutus, 27
Bull, Peter, 183n8
Burke, Edmund, 52–4, 92, 110, 178n8
Burke, Kenneth, 8, 18, 25, 37, 55, 68,
   75–8, 80, 155, 162, 164, 171,
   180n16
Bush, President George W., 14, 41, 44,
   49, 97, 107–8, 111–17, 118, 125,
   126, 129, 130–1, 135–6, 145, 147,
   150, 183n9, 185n13

Caesar, 27
*Cambridge History of Western Music
   Theory, The* (Christensen), 177n10
Camic, Charles, 83
Campbell, George, 6, 174n4
Capra, Fritjof, 157
Cassius, 27
Center for Rhetoric Studies, 176n1
Chamberlain, Prime Minister Neville,
   15, 45
Changing English: Essays for Harold Rosen
   (Meek and Miller), 174n10
Chicago Tribune, ix, 132, 183n7, 184n2
Christensen, Thomas, 177n10
Chronicle of Higher Education, 20, 187n11
Churchill, Winston, 15, 34, 43–4, 49,
   51, 108, 110, 178n6, 181n9

Cicero, 4, 26, 73, 174n13

Clark, Attorney General Ramsey, 125

Clark, Gregory, 82

Classical Rhetoric and Its Christian and Secular Tradition from Ancient to Modern Times (Kennedy), 176n3

Clinton, President William, 126, 137, 140

Clueless in Academe (Graff), 174n7, 182n15

Coetzee, J. M., 49, 50, 90, 178n9

Collapse of the Fact/Value Dichotomy, and Other Essays, The (Putnam), 173n3

Collected Works of Richard Jebb, 176n9

Collection of Essays, A (Orwell), 107

College Composition and Communication (*CCC*), 11, 175n1

College English, 182n15

Collingwood, R. G., 61, 62, 65

Colomb, Gregory, 102

Common Faith, A (Dewey), 159

"Communication and the Human Tradition" (K. Burke), 76, 180n15

Compagnon, Antoine, 34, 176n3

Comte, Auguste, 56, 57, 83

Conley, Thomas, xvi, 89, 176n1

Constable, John, 70

"Contemporary Rhetoric" (Kinneavy), 177n11

Covey, Stephen, 45, 72

Craft of Research, The (Williams, Colomb, and Booth), 102

Crick, Francis, 57, 178n3

"Crippled Servant: Rhetoric as an Essential Problem of Modernity, The" (Torn), 173n2

Cromwell, Oliver, 91

Crooked Timber of Humanity, The (Berlin), 184n14

Crucial Conversations: Tools for Talking When Stakes Are High (Paterson), 121, 184n15

Csikszentmihalyi, Mihaly, 181n2

Culture Studies (journal), 19

Daedalus: The Journal of the American Academy of Arts and Sciences, 98, 175n15

Damasio, Antonio R., 178n2

"Dancing with Tears in My Eyes" (K. Burke), 75

Darwin, Charles, 34

Davies, Paul, 186n7

De Copia (Erasmus), 28

De Doctrina Christiana (Augustine), 176n4

De Inventione (Cicero), 174n13

De Landtsheer, Christ'l, 183n8

De Man, Paul, 35, 37, 82

"Deaths of the Intellectual: A Comparative Autopsy" (Ignatieff), 184n5

Defending Science – Within Reason: Between Scientism and Cynicism (Haack), 64, 178n3

Denham, Robert, xvi

Dennis, Carl, 179n11

Derrida, Jacques, 8, 77–80, 163, 180n17, 180n18, 187n17

Descartes, René, 29, 61, 73, 176n5

Descartes: An Intellectual Biography (Gaukroger), 176n5

Descartes' Error: Emotion, Reason, and the Human Brain (Damasio), 178n2

Dewey, John, 69, 81, 159

Dialogical Turn: New Roles for Sociology in the Postdisciplinary Age, The (Camic and Joas), 83

Dialogues of Plato, The (trans. Jowett), 174n9

Doing Our Own Thing: The Degradation of Language and Music and Why We Should, Like, Care (McWhorter), xv

Draper, John William, 186n7

Dreams of a Final Theory (Weinberg), 167

Drudge, Matt, 142, 143

Eagleton, Terry, 26, 176n3

"Early Voices: The Leap to Language,"180n3

Eberly, Rosa, 82

Éclipse (Compagnon), 176n3

Eco, Umberto, 8, 121, 173n1, 174n6, 182n1, 184n16

Economist, The, 20, 132

Edwards, Paul, 178n1

Einstein, Albert, 34, 57, 153

Eisenhower, President Dwight D., 107, 183n6

Elbow, Peter, 82, 102, 182n15

Elements of Rhetoric (Whately), 176n9

Eliot, T. S., 34, 120

Empson, William, 70

Encyclopedia of Rhetoric, The (Sloane), 174–5n13

Ends of Rhetoric: History, Theory, Practice, The (Bender and Wellbery), 174n8, 177n12

Erasmus, 28, 38

Essay Concerning Human Understanding (Locke), 3, 6–7

Essay on Metaphysics (Collingwood), 61

Ethics of Rhetoric, The (Weaver), 179n10

Europe in the Media: A Comparison of Reporting, Representation, and Rhetoric in National Media Systems in Europe (Kevin), 184n1

"Faith and the Right to Believe" (W. James), 179n9

Faith of a Physicist: The Reflections of a Bottom-Up Thinker, The (Polkinghorne), 186n8

Ferris, Timothy, 186n5

Fish, Stanley, 69

"Fixation of Belief, The" (Peirce), 68

Flow: Studies of Enjoyment (Csikszentmihalyi), 181n2

Fox, Helen, 175n14

Frege, Gottlob, 31

"French Follies: A 9/11 Conspiracy Theory Turns Out to Be an *Appalling Deception*" (Hagen), 182n12

"From Antistrophe to Apostrophe through Catastrophe" (Sutton and Misfud), 174n5

Frye, Northrop, 179n11

Fuller, Jack, 132, 184n3

Fuller, Steve, 38, 82

Fumaroli, Marc, 8, 26, 82, 176n3

Funkenstein, Amos, 186n7

Gage, John T., 36, 82

Galilei, Galileo, 151

Galles, Gary M., 95, 96

Gardner, Howard, 82, 98

Garrett, Mary, 175n14

Garver, Eugene, xvi, 39, 183n13

Gaukroger, Stephen, 176n5

Geertz, Clifford, 178n5

Genesis, 86

Genette, Gérard, 177n11

Get Anyone to Do Anything and Never Feel Powerless Again (Lieberman), 179n5

Gift of Death, The (Derrida), 79, 187n17

Gilkey, Langdon, 186n7

Gimson, Andrew, 184n7

Gitlin, Todd, 138
Giving Offense: Essays on Censorship (Coetzee), 49, 178n9
"Gnostic Scientism and the Prohibition of Questions" (Lessl), 185n2
God and the New Physics (Davies), 186n7
Goebbels, Paul Josef, 129
Goffman, Erving, 55, 68
Goldberg, Bernard, 144, 145, 185n14
Goldberg, Homer, xvi
Goldin-Meadow, Susan, 173n2
Gore, Vice President Al, 139
Gorgias (Plato), 4
Gould, Stephen Jay, 158
Graff, Gerald, 82, 96, 174n7, 182n11
Grammar of Assent (Newman), 156
Grass, Gunter, 118
Grassi, Ernestor, 82
Great Expectations (Dickens), 91
Gregory, Marshall, xvi, 82
Greider, Katherine, 182n16
Gross, Alan G., 153, 178n3, 185n4

Haack, Susan, 64, 178n3
Habermas, Jürgen, 82
Hagen, Kirk, 182n12
Halden-Sullivan, Judith, 174n7
Hall-Jamieson, Kathleen, 83
Hamlet (Shakespeare), 92
Hans, Dennis, 136
Hardin, Russell, 178n5
Harré, Rom, 82
Hartshorne, Charles, 159
Hauser, Gerald, 82
Havel, President Vaclav, 126–7
Hearing Gestures: How Our Hands Help Us Think (Goldin-Meadow), 173n2
Heilman, Robert, 70
Henry V, 110–12, 114
Herder, Johann Gottfried, 121

Hernadi, Paul, 82–3
Herrick, James A., 176n3
Histoire de la rhétorique dans l'Europe moderne (Fumaroli), 176n3
History and Theory of Rhetoric, The (Herrick), 176n3
History of the Conflict Between Religion and Science (Draper), 186n7
Hitler, Adolf, 14, 49, 110, 136, 138
Hochschild, Jennifer, 175n15
Holy Terrors: Thinking about Religion after September 11 (Lincoln), 183n3
Hopkins, Brandon, xvi
Horner, Winifred Bryan, 83, 177n11
How to Do Things with Words (Austin), 67
"How to Make Our Ideas Clear" (Peirce), 68
Howell, Samuel, 83
H-Rhetor (website), 175n1
Huckleberry Finn (Twain), 95
Hume, David, 60, 62, 65, 69, 80, 81
Hussein, Saddam, 15, 44, 46, 49, 97, 108, 112, 115, 118, 120, 131, 135

Idea of the Holy: An Inquiry into the Non-Rational Factor in the Idea of the Divine and its Relation to the Rational, The (Otto), 187n17
Ideas Have Consequences (Weaver), 179n10
Ignatieff, Michael, 134
Inchausti, Robert, 187n15
Inquiry into the Nature and Causes of the Wealth of Nations, An (A. Smith), 28, 176n6, 177n2
"Is There a Place for 'Scientific' Studies in Religion?" (Wuthnow), 159
Ivins, Molly, 126

"Jacques Derrida on Rhetoric and Composition: A Conversation," 77–9, 180–18

Jaki, Stanley L., 186n7

James, Henry, 85

James, William, 68, 160

Jamieson, Kathleen Hall, 139

Jebb, Richard Claverhouse, 30, 176n9

Jefferson, Thomas, 37, 42–3

Jenkins, Roy, 178n6

Joas, Hans, 83

Johnson, President Lyndon B., 17, 108

Jost, Walter, xvi, 36

Journal of Economics, 20

Kaku, Michio, 158

Kamikaze, Cherry Blossoms, and Nationalism: The Militarization of Aesthetics in Japanese History (Ohnuki-Tierney), 178n4

Kant, Immanuel, 62

Kastely, Jay, 83, 174n8

Kempton, Murray, 141

Kennedy, George A., 26, 83, 176n3

Kennedy, President John F., 15, 17, 108

Kerry, Senator John, 112, 135

Kevin, Deirdre, 184n1

Kinneavy, James L., 83, 177n11

Kissel, Adam, xvi

Krakauer, Jon, 177n3

Kraus, Karl, 129

Kristof, Nicholas, 90

Krugman, Paul, 130–1, 139, 141

Laden, Osama bin, 97, 135

Langer, Susanne, 65–6, 70

Language Police: How Pressure Groups Restrict What Students Learn, The (Ravitch), 95

Le Monde, 131

Lectures on Rhetoric and Belles Lettres Delivered in the University of Glasgow by Adam Smith. Reported by a Student in 1762–63, 28, 176n7

Ledbetter, James, 139, 184n8

Lehrer, Jim, 97

Leibniz, Gottfried Wilhelm, 187n12

Lenin, Vladimir Ilyich, 145

Lessl, Thomas M., 185n2

Levi, Haskel, xvi

Levin, Richard, xvi

Lichanski, Jakub, 176n1

Lieberman, David J., 179n5

Lightman, Alan, 187n16

Limbaugh, Rush, 117, 136

Lincoln, Bruce, 183–4n3

Liss, Neil J., 94

Literature and Dogma: An Essay Towards a Better Apprehension of the Bible (Arnold), 187–14

Locke, John, 3, 6, 7, 28, 60

Logo: Revista de Retorica y Teoria de la Communicacion (journal), 176n1

Love's Labour's Lost (Shakespeare), xi

Lukács, Georg, 177n14

Lunsford, Andrea, 8

Lynch, Jessica, 130

Machiavelli, Niccoló, 120, 143

Machiavelli and the History of Prudence (Garver), 183n13

McCloskey, Deirdre (Don), 35, 71, 85

McCreless, Patrick, 177n10

McEwan, Ian, 141

MacIntyre, Alasdair, 65, 83, 179n6

McKeon, Richard, 55, 79, 80, 81–2, 180n19

McVeigh, Timothy, 184n19

McWhorter, John, xv

Mad Anthony Wayne, 91

Mailloux, Steven, 83

Malcolm, Norman, 67

Mandela, Nelson, 45, 126

Mandelstam, Osip, 54

Mangakis, George, 49, 50

Mauthner, Fritz, 67

Mayr, Ernst, 57

"Media Inspire Distrust, The" (Allen),
    132, 184n2

Merton, Thomas, 187n15

Metaphysics as a Guide to Morals
    (Murdoch), 179n6, 186n7

Meyssan, Thierry, 182n12

*Middle Minds: Why Americans Don't
    Think for Themselves, The* (White),
    89

Mifsud, Mari Lee, 174n5

Mill, John Stuart, 101, 102

Miller, David, 185n13

*Mimesis: The Representation of Reality
    in Western Literature* (Auerbach),
    179n11

Mind: An Essay on Human Feeling
    (Langer), 65

Mirel, Jeffrey, 99

Modern Dogma and the Rhetoric of Assent
    (Booth), 173–4n3

Modern Language Association (MLA),
    79

"Modernist Return of Rhetoric"
    (Bender and Wellbery), 177n12

Morality: An Introduction to Ethics
    (B. Williams), 179–6

Murdoch, Iris, 65, 179n6, 186n7

Murphy, James, 83

"Music and Rhetoric" (McCreless),
    177n10

"Mystery of Rhetoric Unveiled:
    A Memoir, The" (Sloane), 173n1

*Naming the Whirlwind: The Renewal of
    God-Language* (Gilkey), 186n7

Narrative (journal), 175n1

Nation, 133

National Association of Scholars (NAS),
    79

"New Labour, New Rhetoric? An
    Analysis of the Rhetoric of Tony
    Blair" (Bull), 183n8

*New Leviathan: Or Man, Society,
    Civilization, and Barbarism*
    (Collingwood), 61

New Rhetoric, The (Perelman and
    Olbrechts-Tyteca), 73, 178n5

*New Science Concerning the Principles of
    Humanity* (A. Smith), 176n8

New York Times, 115, 130, 133, 134,
    140, 180n3, 181n4, 183n5, 184n4

New Yorker, 18

Newfield, Jack, 141

Newman, Cardinal Henry, 156, 159

News Values: Ideas for an Information Age
    (Fuller), 184n3

Newsweek, 133

Nixon, President Richard, 17

Noonan, John T., Jr., 187n18

Observer, 142

"Of the Standard of Taste" (E. Burke),
    69

Office of Global Communications
    (OGC), 113

Ogden, C. K., 83

Ohmann, Richard, 83

Ohnuki-Tierney, Emiko, 178n4

Olbrechts-Tyteca, L., 73

"Old Rhetoric: An Aide-Mémoire,
    The" (Barthes), 180n18

Olson, Gary, 83

"On American Taxation" (E. Burke),
    52

"On Conciliation with the Colonies"
    (E. Burke), 52–3

On Liberty (Mill), 101
"On the Social Science Wars" (Hochschild), 175n15
One for All: The Logic of Group Conflict (Hardin), 178n5
Ong, Walter, 83
Orwell, George, 107, 118
Otto, Rudolf, 187n17

"Patient Compliance, The Rhetoric of Rhetoric, and the Rhetoric of Persuasion" (Segal), 173n1
Patterson, Kerry, 184n15
Pauling, Linus, 58
Payne, E. J., 53
Peck, M. Scott, 163
Peirce, Charles Sanders, 68, 179n8
Perelman, Chaim, 3, 55, 73, 74, 178n4, 180n14
Perpetual War for Perpetual Peace: How We Got to Be So Hated (Vidal), 126
Personal Knowledge: Towards a Post-Critical Philosophy (Polanyi), 63
Phaedrus (Plato), x, 171, 174n9
Phelan, James, xvi
Philosophy and Literature (journal), 175n1
Philosophy in a New Key (Langer), 65
Philosophy of Rhetoric, The (Richards), 70, 173n3
Philosophy of Rhetoric, The (Campbell), 174n4
"Physicist Experiments with Cultural Studies, A" (Sokal), 175n17
Picture of Dorian Gray, The (Wilde), 3
Pirsig, Robert M., 180n19
Plato, x, 4, 13, 31, 71, 78, 174n9
Poetic Closure: A Study of How Poems End (B. Smith), 179n11
Poetry as Persuasion (Dennis), 179n11
Poirier, Richard, 83

Polanyi, Michael, 63–4, 72, 82, 85, 178n4
"Political Language: The Use and Abuse of Rhetoric" (Eco), 173n1, 174n6, 182n1, 184n16
Polkinghorne, John, 159, 186n8
Popper, Karl, 33
"Post-Nietzschean Anthropology: The Idea of Multiple Objective Worlds" (Shweder), 187n10
Poster, Carol, 176
Potter, Jonathan, 174n11
Poulakos, Takis, 36, 83
Powell, Secretary of State Colin, 113
Practical Criticism: A Study of Literary Judgment (Richards), 70
Present State of Scholarship in Historical and Contemporary Rhetoric, The (Horner), 177n11
Presentation of Self in Everyday Life, The (Goffman), 55, 68
Princess Diana, 140
Principles of Literary Criticism (Richards), 107
Project on Rhetoric of Inquiry (*POROI*), 175n1
Protestant Ethic and the Spirit of Capitalism, The (Weber), 179n7
Public Discourse in America: Conversation and Community in the Twenty-First Century (Rodin and Steinberg), 182n2
"Pursuit of the Ideal, The" (Berlin), 184n14
Putnam, Hilary, 173n3

Quest for Certainty: A Study of the Relation of Knowledge and Action (Dewey), 69
Quine, W. V., 67
Quinn, Arthur, 83
Quintilian, 4, 6, 26, 39, 73

Rabinowitz, Peter, xvi
Radical Pluralism and Truth (Tracy),
  185n1
Ransom, John Crowe, 70
Rather, Dan, 90
Ravitch, Diane, 95, 96, 98
Realm of Rhetoric, The (Perelman),
  180n14
*Reasoning and the Logic of Things: The
  Cambridge Conferences Lectures of
  1898* (Peirce), 179n8
*Reconciling Science and Religion: The
  Debate in Early Twentieth-Century
  Britain* (Bowler), 186n7
*Relativism: Interpretation and
  Confrontation* (Shweder),
  187n10
*Religion and Science: Historical and
  Contemporary Issues* (Barbour),
  186n9
*Religion and Science: History, Method,
  Dialogue* (Richardson and
  Wildman), 186n7
"Religion as a Conversation Stopper"
  (Rorty), 153
Religion in an Age of Science (Barbour),
  186n7
*Representing Reality: Discourse, Rhetoric,
  and Social Construction* (Potter),
  174n11
Rhet-Net (website), 175n1
Rhetoric and Public Affairs (*R&PA*),
  175n1, 182n1
Rhetoric of Economics, The (McCloskey),
  35, 71
Rhetoric of Motives, The (K. Burke), 25,
  75
*Rhetoric of Music: Harmony, Counterpoint,
  Musical Form, The* (Wilson), 25
"Rhetoric of Practical Choice, The"
  (Gendlin), 69

Rhetoric of Religion, The (K. Burke), 76,
  155, 164
Rhetoric of Science, The (Gross), 153,
  178n3, 185n4
"Rhetoric Restrained" ("La
  Rhétorique restreinte") (Genette),
  177n11
Rhetorica (*International Society for History
  of Rhetoric*), 175n1, 176n1
*Rhetorica Movet: Studies in Historical and
  Modern Rhetoric in Honour of
  Heinrich F. Plett* (Oesterreich and
  Sloane), 173n1
Rhetorica (queen of the sciences and
  arts), 5, 27, 28, 34
"Rhetorical Situation Revisited, The"
  (Garret and Xiao), 175n14
"Rhetorical Stance, The" (Booth), 11
Richards, I. A., x, 7, 37, 69, 70, 75, 94,
  107, 149, 179n12
Richardson, W. Warrant, 186n7
Richter, David, 83
Ricoueur, Paul, 83
*Risk and Reason: Safety, Law, and the
  Environment* (Sunstein), 178n5
Road Less Traveled, The (Peck), 163
*Rocks of Ages: Science and Religion in the
  Fullness of Life* (Gould), 158
Roosevelt, Eleanor, 34
Roosevelt, Franklin Delano, 49
Rorty, Amélie Oksenberg, 83
Rorty, Richard, 69, 83, 153
Rosen, Harold, 83
Royster, Jacqueline, 83
Rumsfeld, Secretary of Defense Donald,
  116, 147
Russell, Bertrand, ix, 75, 81
Russert, Tim, 142

Sacks, Sheldon, 83
Safire, William, 133

Index of Names and Titles

St. Augustine, 6, 26

Saint-Simon, Claude Henri de Rouvroy, comte de, 56

Saintsbury, George, 83

Samson, 48

Schell, Jonathan, 123, 184n17

Science and Creation: From Eternal Cycles to an Oscillating Universe (Jaki), 186n7

Science and Human Values (Bronowski), 186n7

Scienza Nuova, La (Vico), 29, 175n14

Segal, Judith, xvi

Semiotic Challenge, The (Barthes), 180n18

Seshadri, Ambika, xvi

Shakespeare, William, xi, 27, 110–11

Shweder, Richard, 186–7n10

Siegel, Daniel, 86, 180n2

Silverstein, Michael, 183n4

Sizer, Theodore, 98

Sledd, James, 83

Sloane, Thomas O., 83, 173n1

Smith, Adam, 28, 71, 177n2, 179n13

Smith, Barbara Herrnstein, 179n11

Social Text (journal), 20, 175n16

Sociology of Religion, The (Weber), 66

Socrates, x, 4, 171

Sokal, Alan D., 20, 175n16

Sophists, x, 4, 51, 78

Sound and Fury: The Making of the Punditocracy (Alterman), 143, 184n11

Sovereignty of Good, The (Murdoch), 179n6

Spender, Stephen, ix

Spinoza, Baruch 79, 81

Stalin, Joseph, 54

Stauber, John, 113, 183n12

Steinberg, Stephen P., 182n2

Steinmann, Martin, 83

Stern, Howard, 116

Stevens, Robert, 181n6

Stimpson, Catherine, 98

Stone, I. F., 141

Stowe, Harriet Beecher, 41

Strachey, Lytton, ix

Sullivan, Dale L., 182n14

Sunstein, Cass, 178n5

Sutton, Jane, 174n5

Swearingen, C. Jan, 83

Tacit Dimension, The (Polanyi), 63

Talking Politics: The Substance of Style from Abe [Lincoln] to "W" [Bush] (Silverstein), 183n4

Tao of Physics: An Exploration of the Parallels Between Modern Physics and Eastern Mysticism, The (Capra), 157, 186n7

Taylor, Charles, 83

Temple Foundation, 157–8

Theology and the Scientific Imagination: From the Middle Ages to the Seventeenth Century (Funkenstein), 186n7

Theory of Moral Sentiments, The (A. Smith), 179–13

They Shoot Writers, Don't They? (Mangakis), 50

This is Biology: The Science of the Living World (Mayr), 57

Thomas Merton's American Prophecy (Inchausti), 187n15

Timaeus (Plato), 71

Time Warner, 137

Times Literary Supplement (*TLS*), 132

Tolstoy, Leo, 34

Torn, Jon Leon, 173n2

Toulmin, Stephen, 18, 83, 159, 183–4n13

Tractatus Logico-Philosophicus
  (Wittgenstein), 67
Tracy, David, 161, 163, 185n1
Treatise of Human Nature, A (Hume), 60
Tribune Publishing Company, 132
Trust and Trustworthiness (Hardin),
  178n5
Turner, Ted, 137

UN Commission on Human Rights,
  140
Unamuno, Miguel de, 35
Uncle Tom's Cabin (Stowe), 41
*Unconquerable World: Power, Nonviolence,
  and the Will of the People* (Schell),
  184n17
*Under the Banner of Heaven: A Story of
  Violent Faith* (Krakauer), 177n3
United Nations Educational, Scientific,
  and Cultural Organization
  (UNESCO), 80
*University to UNI: The Politics of Higher
  Education in England Since 1944*
  (Stevens), 181n6
"Uses of Fear, The" (Rampton and
  Stauber), 183n12

Vallas, Paul, 99, 182n13
*Value of the Individual: Self and
  Circumstance in Autobiography*
  (Weintraub), 177n14
Varieties of Religious Experience, The
  (W. James), 69, 160
Venus and Adonis (Shakespeare), 27
Vickers, Brian, 83
Vico, Giambattista, 29, 51, 121, 175n14
Vidal, Gore, 126
Villette (C. Brontë), 89
*Visions: How Science Will Revolutionize
  the Twenty-First Century* (Kaku),
  158

Waldman, Paul, 139
Wall Street Journal, 135
Wallace, Karl, 83
*Walter Benjamin: Or Towards a
  Revolutionary Criticism* (Eagleton),
  176n3
Warren, Robert Penn, 70
Washington Post, 134
Watson, James D., 57, 178n3
Watson, Walter, 175n13
Weapons of Mass Deception (Rampton
  and Stauber), 113, 183n12
Weaver, Richard, 8, 83, 179n10
Weber, Max, 66, 179n7
Weinberg, Steven, 167
Weintraub, Karl, 177n14
Wellbery, David E., 174n8,
  177n12
"What Is a Discourse Community?"
  (Bizzell), 175n14
*What Liberal Media? The Truth About
  BIAS and the News* (Alterman),
  145
Whately, Richard, 30, 176n9
White, Curtis, 89
White, Hayden, 83
White, James Boyd, 83
Whitehead, Alfred North, 159
Whittemore, Reed, 83
*Whole Shebang: A State-of-the-Universe(s)
  Report, The* (Ferris), 186n5
"Why Rhetoric Needs Ethos," in
  *Aristotle's Rhetoric: An Art of
  Character* (Garver), 177n1
Wicken, Jeffry, 153
Wilde, Oscar, 3
Will to Believe, The (W. James), 69
Williams, Bernard, 65, 83, 179n6
Williams, Joseph, xiii, 83, 102
Williams, William Carlos, 36
Williamson, George, 83

Index of Names and Titles

Wilson, Mortimer, 25
Wimsatt, William, 70
Winfred, George, 25
Winterowd, Ross, 83
Wittgenstein, Ludwig, 34, 67
Woolf, Virginia, 34

Wuthnow, Robert, 159

Xiao, Xiaosui, 175n14

Zen and the Art of Motorcycle Maintenance
(Pirsig), 180n19

Index of Subjects

accommodation to audience, 50–4, 108, 113–15, 125–8
Al Qaeda, 97
alchemists, 166
American Revolution, 43, 53, 124
anthropology, 26, 178–5
anti-Semitism, 136
AOL Time Warner, 134
argument, productive
   as destroyed by the media, 129–47
   as goal of education, 89–106
   illustrated, 100–2
   as lost in politics, 107–28
art as rhetoric, 11, 69–71
authority, scientists' reliance on, 58
   see also Polanyi, Michael

Baghdad, 142
bias
   as affecting education, 95–6
   as affecting the media,141–6
   of Booth, 136
   as exhibited in politics, 108, 116–17
   as problem for judging rhetoric, 41–2, 107–8, 183–9
Buddhism, 19, 161
business management, rhetoric of, 47, 52

casuistry, 119–22
Catholicism, 149, 156, 161
causes of decline in status of rhetoric, 30–4
celebrity, quest of, 140–1
CEOs, 17, 54, 99
certainty, Cartesian quest for, 23–34, 61–2, 176–5
choice among lesser evils or "greater goods," *see* casuistry; *phronesis*, situation ethics
Christian-Judaic tradition, 169
Christianity, 26, 97, 149, 159, 160, 164, 182–3n3
CNN, 106, 137, 138
Communism, 103, 136, 138
"composition," "communication," and other synonyms for rhetorical studies, 23–4
conviviality, 64–5
   see also Polanyi, Michael
cosmic conflicts among "truth," "goodness," and "beauty," 167
creationism, 97
Czech Republic, 126–7

Declaration of Independence, 42, 92
deconstruction, 19

deconstruction (*Continued*)
  see also De Man, Paul; Derrida,
    Jacques
Deism, 160
deliberative rhetoric, 17, 107–28
Demiurgos, 166
dialectic, as sibling of rhetoric, 4, 7
dialogue, *see* listening-rhetoric; trust
dialogue, intellectual, 83
domains, rhetorical (discourse
    communities), 18–21
Dubious Data Awards, 135

economics, 71–2
  see also business management, rhetoric
    of
education, 89–106
  dropout rates, 91–2, 181n3, 181n4
  equality, right to, 93
  facts, overemphasis on memorized,
    91, 93–4
  failures of, 89–93
  miseducation outside classroom, 96–8
  students' hatred of, 91, 181n2
  threat of rote testing, 93–4
  underfunding of, 90–1
elocutio (elocution, sometimes mere
    prettifying), 6
eloquence, 60
English, as synonym for rhetorical
    studies, 23
Enlightenment, 1, 6, 28
  see also certainty, Cartesian quest for
enthymemes, 57
epideictic rhetoric, 17
ethics, 39–54
ethos (character), 17–18, 58, 99
  see also Polanyi, Michael
Europe, xii, 23, 97, 135, 184n1

fact–value distinction, 6, 173n3

  see also pluralism
Fall, the (in Genesis), 164
Fascism, 104, 136, 138
fiction authors, as key critics of bad
    rhetoric, 141
forensic rhetoric, 17
FoxNews, 134, 137, 140
France, 34, 37, 51, 103, 112, 132, 176,
    178, 182n12
Freudians, 85
fundamentalism, 96–7, 187n18

Germany, 30, 110, 132, 138, 177n10
gesture as rhetoric, 4, 173n2
gnosticism and science, 153–4
God, 26, 48, 71, 76, 77, 86, 97, 110–11,
    118, 142, 151, 157, 164, 166, 167,
    168–9, 180n16, 187n18
Golden Mean, 120
  see also casuistry
Greek rhetoric, 43, 49
Gulf War, 138, 139
gullibility of public, 96–7, 130–1

hermeneutics, 10
Homo sapiens, 128, 149
honesty, 39–54
  see also Burke, Edmund
hypocrisy
  defensible, 50–2
  indefensible, 52

identification (K. Burke's key term for
    listening-rhetoric), 75–6
images as rhetoric, xi, 129–47
Internet, 139, 180n17
invention (*inventio* as *discovery*), 4, 6,
    174–5n13, 175n1
Iraq, 4, 8, 9, 15, 44, 49, 97, 107, 109,
    111–18, 120, 125, 130–1, 138,
    150, 183n3, 187n18

Index of Subjects

Ireland, 132
Islam, 182–3n3

Jesuits, 120
Jesus, 160, 186n6
Jews, 97, 135–6, 161, 164, 166
journals dealing with rhetoric and its synonyms, 175n1

law rhetoric, 178–9n5
listening-rhetoric
  as central to good war rhetoric, 107–28
  as cure for political rhetrickery, 127–8
  as goal of education, 89–106
  kinds distinguished, 46–9
  opponents confirmed in their bias, 116
  problems with, 50–4
  rising anger, 116–17
  rising self-censorship and deception, in and out of the media, 117–18
  rising skepticism about *all* appeals, 116
logology, 180n16

Manhattan Project, 167
Marxists, 16, 85, 149
media, 129–47
  ambiguity of term, 131
  deliberate distortions by, 130, 136–43
  physical threats against journalists, 131
  progress in, 146–7
  revolution in, 111–12, 128
  self-critique in, 132–6
  skepticism about, in America, 134
  technical improvement in, 131–2
  unconscious deception by, 134–6
metaphor, 57, 70–1

metonymy, 72
Millennium Dome, 15, 16
miseducation
  in classroom, 89–106
  intended, 130, 136–43
  by media, 96–8, 129–47
  motives for, 137–43
  outside America, 182n12
  unintended, 134–6
Mormons, 48, 149, 160, 166, 177n3
Munich Accord, 45
Muslims, 113, 114, 149, 161, 182–3n3
mutual understanding, *see* listening-rhetoric; trust
mysterium tremendum, 168, 187n17

National Anthem, the, 124
nature, 14, 167
Nazism, 51, 52, 129, 138
NBC, 142
New Criticism, 70
Nigeria, 15, 130
North Korea, 112, 113, 114

objectivity and subjectivity, *see* bias
Occam's razor, 31
ordinary language, 66–8
organizations dealing with rhetorical studies, 175n1
Oxford, viii, ix, 24

panentheism, 159
Parliament, 5, 52, 53
pathos, 65–6
photographic deception, 135
phronesis, 120
  see also casuistry
Platonists, 13, 80, 81
pluralism, 186–7n10
poetry as rhetoric, xi

polarization of public, effect on
  rhetoric, 90
political correctness, exaggerated, 95–6,
  98
political rhetoric, 107–28
  attempts to produce listening, 113–14
  defensible and indefensible
    distinguished, 109–11
  problems in such distinctions, 111–15
  remedies for rhetrickery, 127–8
  success with *local* audience, as
    standard of judgment, 110–11
  see also protest rhetoric
positivism, 56, 61–3
pragmatism, 68–9
protest rhetoric, 108, 116, 123–7,
  185n13
Protocols of Zion myth, 135–6
psychology, 26, 178–9n5

quadrivium, 26–7

realities created by rhetoric, 14–16 and
  passim
reason vs. rhetoric, 56, 153–70
relativism, 186n10
religion, definitions of, 160–1
  books about religion and science,
    186–7
  multiple blessings of, 168–9
  and rhetoric, 154–5
  and science, 153–70
religionist, problems with term, 185n3
Renaissance, xiii, 4, 27–8
research, relevance of rhetorical studies
  to, 102–3
Revolutionary War, 42–3, 52–3
rhetoric
  effect on quality of life, viii–xv,
    171–2
  inescapability of, 56–62

neglect of issues, in other academic
  fields, 24
neglect of terms, in other academic
  fields, 24, 55–84
rise of status, 23–38
studies of, in other fields, 29–38
synonyms for, 11–12
technical resources of, 72–4; *see also*
  Perelman, Chaim; Sloane,
  Thomas O.; Smith, Adam
rhetoric, defined, 3–11
  affirmatively, 4–6, 7–8; *see also*
    argument, productive
  as altar boy to religion, 154–5
  as confined to males, 4
  as creator or maker of reality, 12–17
    and *passim*
  dictionary definition, x
  as enemy of truth, 55–9; *see also*
    positivism
  as escape from misunderstanding, see
    Richards, I. A. and *passim*
  pejoratively, 6–7
  as queen of the sciences and arts, 4, 5,
    6, 27
  as related to all other fields, viii–xv,
    7–8
  as related to other rhetorical terms,
    10–11
  as sibling of dialectic, 7
rhetoric, kinds of
  architectonic (McKeon) 80, 82
  deliberative, 17, 40, 107–28
  epideictic, 17, 40
  forensic, 17, 40
rhetoric, motives for, distinguished
  bargain-rhetoric, 45–6, 71–2
  listening-rhetoric, 46–50, 71–2, 138
  win-rhetoric, 43–5, 71–2, 141
rhetorical studies, revival of, 23–38,
  55, 73

rhetorical study
as claiming to demonstrate one unique religious denomination, 156, 159–60
status of, viii, 1–2, 23–38, 55–84
rhetorology
defined, 10
as hope for all rhetorical inquiry, 169–70, 171–2
as not complete cure of controversy, 156–8
as "solution" of warfare betweens science and religion, 153–70
rhetrickery (as cheating rhetoric)
in advertising and marketing, 44–5
in the media, 129–47
near universality of, 41
in politics, 107–28

Satan, 86, 97, 125
scene of rhetoric, *see* domains, rhetorical
science, 30
books on relation to religion, 186–7
and gnosticism, 153–4
and religion, 153–70
and rhetoric, 155
self-censorship, *see* surrender rhetoric
sincerity, political limits on, *see* casuistry; *phronesis*; situation ethics
situation ethics, 120
60 Minutes, 160
slavery, 13, 41
sociology, 26, 67–8, 83
"Sokal Hoax," 20
South Africa, 45, 126
Soviet Union, 54, 126
standards, 39–54
differences among, *see* domains, rhetorical
influence of bias, *see* bias
technical choices, 39

statistics, unreliability of, 136
surrender rhetoric (self-censorship), 48–54, 138–40
synecdoche, 72

talk shows on TV, 106, 140–1, 146
terrorism as limit to listening-rhetoric, 49
theology, 180n16
topoi, as synonym for commonplaces, places, assumptions, *see* warrants
trivium, 26–7
trust, 40, 178n5
truth, non-contingent, 12–14

UFOs, 97
United Kingdom, 11, 18, 19, 42, 90, 92, 93, 103, 107, 114–15, 124, 130, 132–4
United Nations, 115, 150
United Nations Declaration of Human Rights, 80
United States, xii, 11, 14, 30, 37, 42, 46, 51–3, 90–2, 97, 103, 109, 111, 113, 114, 116, 117, 118, 120, 124, 130–1, 131, 132, 133, 134–5, 146
University of Chicago, 92, 181–7
University of Copenhagen, 176n2
University of Illinois at Chicago, 132
US Congress, 111, 126, 133, 161
US House of Representatives, 114, 115
US Library of Congress, 25

value judgments, contingent and non-contingent, 39–54
Vietnam War, 17, 38, 139
violence, threat of, as limit on listening-rhetoric, 48

war, effect on rhetoric, 117–19
warfare among religions, 182–3n3

warfare between science and religion, synonyms for, 158

warrants, 18–20, 56
  defined, 18
  explored, 161–8
  religious warrants, shared with science: world is flawed, 161–2, 163–4; truth exists, both factual and ethical, 162; a "cosmos" exists, call it supreme Being or just Nature, 161–3; each of us is flawed, 165; each of us *ought* to do something about the flaws, 165–6; when my desires conflict with what I know is right, I should follow the right, 166–7; my deepest beliefs yield *feelings* of attachment to the "whole of things," 167–8

weapons of mass destruction (WMD), 115, 116–17, 128
  rhetorical revolution produced by, 112

whistle-blowing, 52, 138–9
White House, 117, 131
win-rhetoric, 43–5
win-win rhetoric, 45
World War II, 14–16, 48
World War III, 128

Zimbabwe, 132
Zion, 136

Blackwell Manifestos

In this new series major critics make timely interventions to address important concepts and subjects, including topics as diverse as, for example: Culture, Race, Religion, History, Society, Geography, Literature, Literary Theory, Shakespeare, Cinema, and Modernism. Written accessibly and with verve and spirit, these books follow no uniform prescription but set out to engage and challenge the broadest range of readers, from undergraduates to postgraduates, university teachers and general readers – all those, in short, interested in on-going debates and controversies in the humanities and social sciences.

Already Published

The Idea of Culture   Terry Eagleton
The Future of Christianity   Alister E. McGrath
Reading After Theory   Valentine Cunningham
21st-Century Modernism   Marjorie Perloff
The Future of Theory   Jean-Michel Rabaté
True Religion   Graham Ward
Inventing Popular Culture   John Storey
Myths for the Masses   Hanno Hardt
The Rhetoric of Rhetoric   Wayne C. Booth
The Future of War   Christopher Coker
When Faiths Collide   Martin E. Marty

Forthcoming

The Future of Society   William Outhwaite
The Idea of English Ethnicity   Robert Young
The Idea of Economy   Deirdre McCloskey
The Battle for American Culture   Michael Cowan
Television: Literate at Last   John Hartley
What Cinema Is!   Dudley Andrew
The Idea of Evil   Petu K. Dews